EASY PIANO

children's
movie favorites

ISBN 0-634-02908-8

HAL•LEONARD®
CORPORATION

7777 W. BLUEMOUND RD. P.O. BOX 13819 MILWAUKEE, WI 53213

Visit Hal Leonard Online at
www.halleonard.com

THE BARE NECESSITIES

from Walt Disney's THE JUNGLE BOOK

Words and Music
TERRY GILKYS

Brightly

Look for the bare ne - ces - si - ties, the

sim - ple bare ne - ces - si - ties; ___ for - get a - bout your

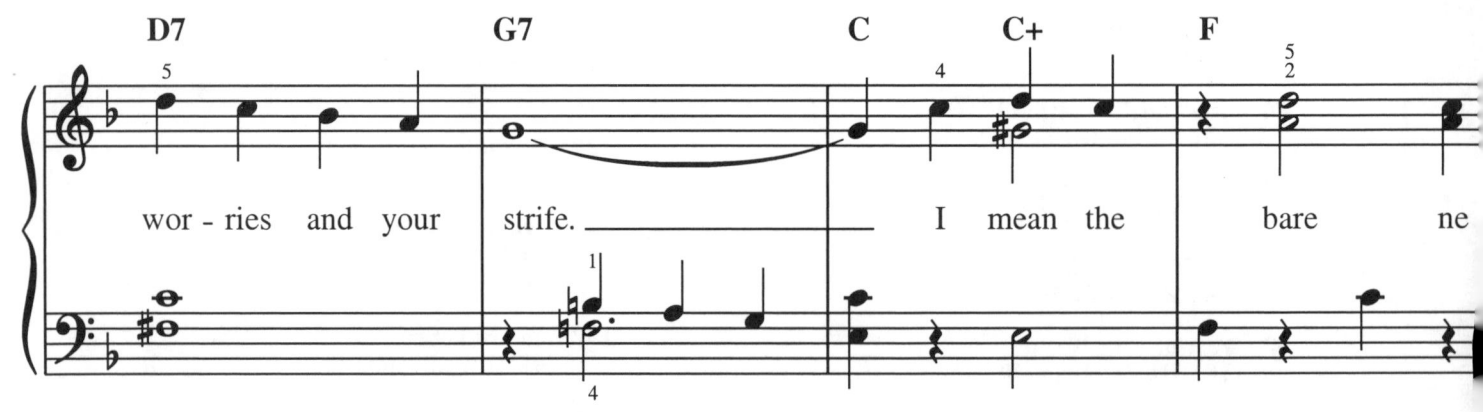

wor - ries and your strife. ___ I mean the bare ne

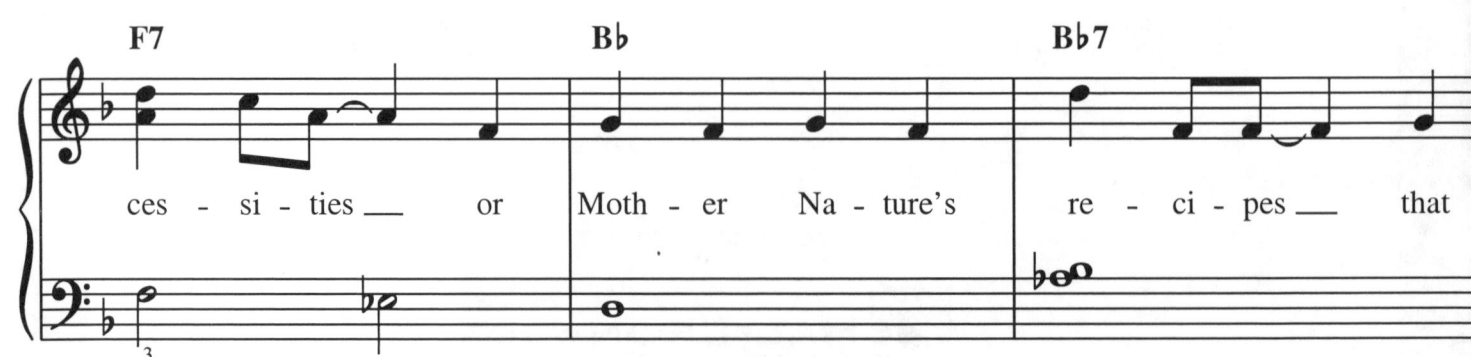

ces - si - ties ___ or Moth - er Na - ture's re - ci - pes ___ that

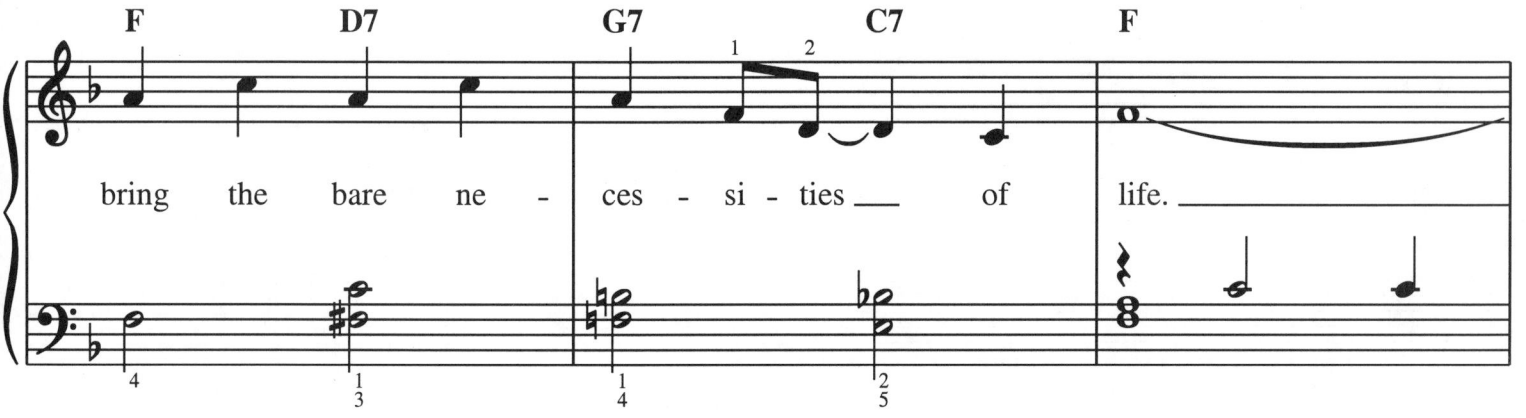

bring the bare ne - ces - si - ties ___ of life. ___

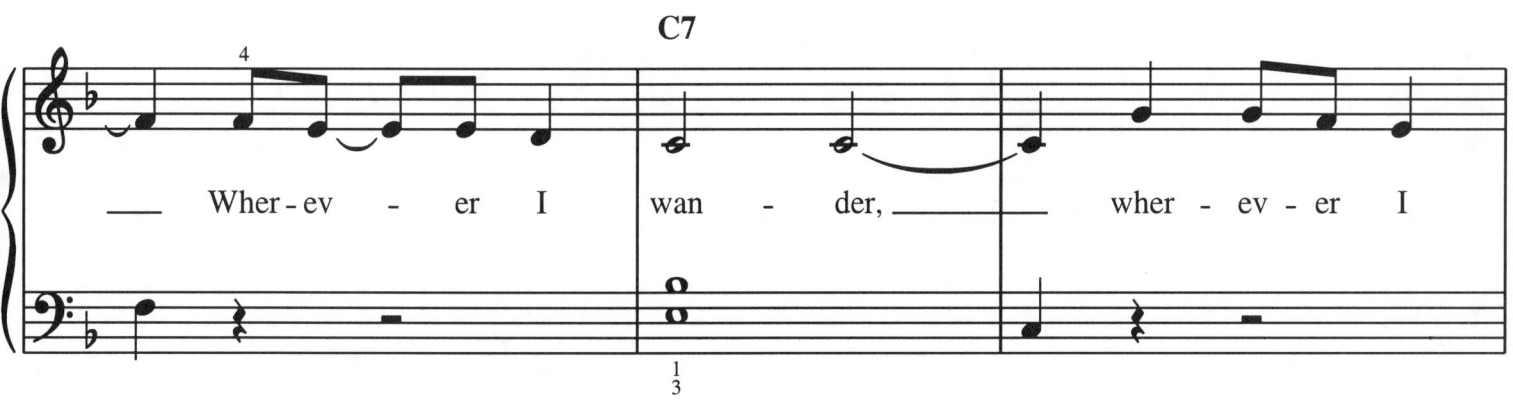

___ Wher - ev - er I wan - der, ___ ___ wher - ev - er I

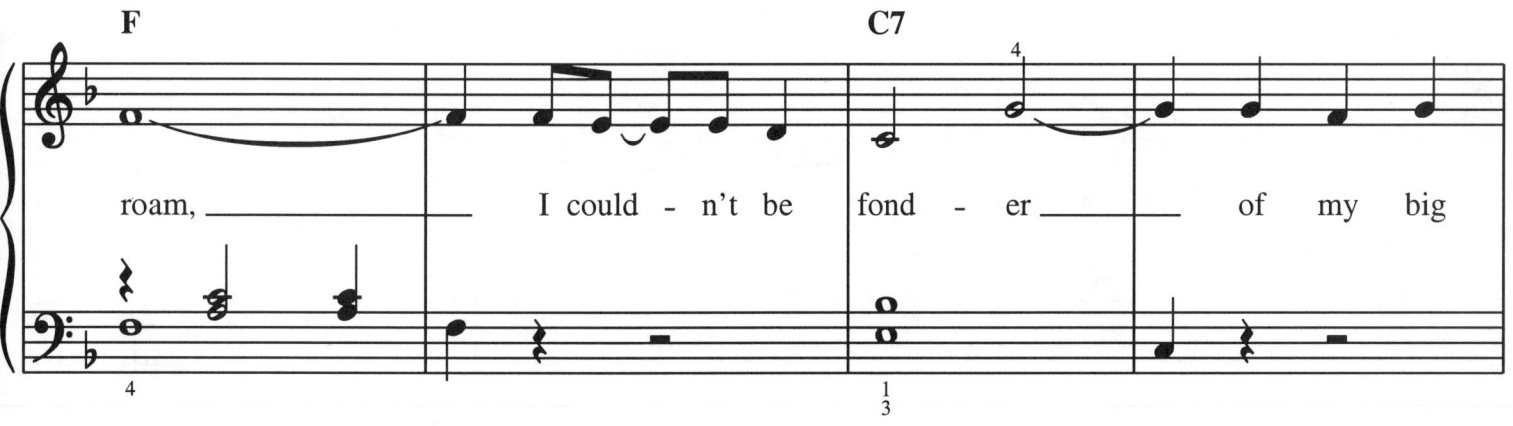

roam, ___ I could - n't be fond - er ___ of my big

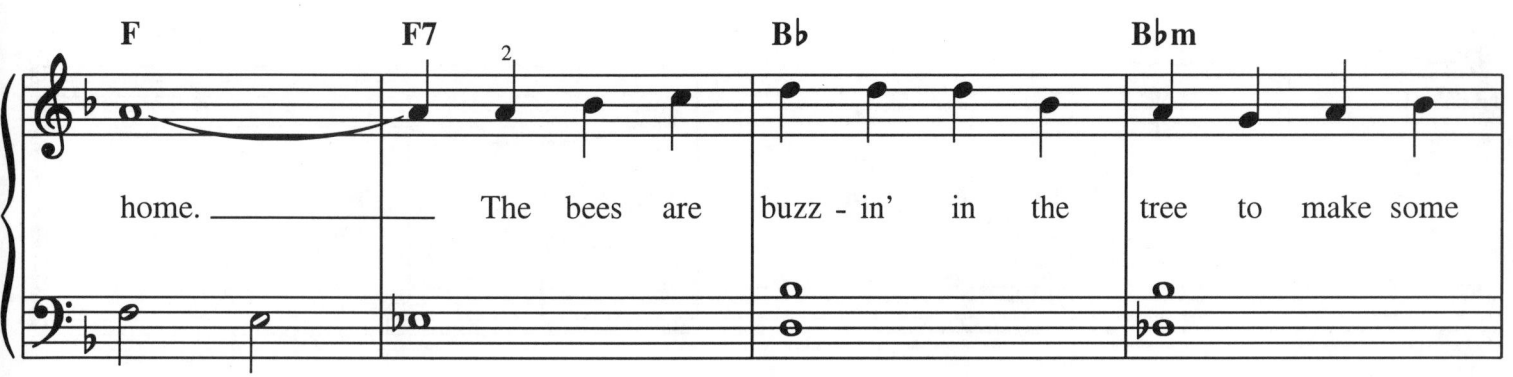

home. ___ The bees are buzz - in' in the tree to make some

4

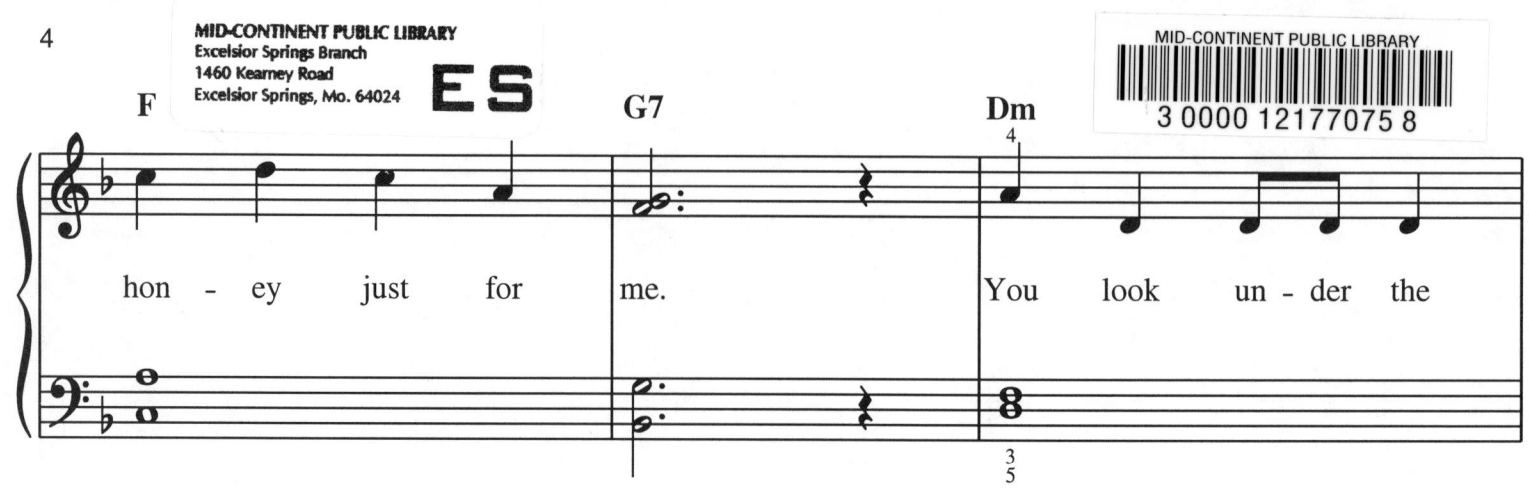

honey just for me. You look un-der the

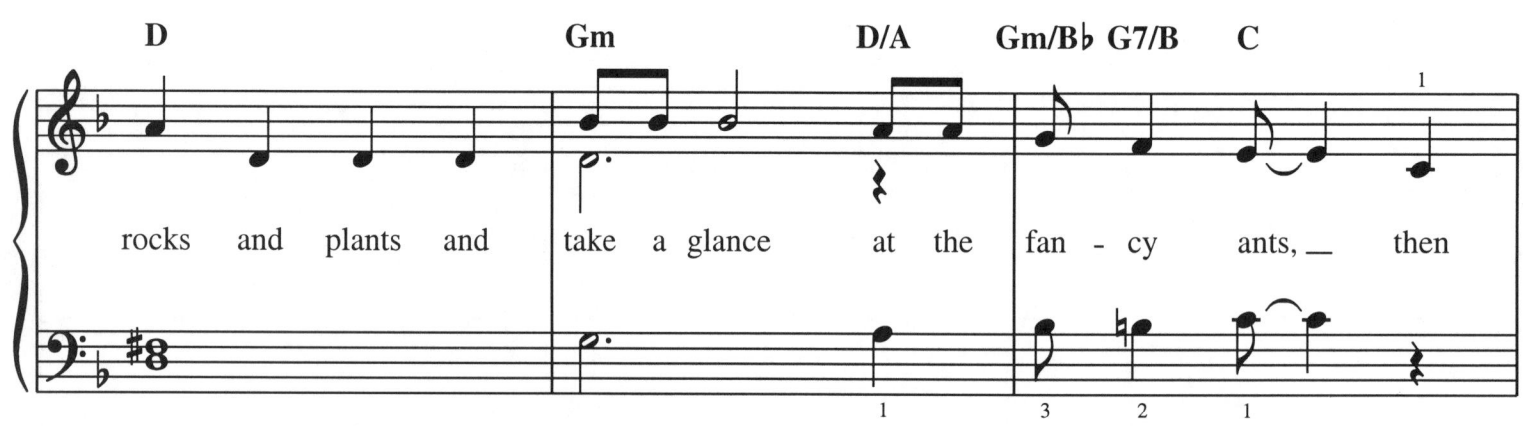

rocks and plants and take a glance at the fan-cy ants, __ then

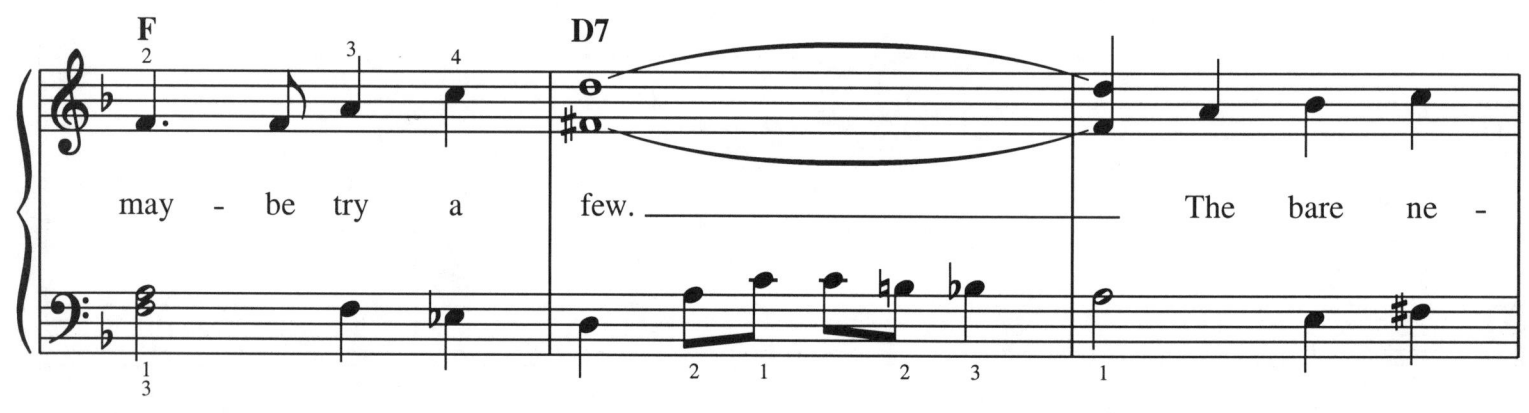

may-be try a few. _____ The bare ne-

ces-si-ties of life will come to you. _____

BEAUTY AND THE BEAST

from Walt Disney's BEAUTY AND THE BEAST

Lyrics by HOWARD ASHMAN
Music by ALAN MENKEN

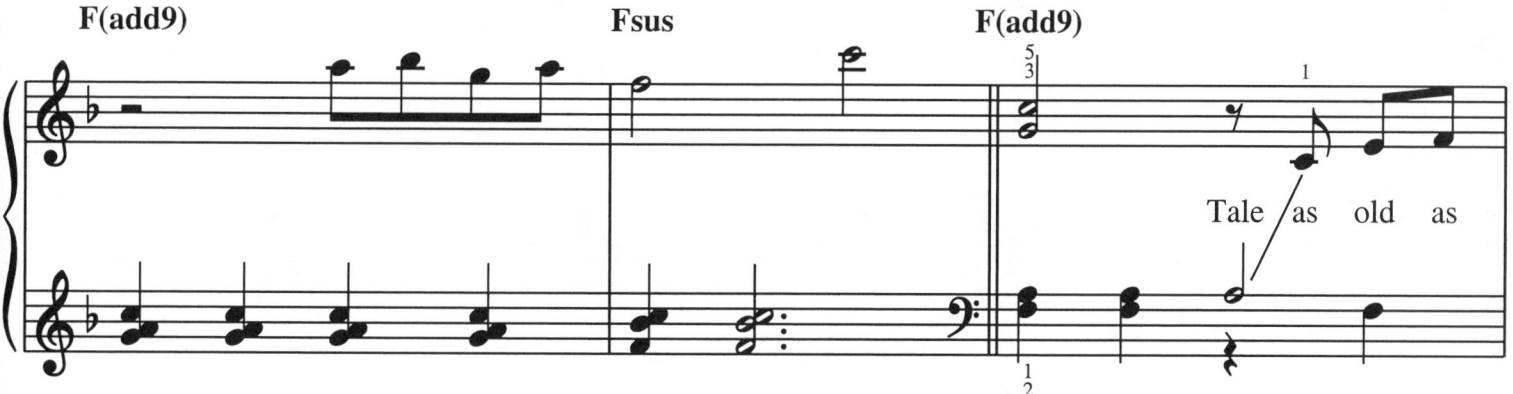

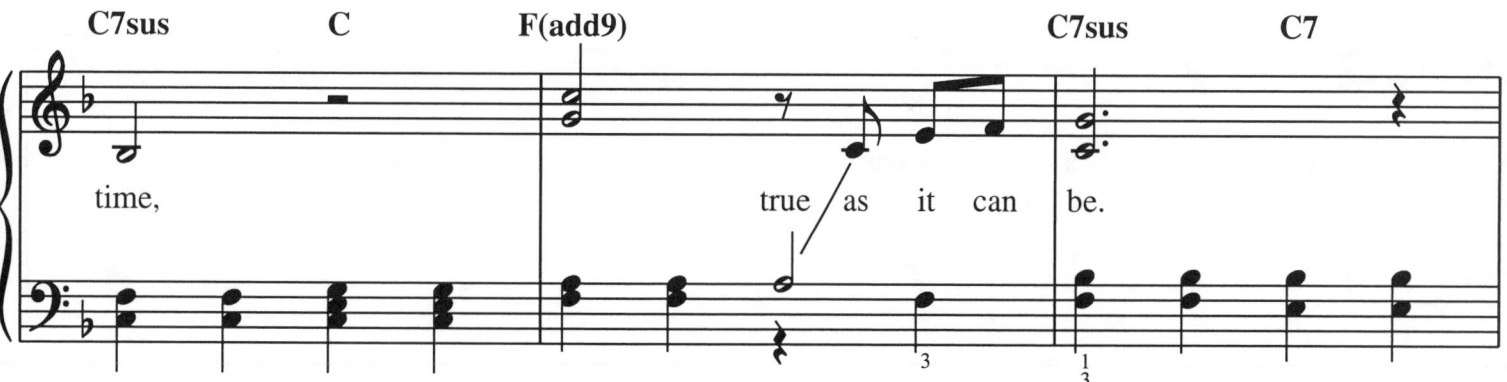

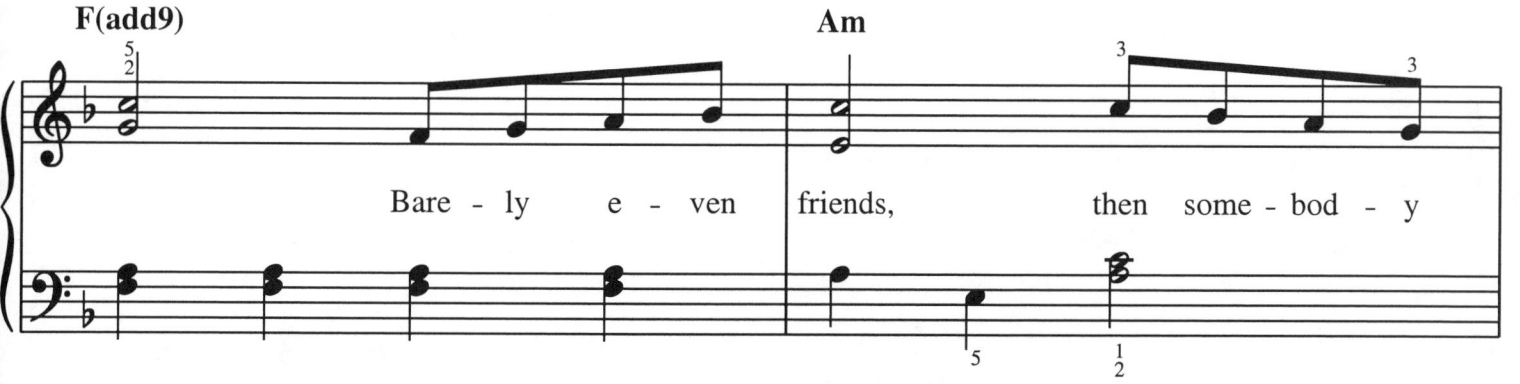

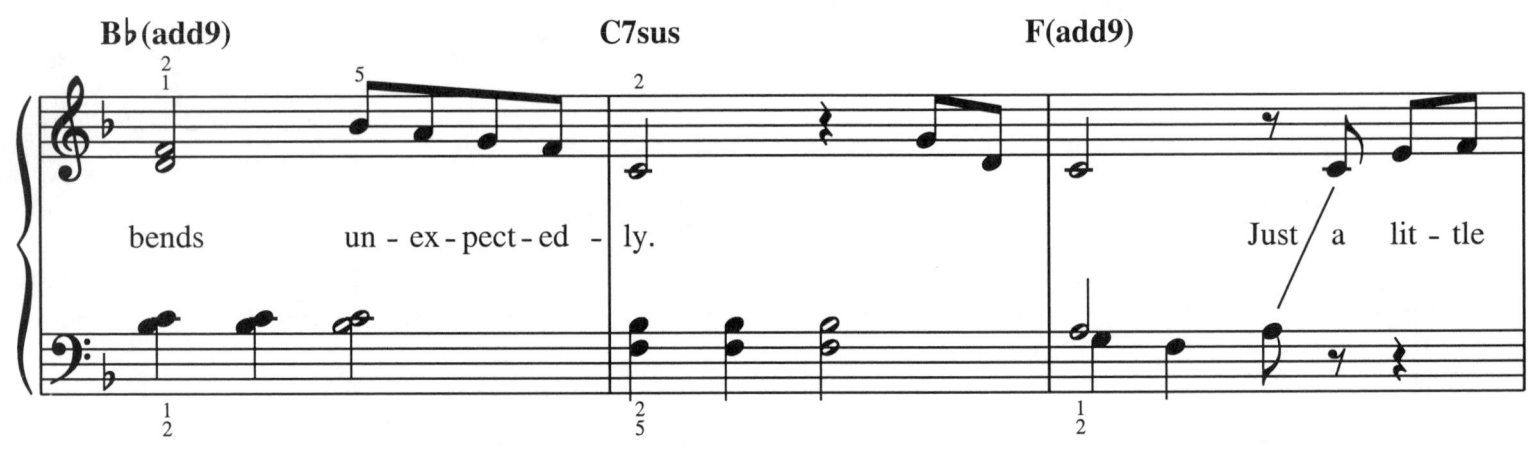

bends   un - ex - pect - ed - ly.   Just a lit - tle

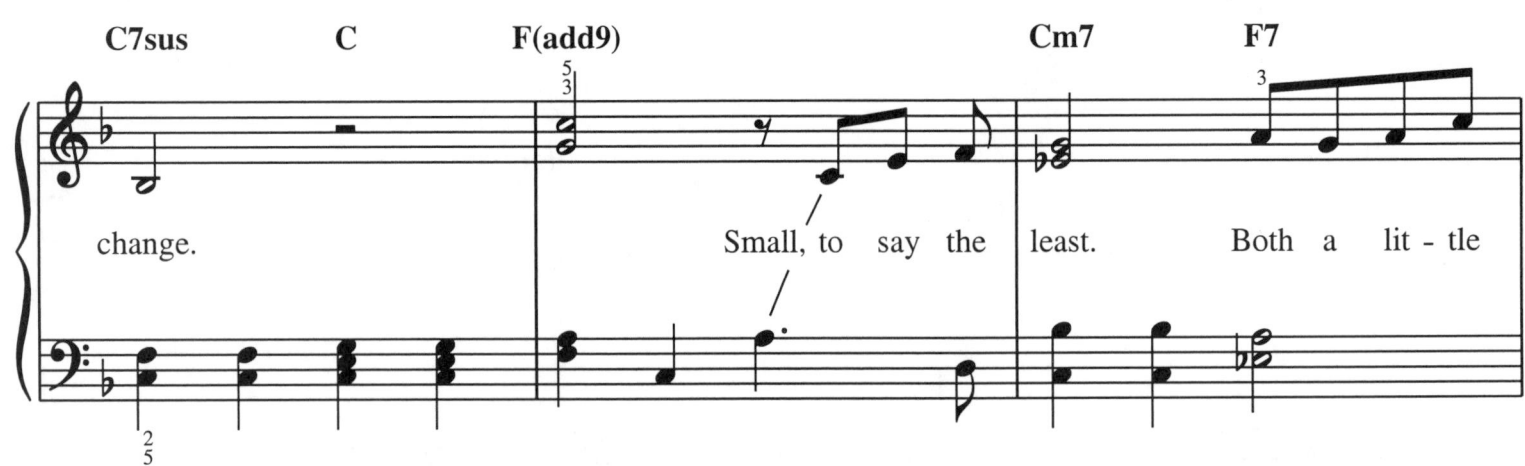

change.   Small, to say the least.   Both a lit - tle

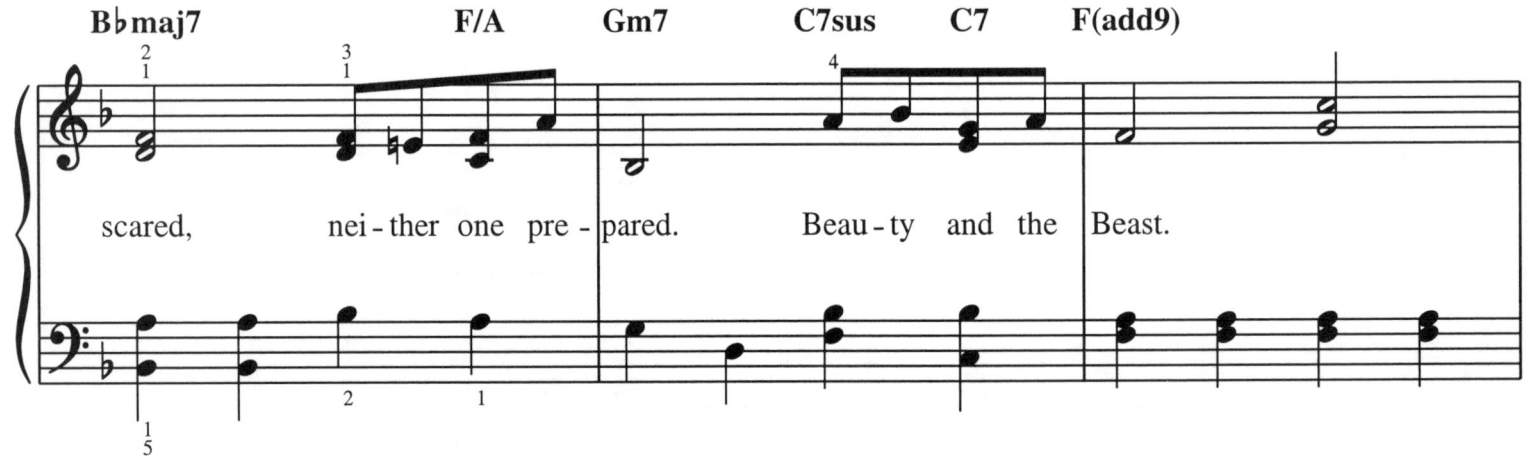

scared,   nei - ther one pre - pared.   Beau - ty and the Beast.

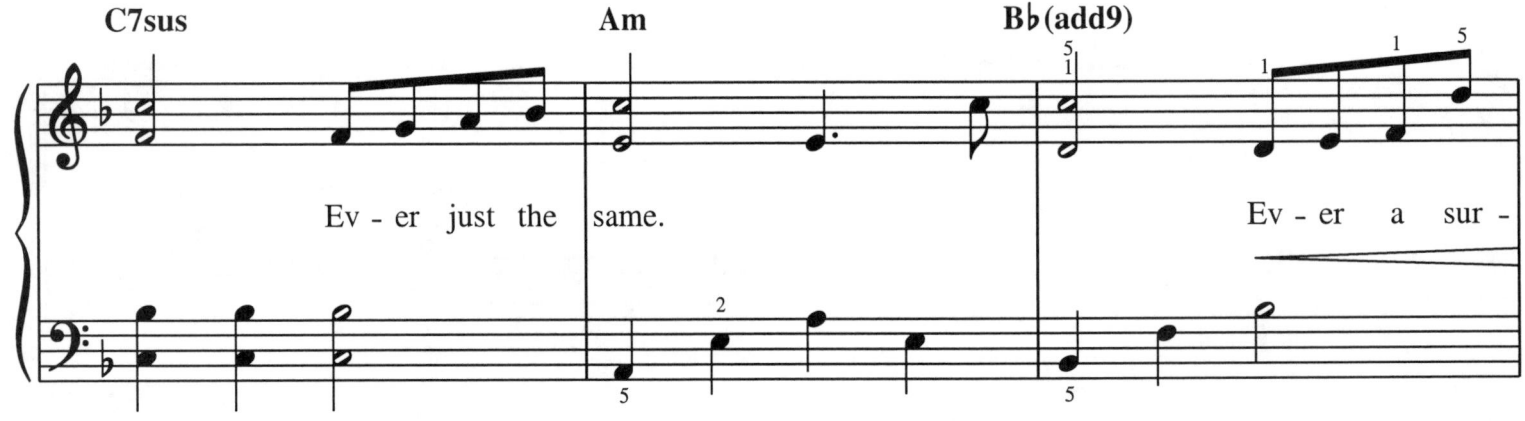

Ev - er just the same.   Ev - er a sur -

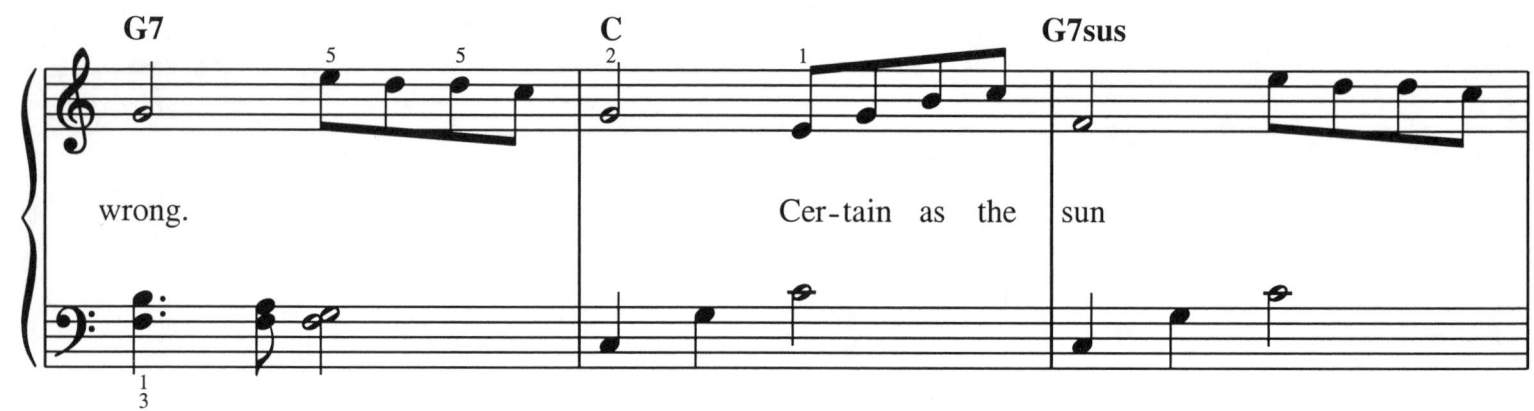

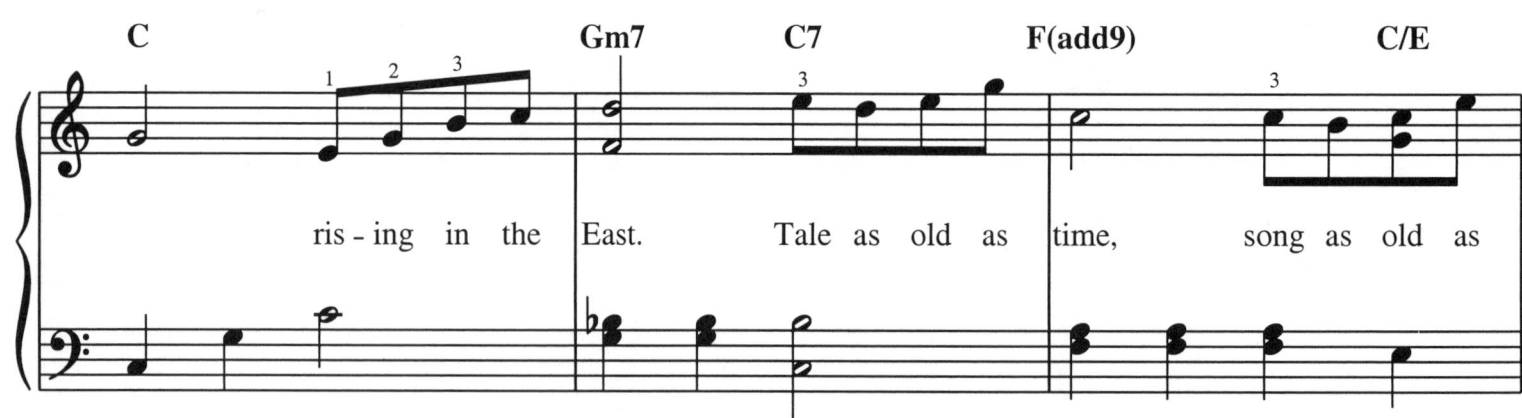

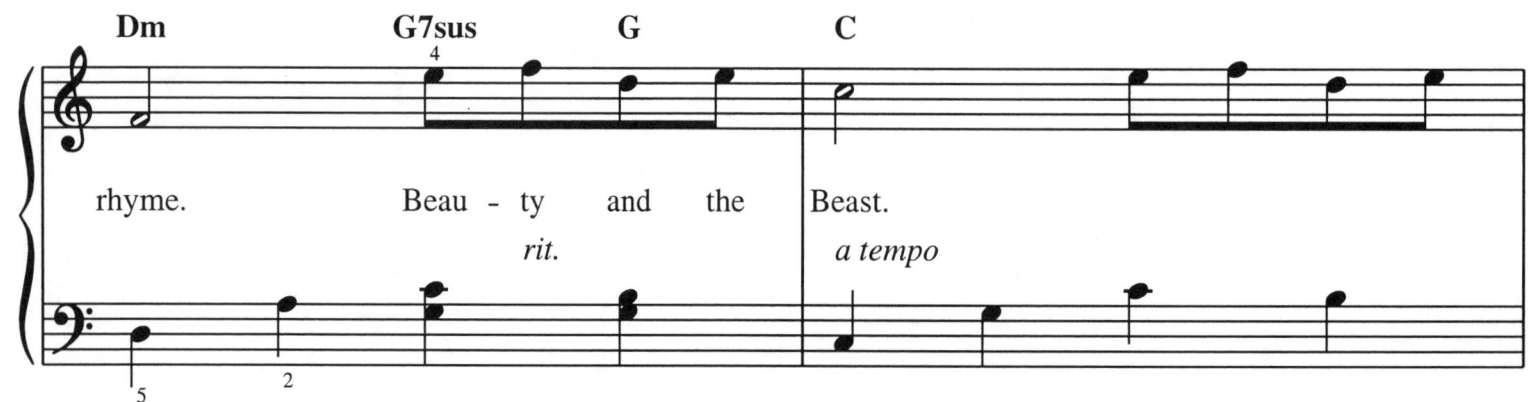

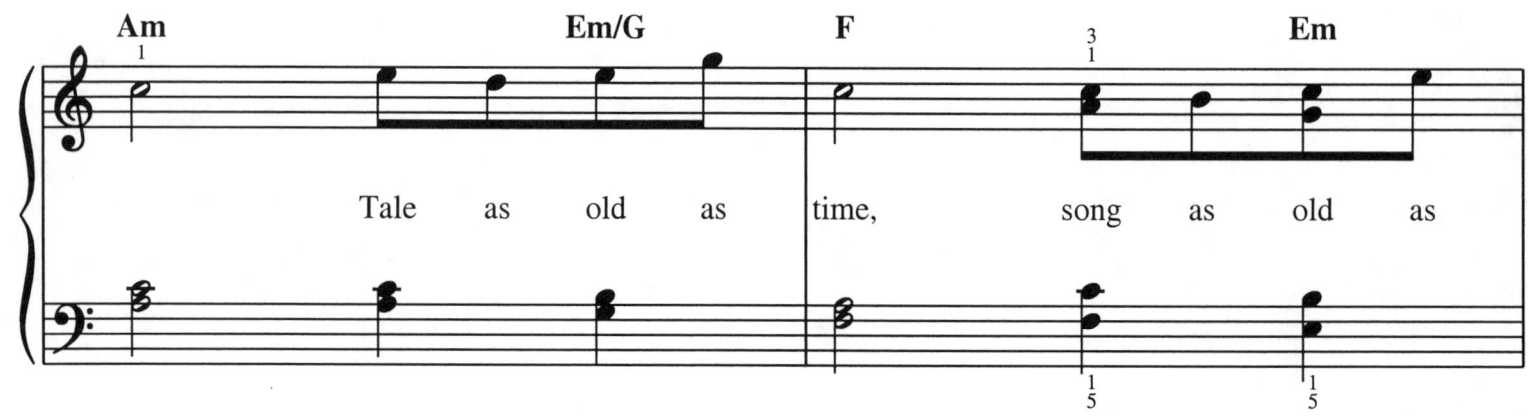

rhyme. Beau - ty and the Beast.

BIBBIDI-BOBBIDI-BOO
(The Magic Song)
from Walt Disney's CINDERELLA

Words by JERRY LIVINGSTON
Music by MACK DAVID and AL HOFFMAN

Sa - la - ga - doo - la men-chic-ka boo - la bib - bi - di - bob - bi - di - boo.

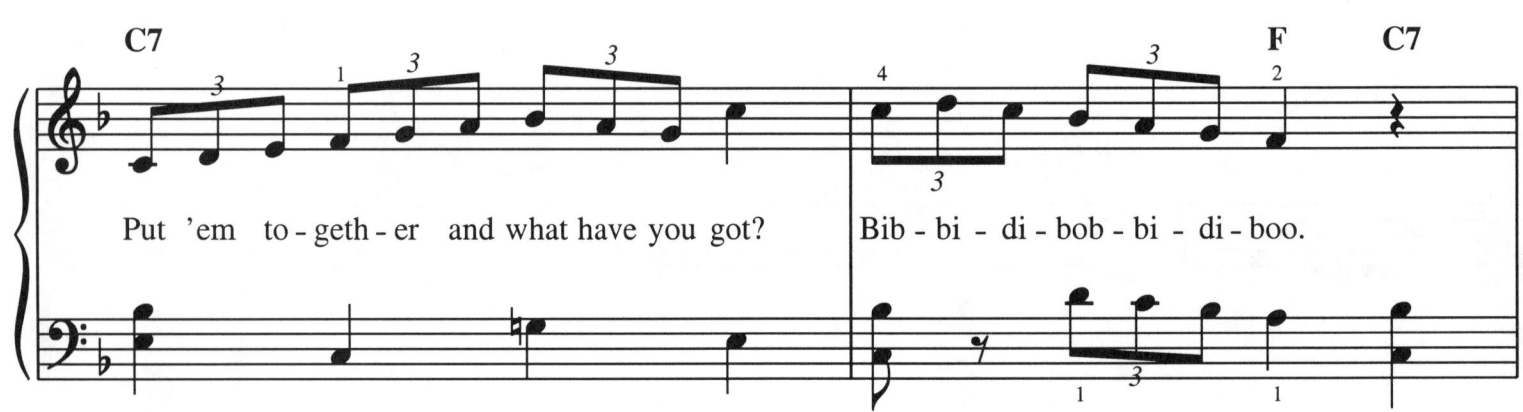

Put 'em to-geth - er and what have you got? Bib - bi - di - bob - bi - di - boo.

CHIM CHIM CHER-EE

from Walt Disney's MARY POPPINS

Words and Music by RICHARD M. SHERMAN
and ROBERT B. SHERMAN

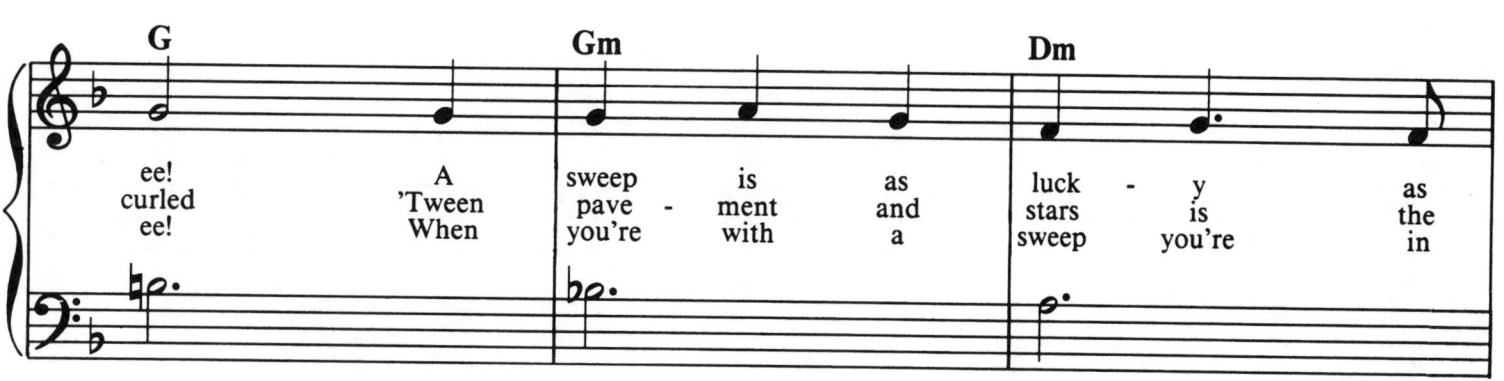

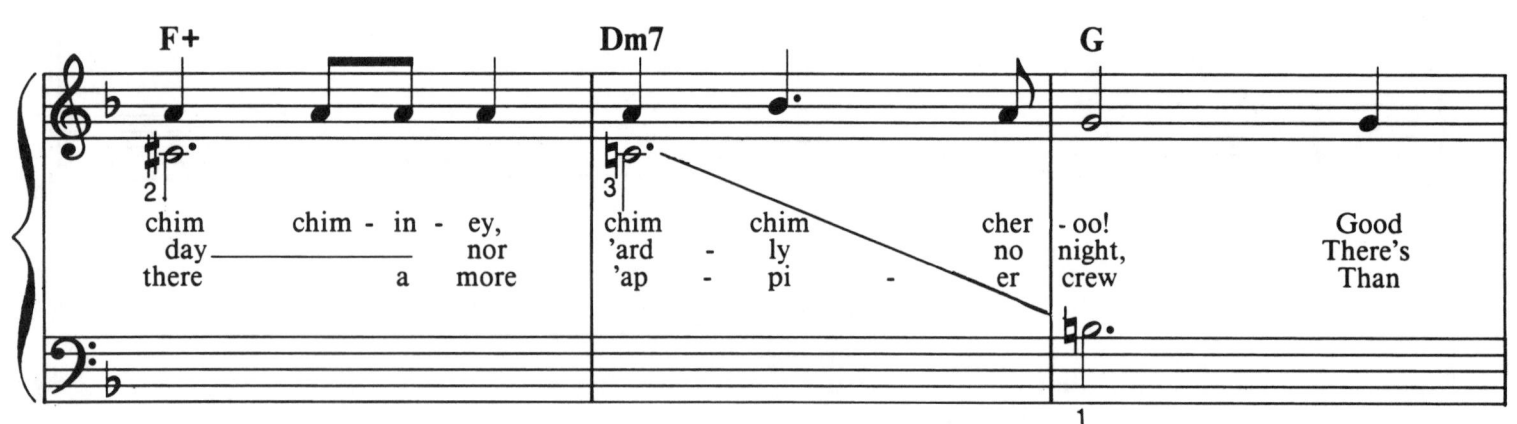

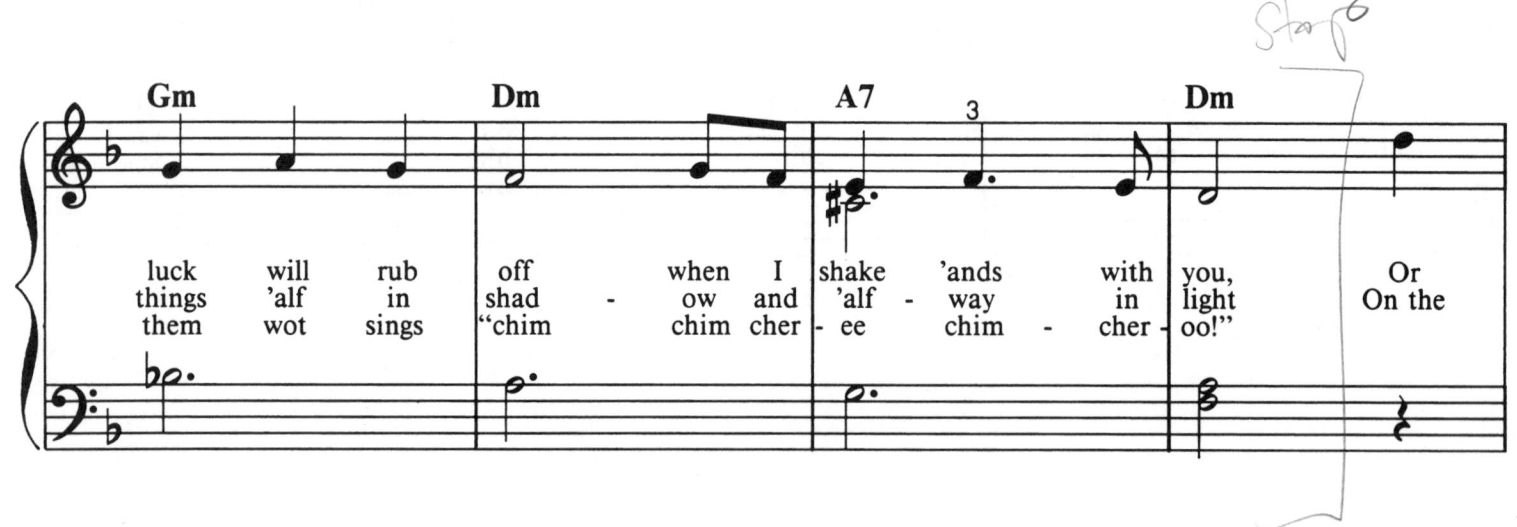

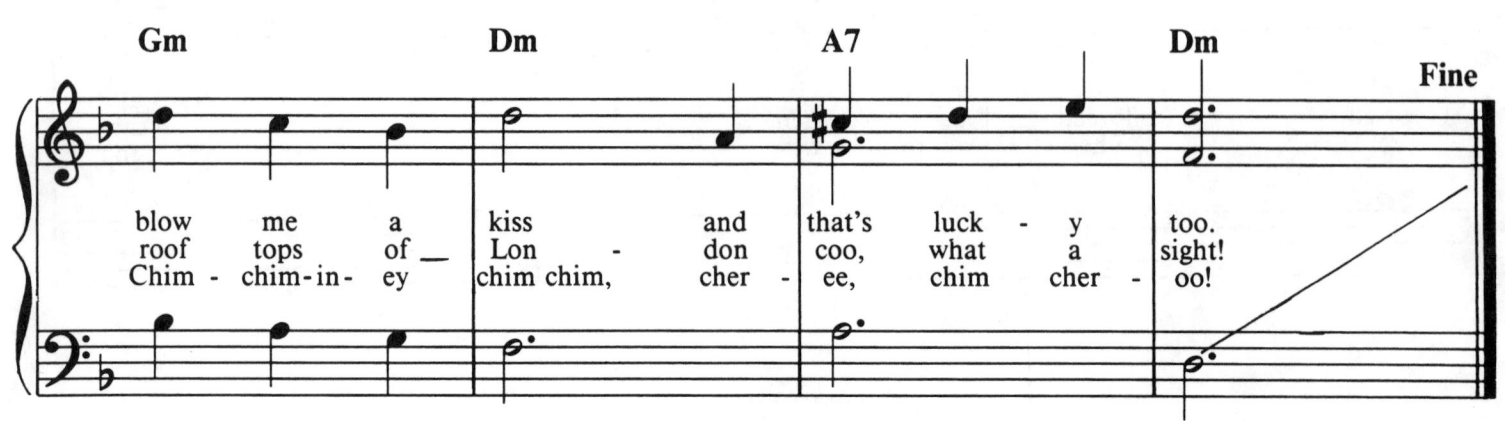

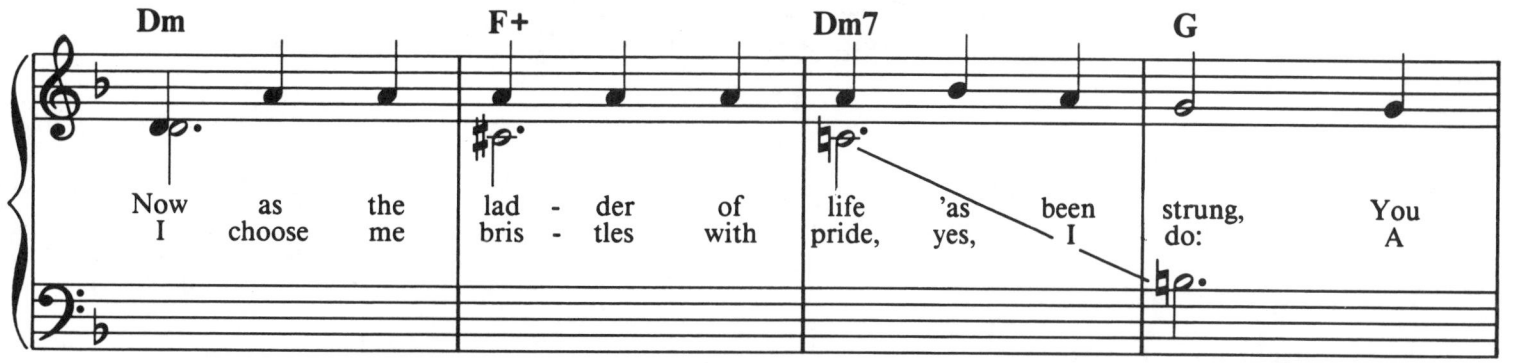

Now as the lad - der of life 'as been strung, You
I choose me bris - tles with pride, yes, I do: A

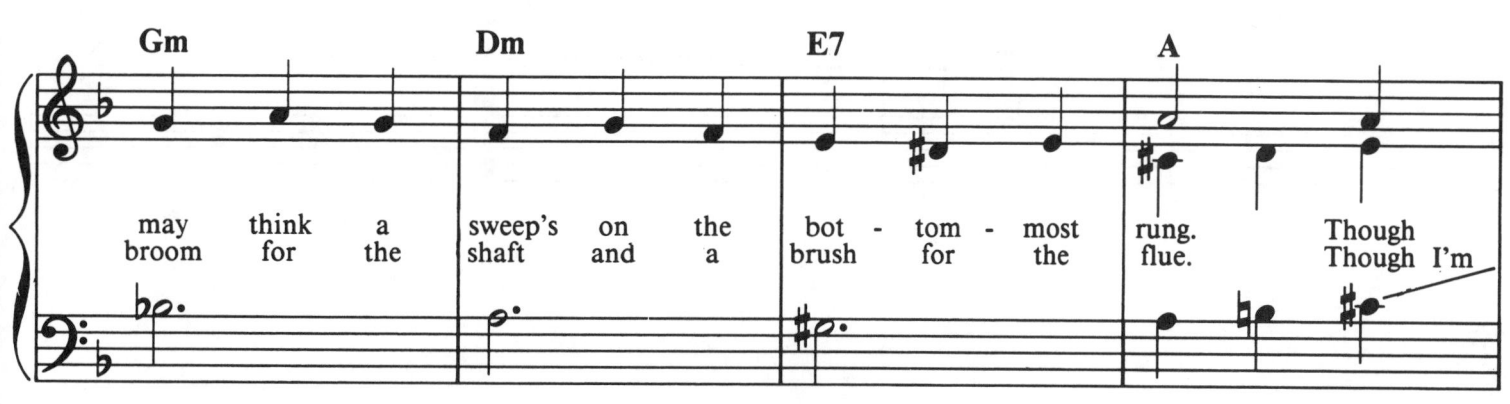

may think a sweep's on the bot - tom - most rung. Though
broom for the shaft and a brush for the flue. Though I'm

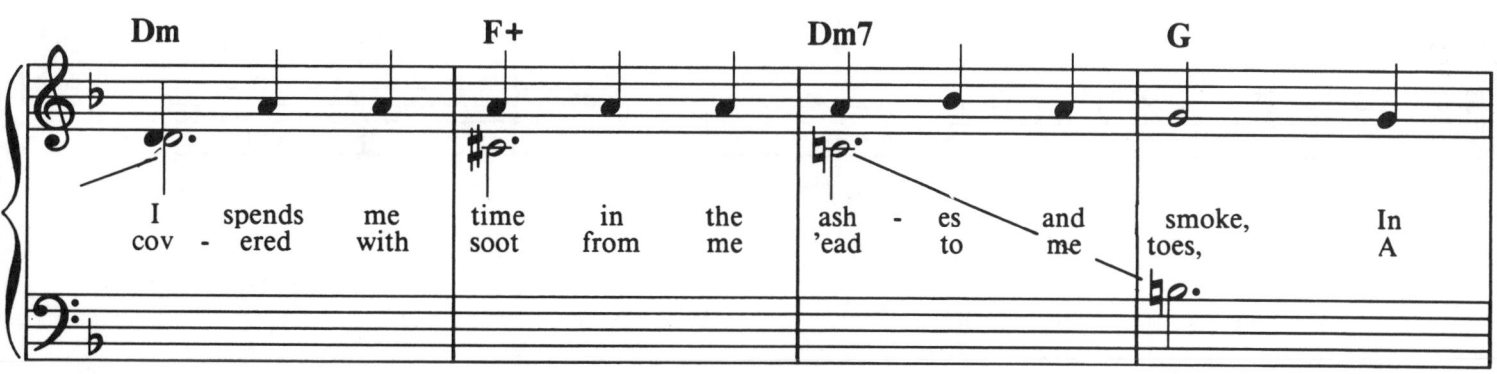

I spends me time in the ash - es and smoke, In
cov - ered with soot from me 'ead to me toes, A

this 'ole wide world there's no 'ap - pi - er bloke.
sweep knows 'e's wel - come wher - ev - er 'e goes.

(D.C.)

DO-RE-MI
from THE SOUND OF MUSIC

Lyrics by OSCAR HAMMERSTEIN II
Music by RICHARD RODGERS

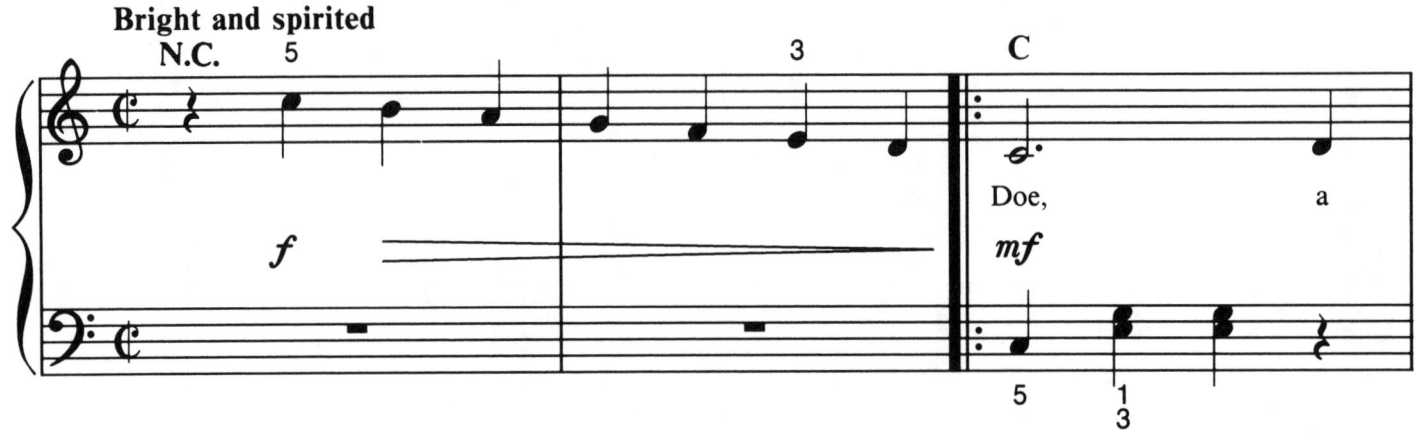

Doe, a

deer, a fe - male deer;

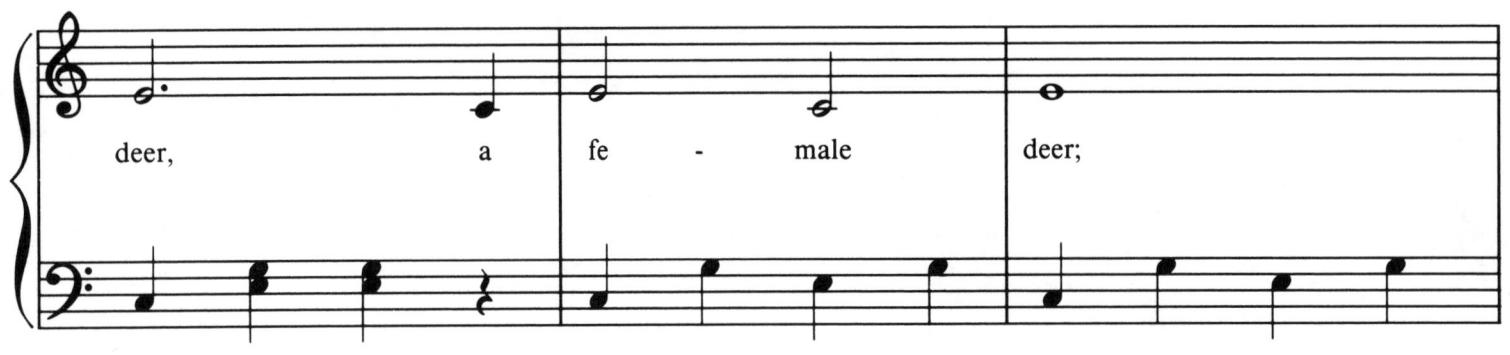

Ray, a drop of gold - en sun; _____

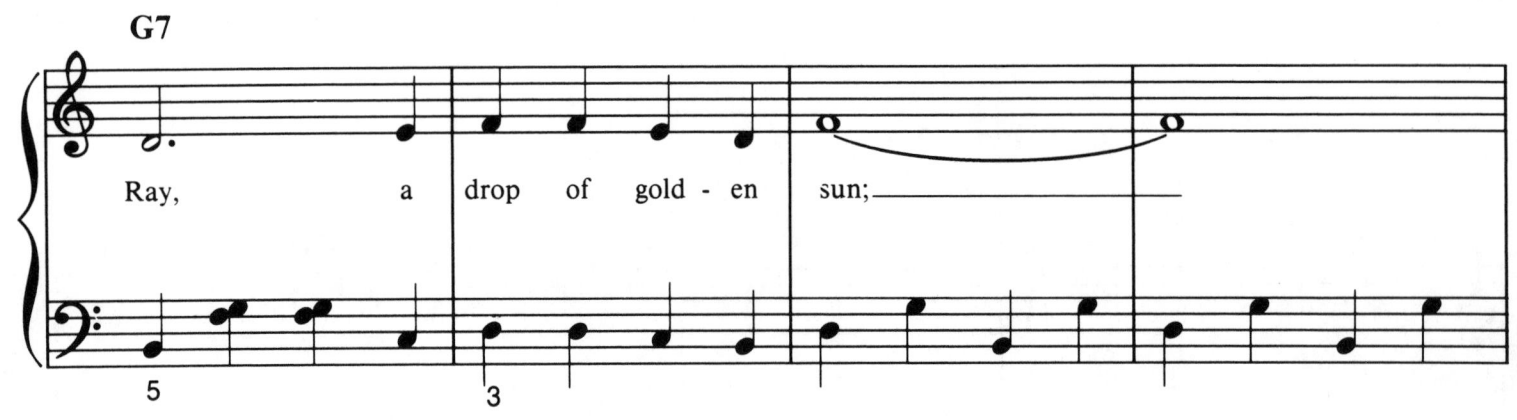

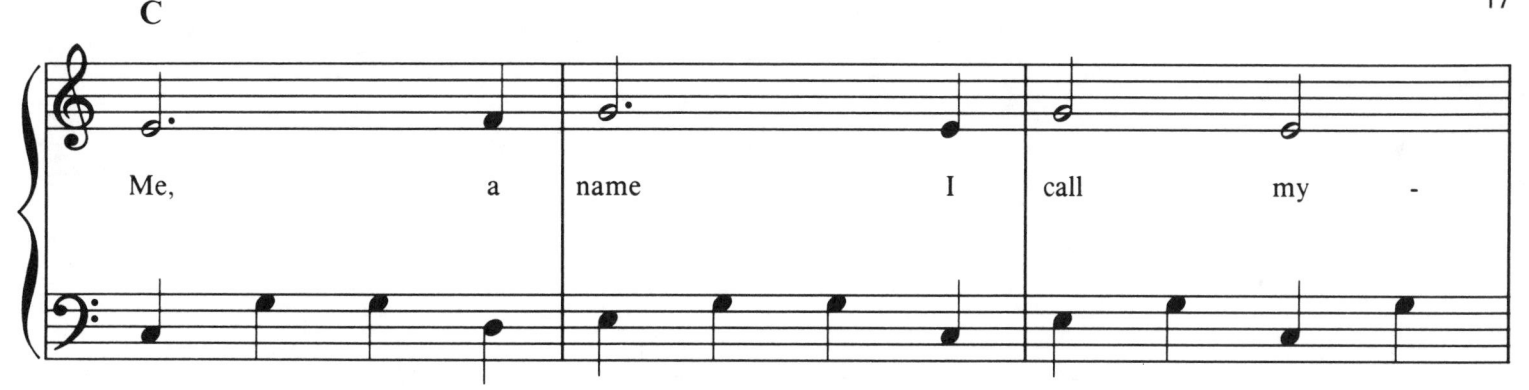

Me, a name I call my -

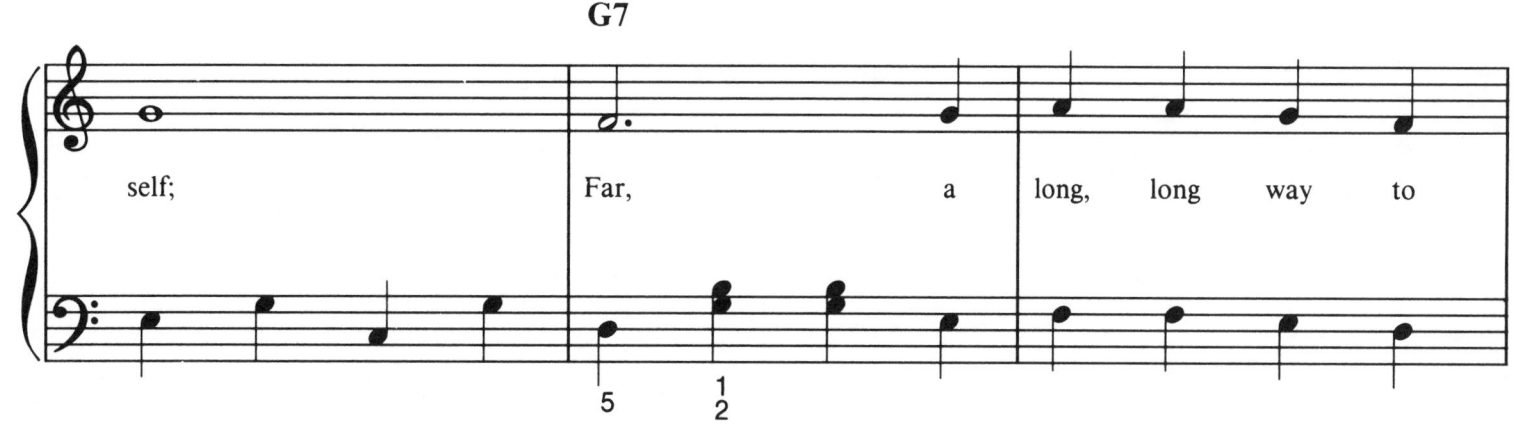

self; Far, a long, long way to

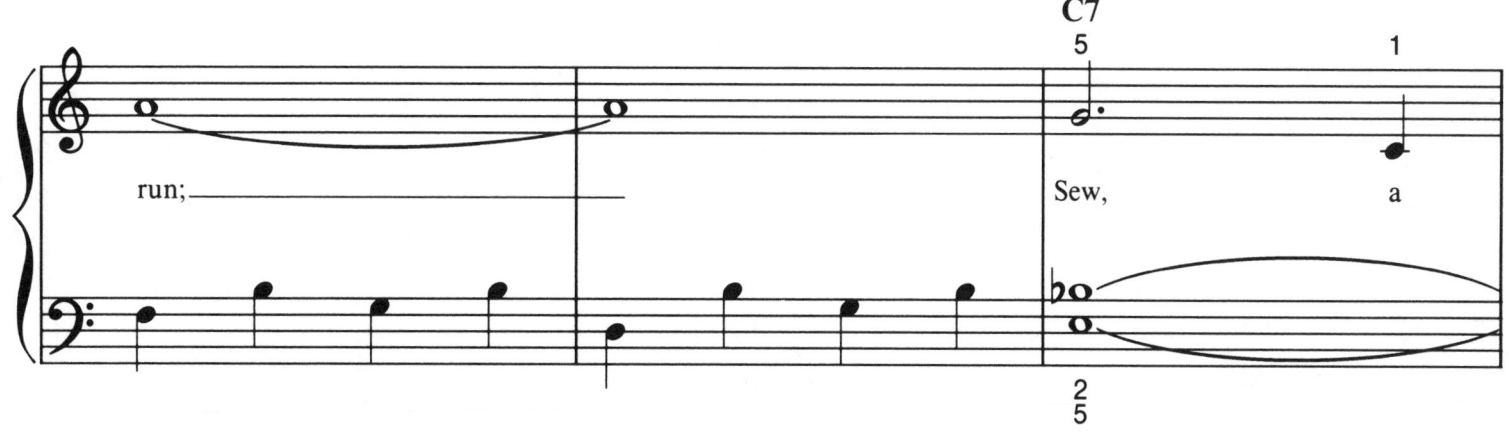

run;_____ Sew, a

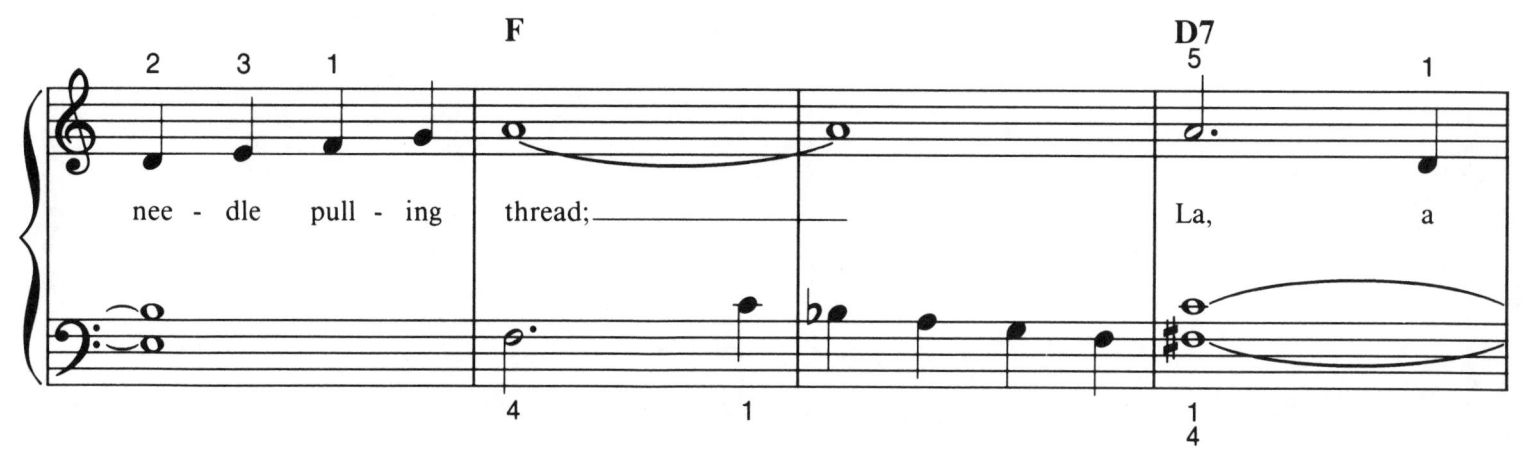

nee - dle pull - ing thread;_____ La, a

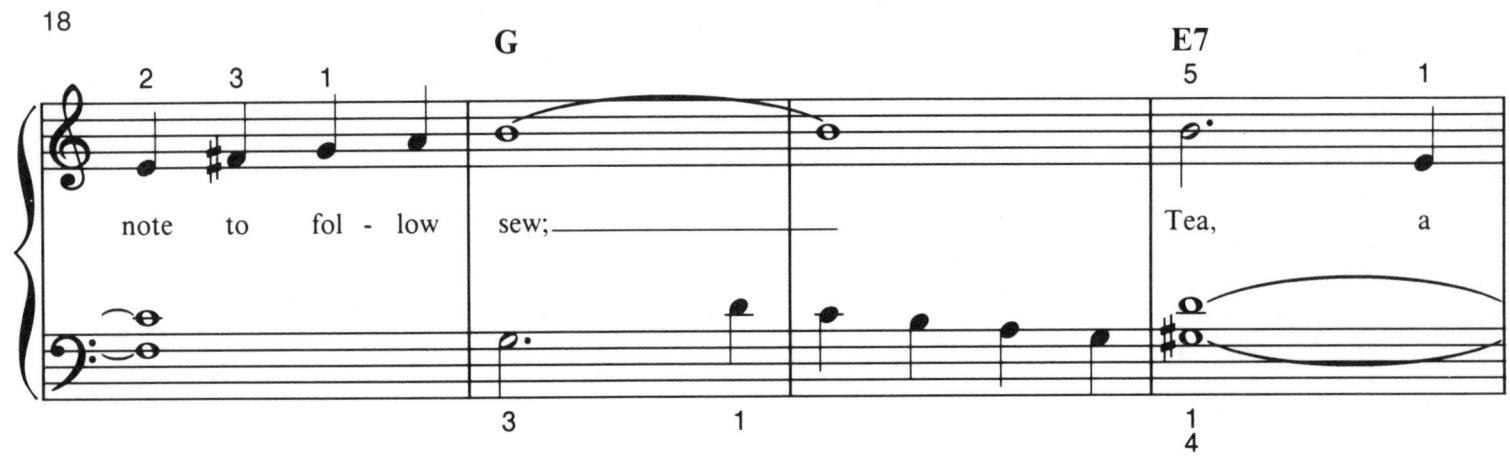

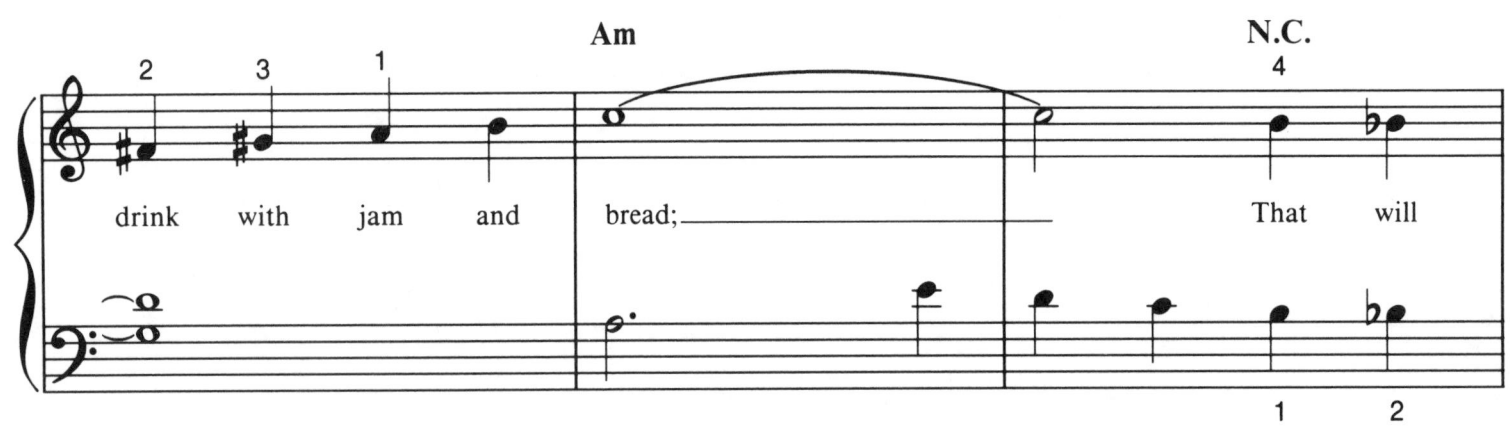

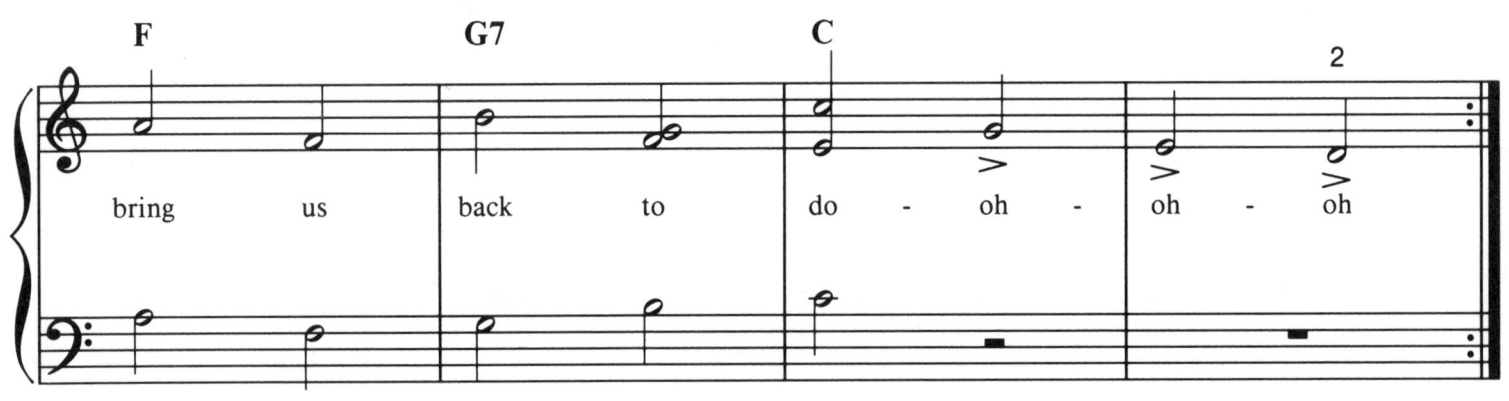

GARY, INDIANA
from Meredith Willson's THE MUSIC MAN

By MEREDITH WILLSON

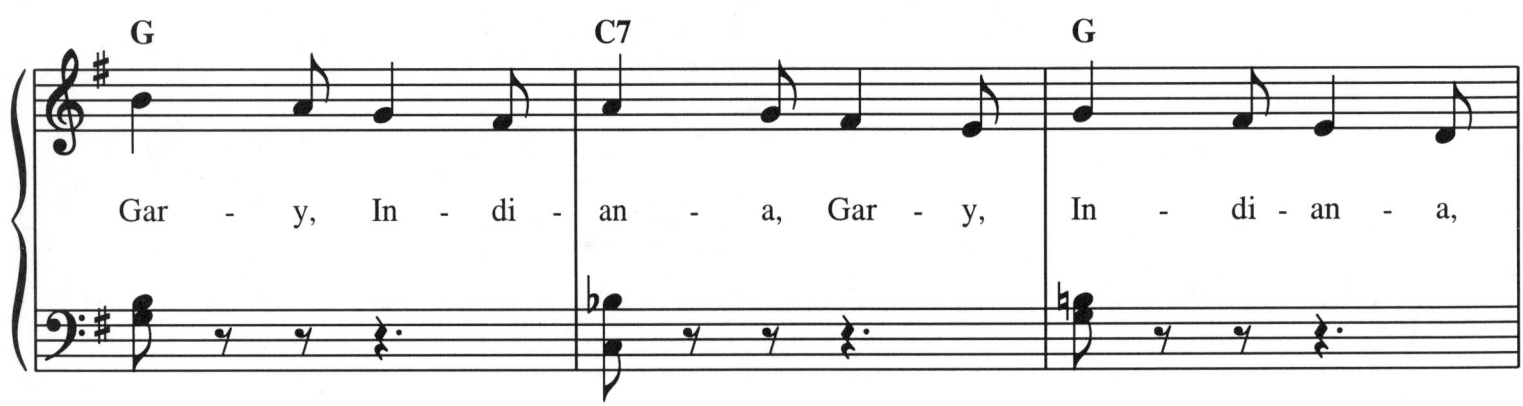

Gar - y, In - di - an - a, Gar - y, In - di - an - a,

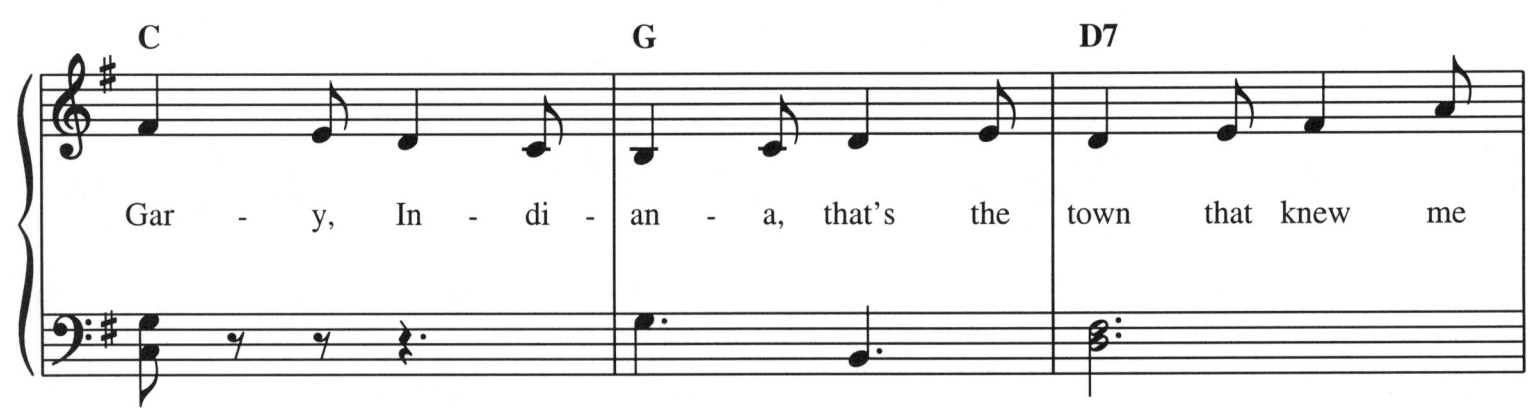

Gar - y, In - di - an - a, that's the town that knew me

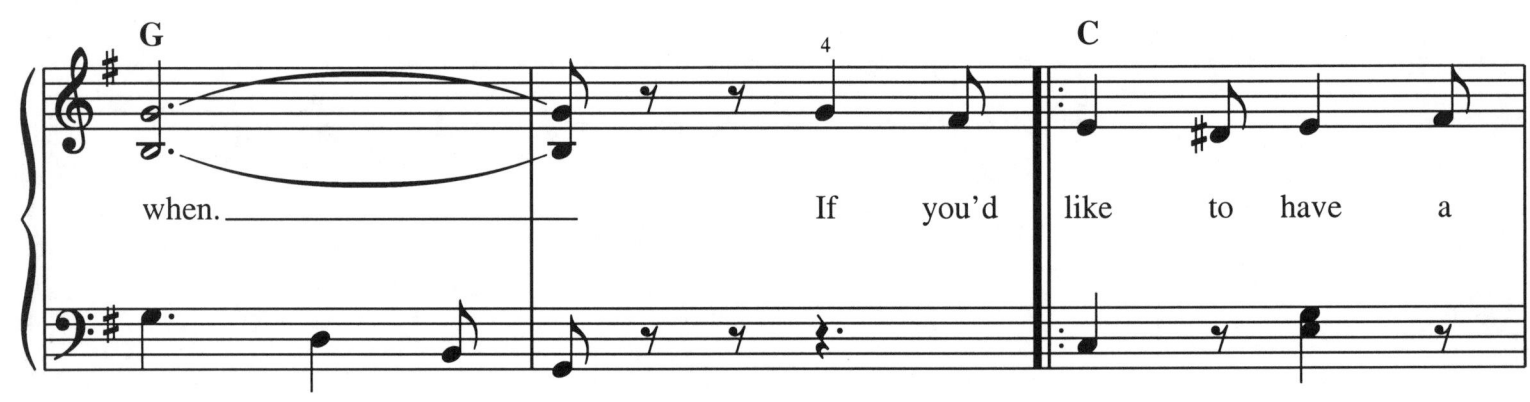

when. _____ If you'd like to have a

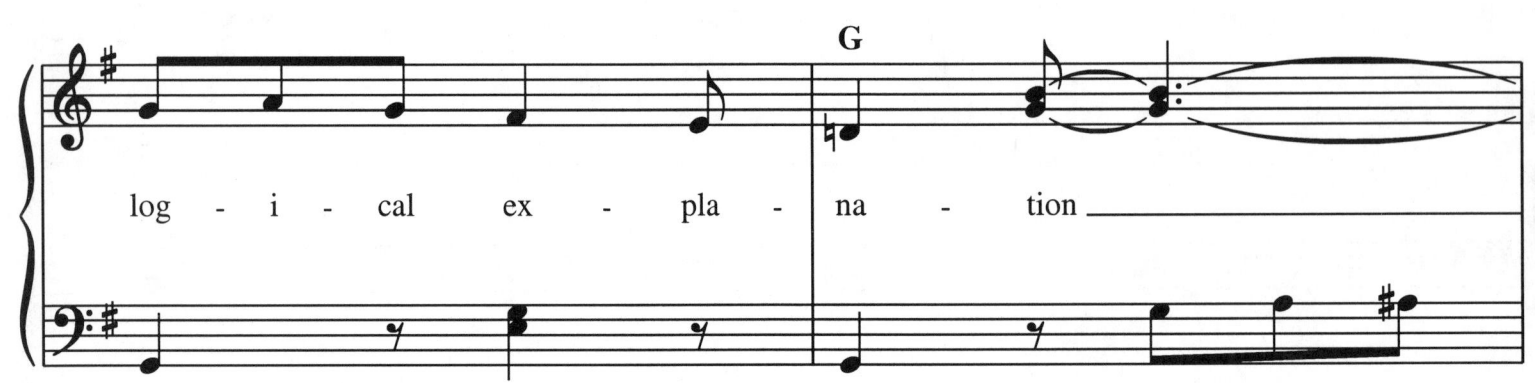

log - i - cal ex - pla - na - tion _____

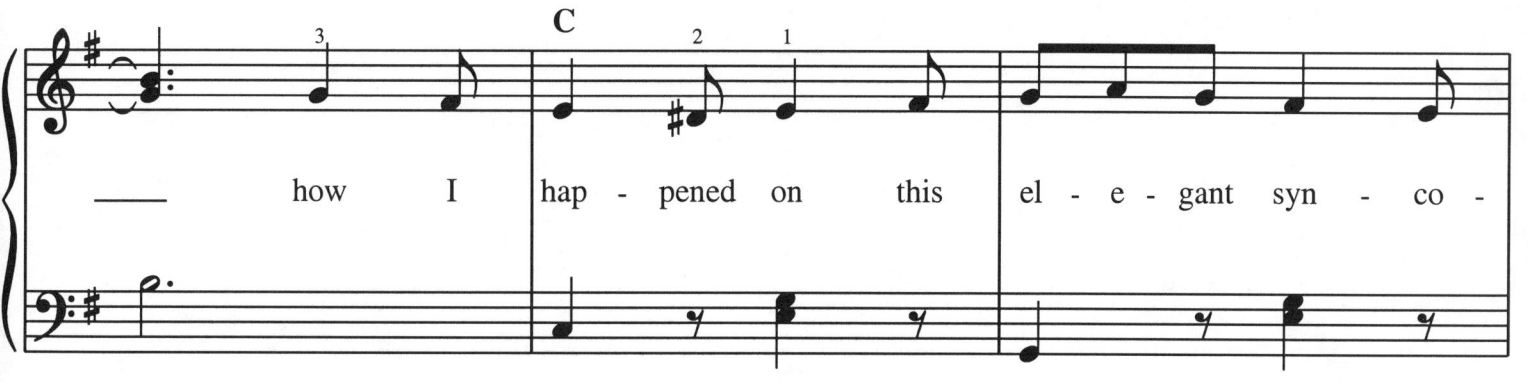

how I hap - pened on this el - e - gant syn - co -

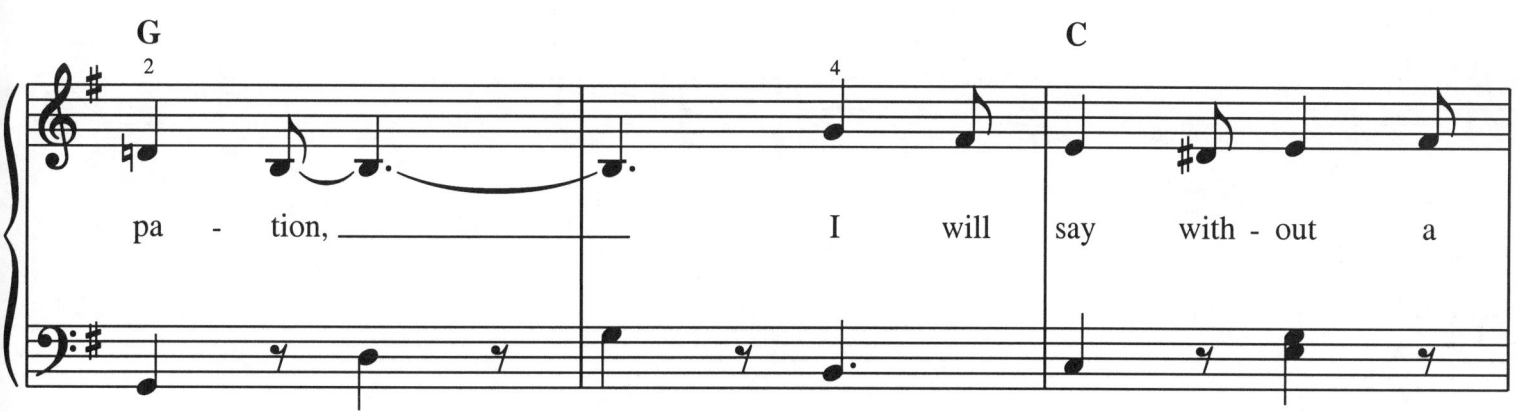

pa - tion, _____ I will say with - out a

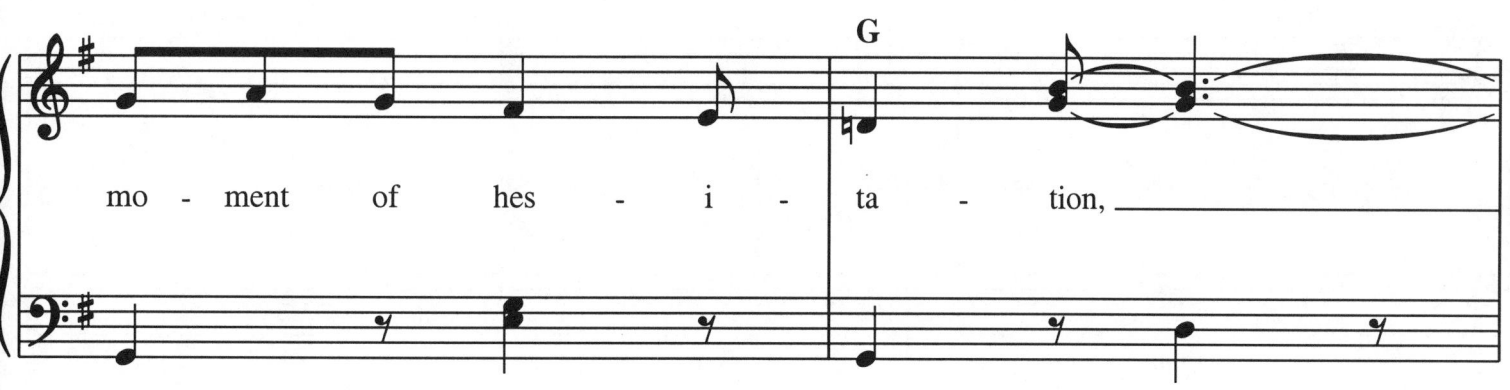

mo - ment of hes - i - ta - tion, _____

_____ there is just one place that can

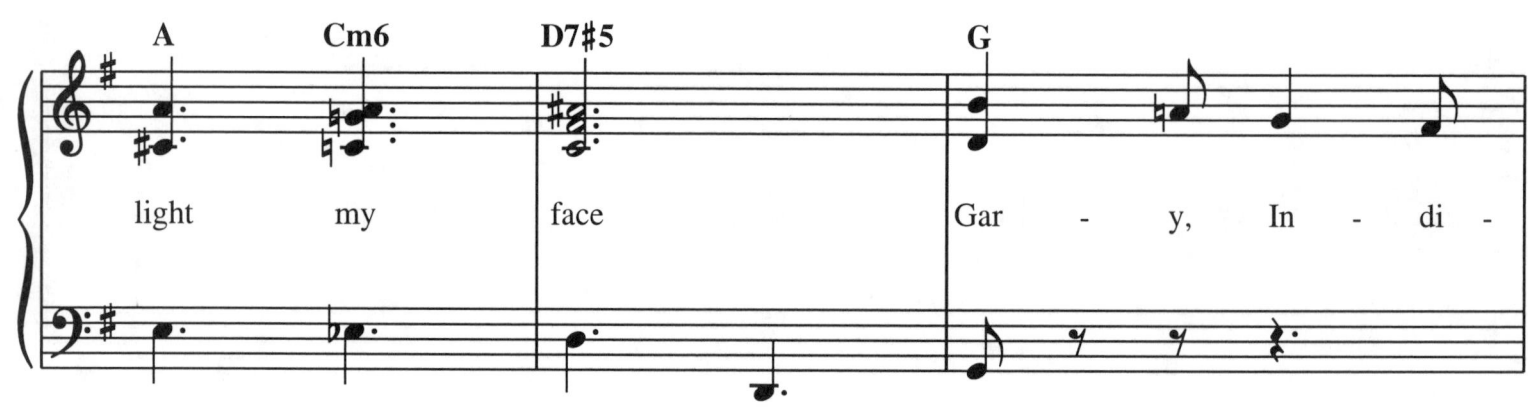

light my face Gar - y, In - di -

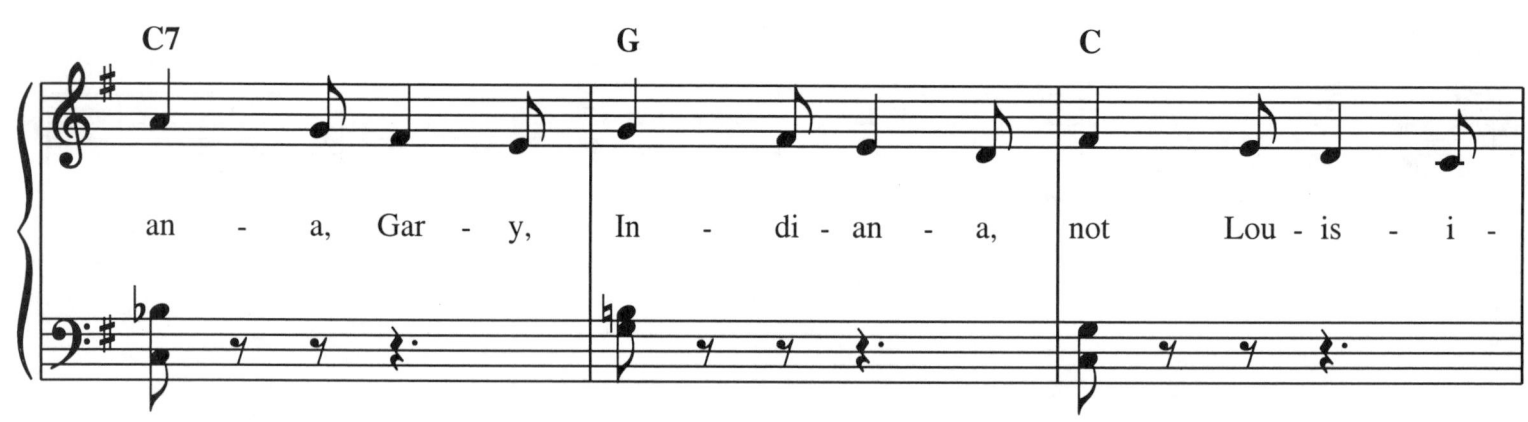

an - a, Gar - y, In - di - an - a, not Lou - is - i -

an - a, Par - is, France, New York or Rome, ___

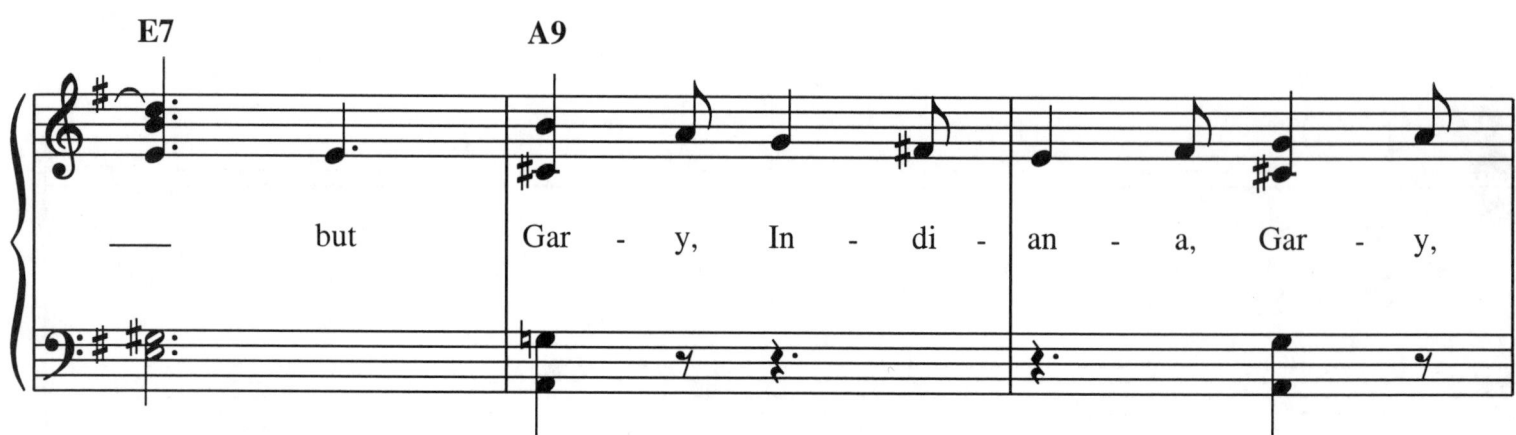

___ but Gar - y, In - di - an - a, Gar - y,

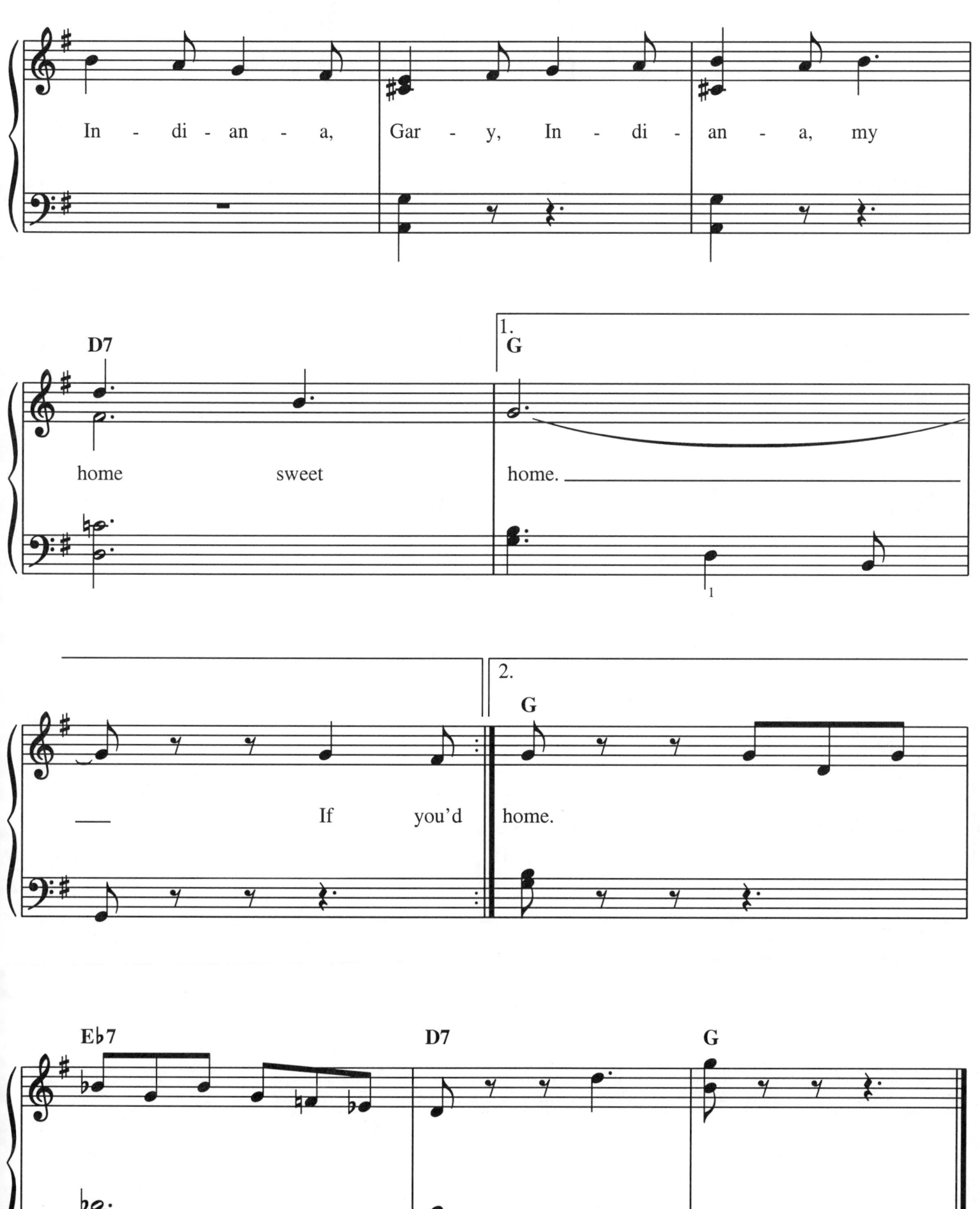

A DREAM IS A WISH
YOUR HEART MAKES

from Walt Disney's CINDERELLA

Words and Music by MACK DAVID,
AL HOFFMAN and JERRY LIVINGSTON

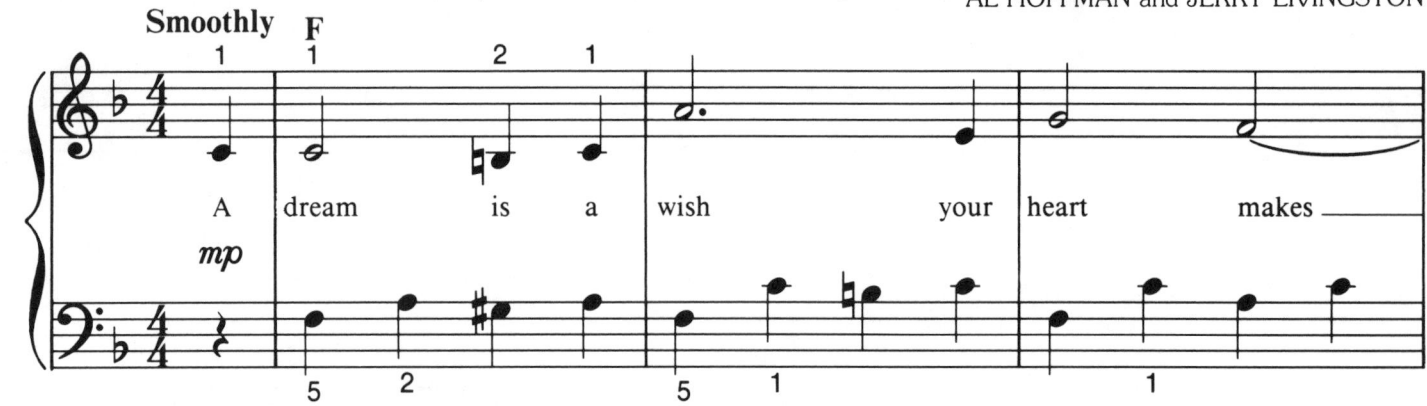

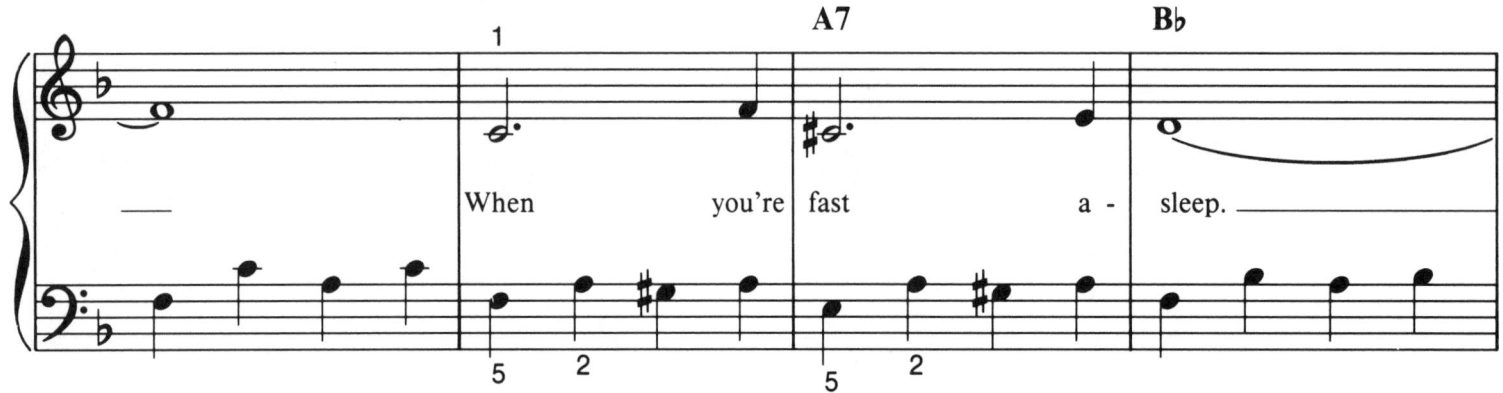

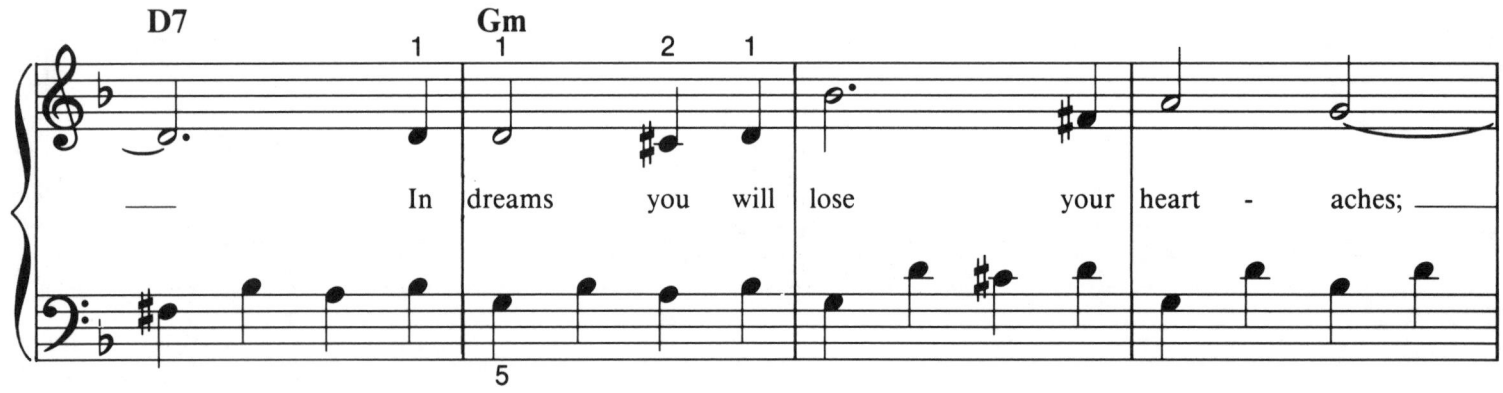

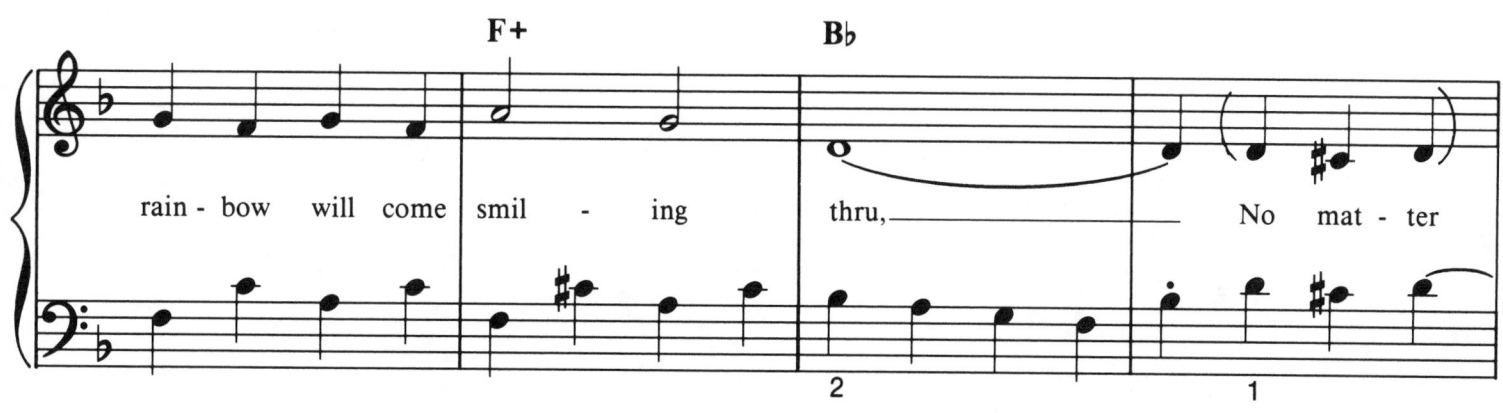

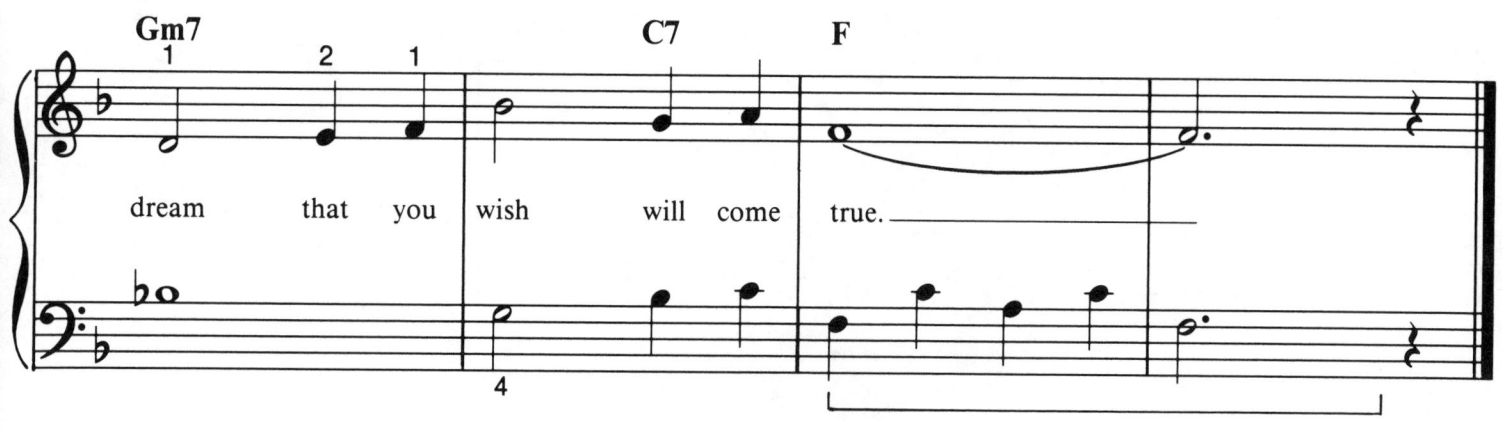

GETTING TO KNOW YOU

from THE KING AND I

Lyrics by OSCAR HAMMERSTEIN II
Music by RICHARD RODGERS

Moderately *(gracefully and not fast)*

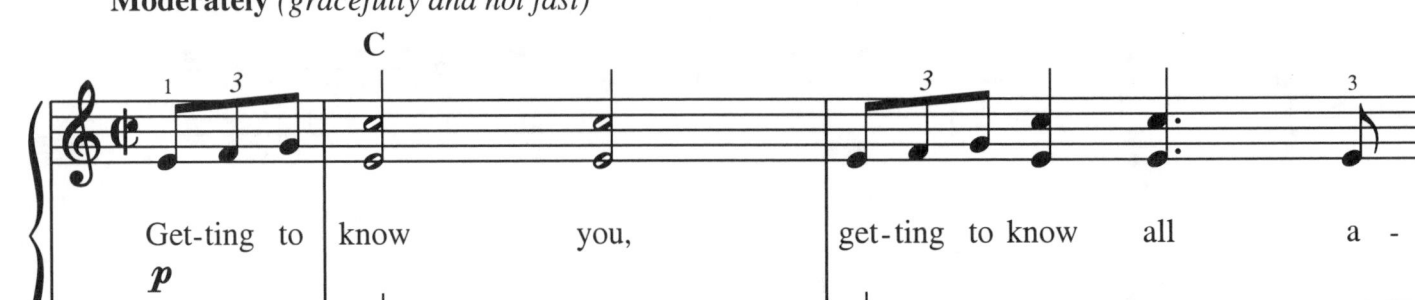

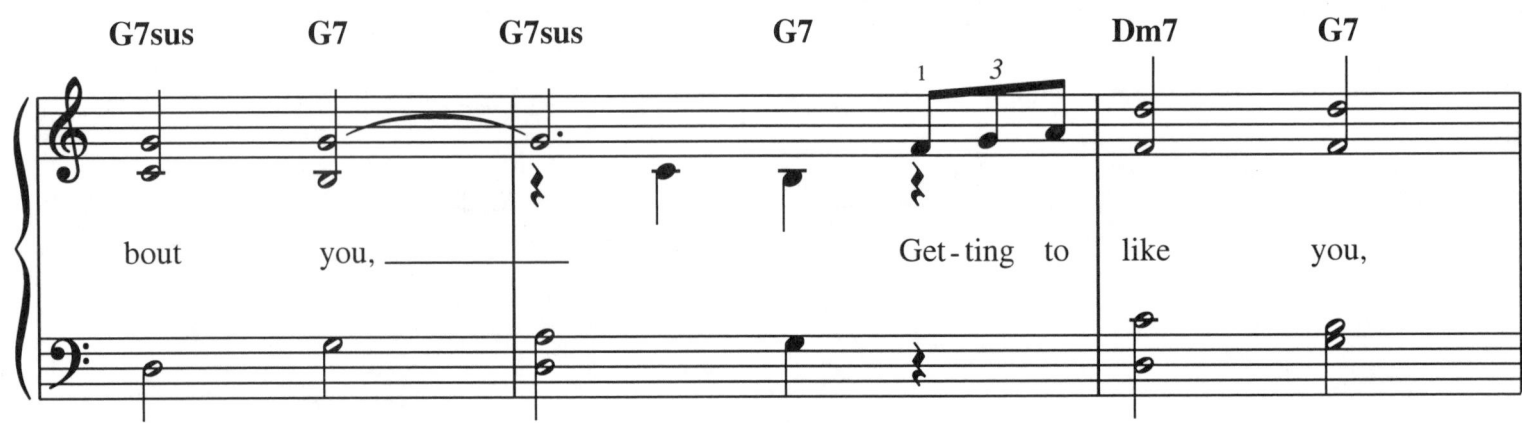

HAKUNA MATATA
from Walt Disney Pictures' THE LION KING

Music by ELTON JOHN
Lyrics by TIM RICE

Freely

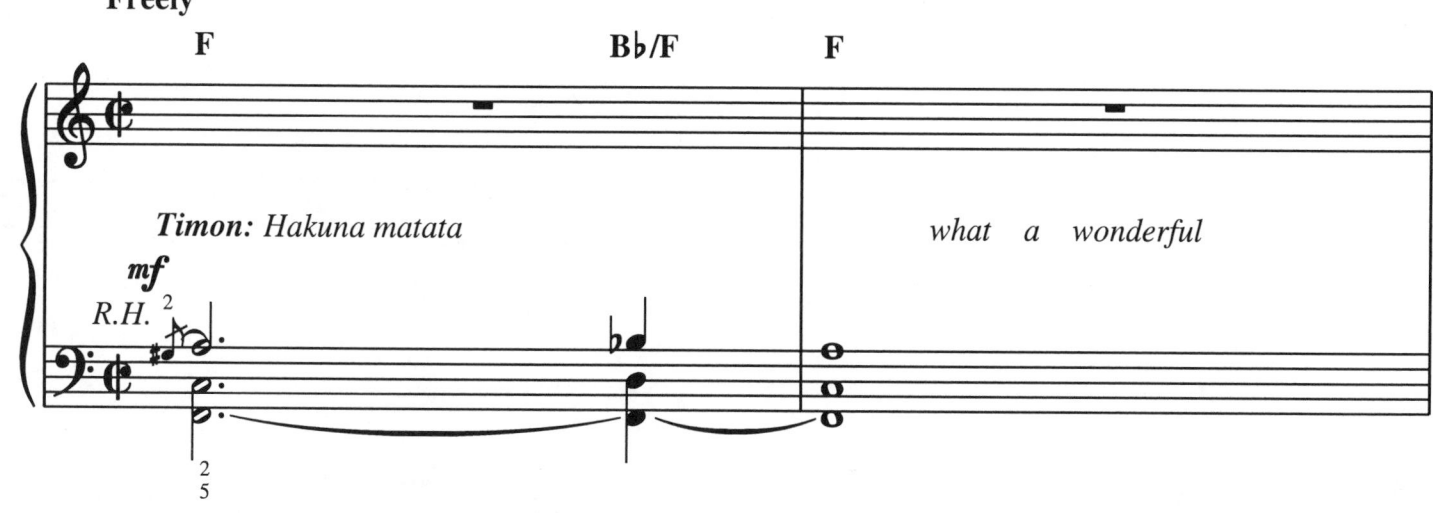

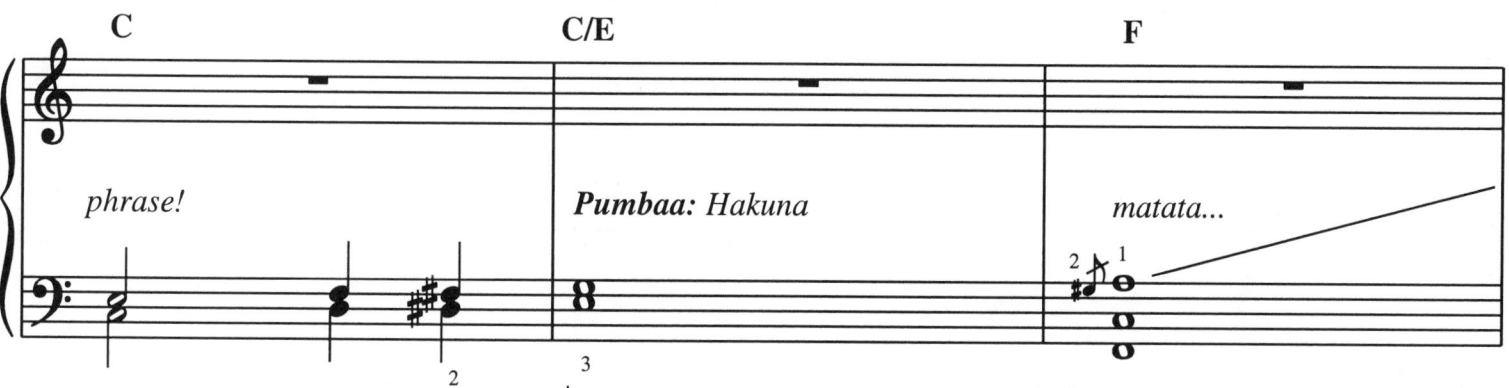

Bouncy shuffle

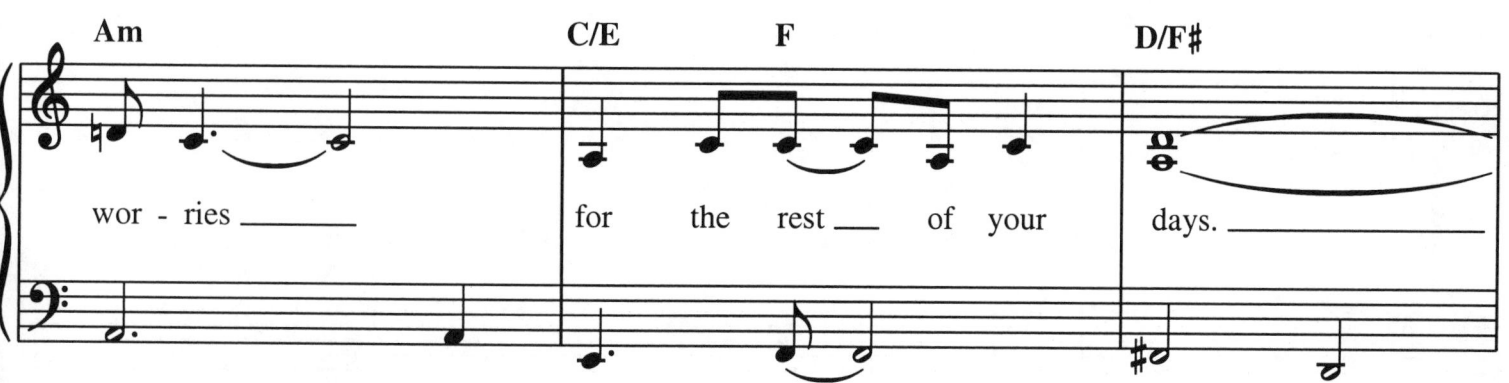

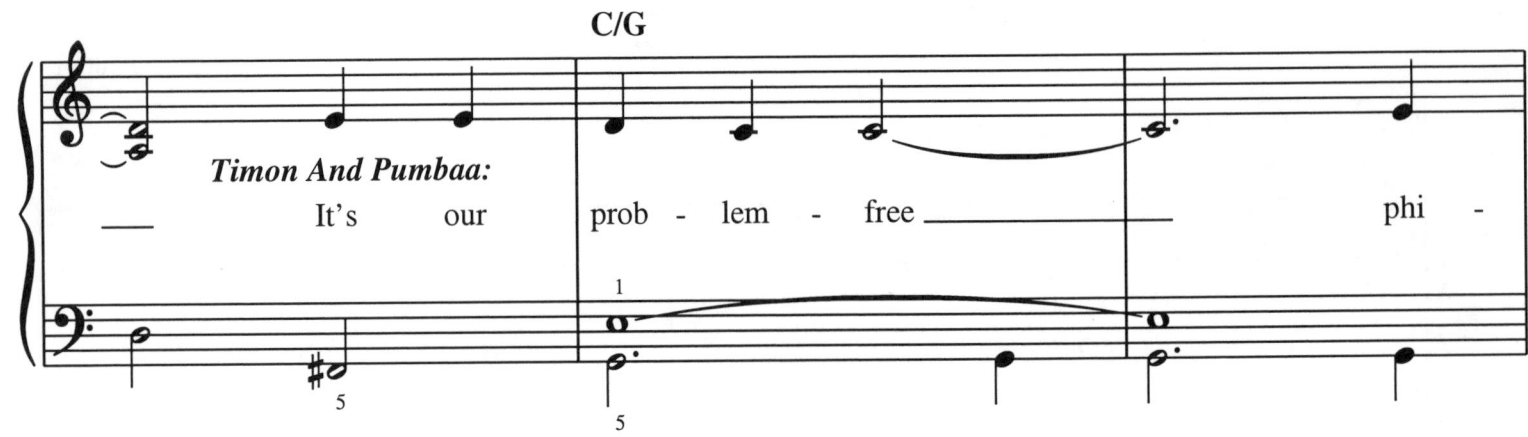

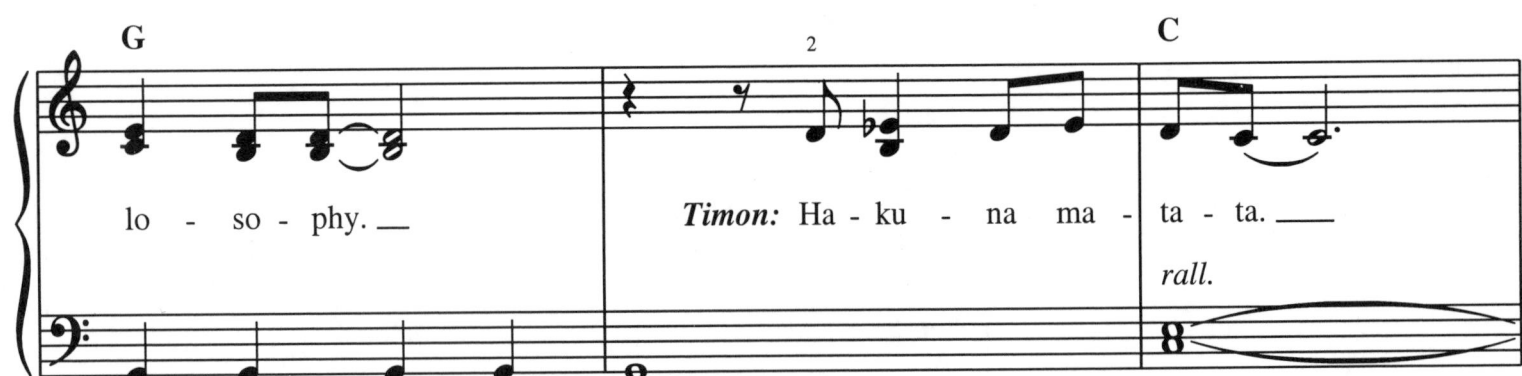

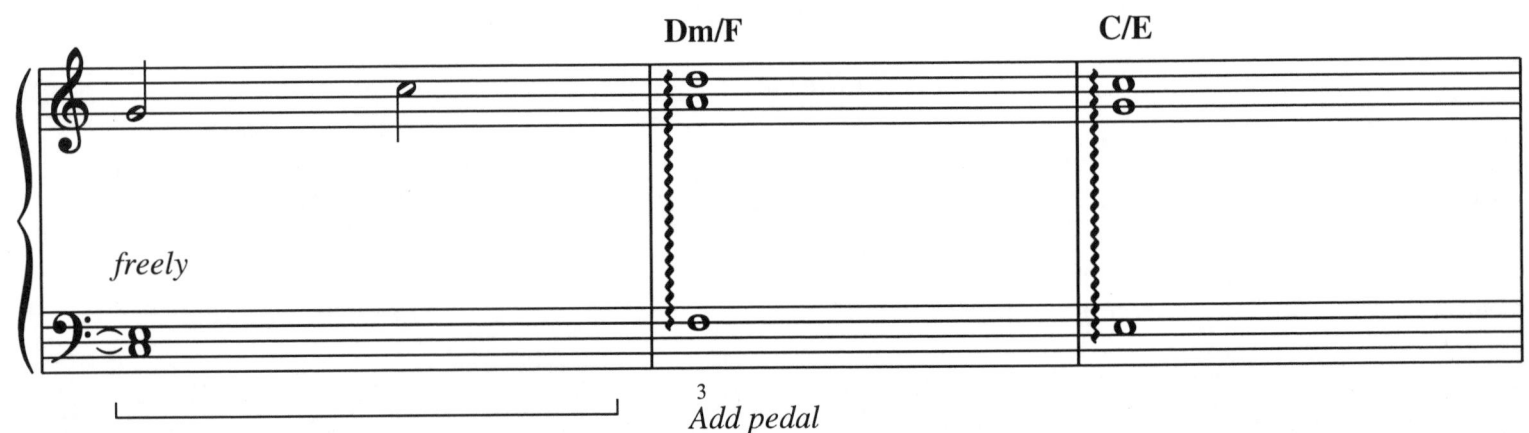

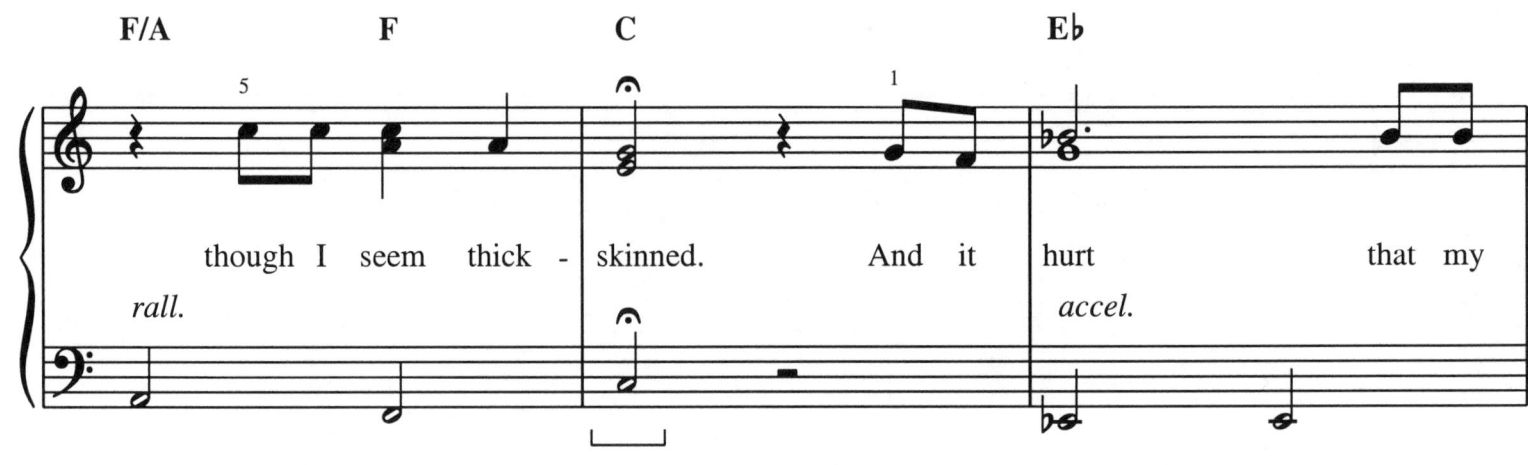

F/A   **F**   **C**   **E♭**

though I seem thick - skinned. And it hurt that my

rall.   *accel.*

F   **G**   **G7sus**

friends nev - er stood down - wind!

(Spoken:) And, oh, ___ the

rit.

C   **F/C** **C**   **G**   **C/G**

Timon: **Pumbaa:**   **Timon:**

shame! He was a - shamed! Thought of chang-in' my name! Oh, what's in a

a tempo

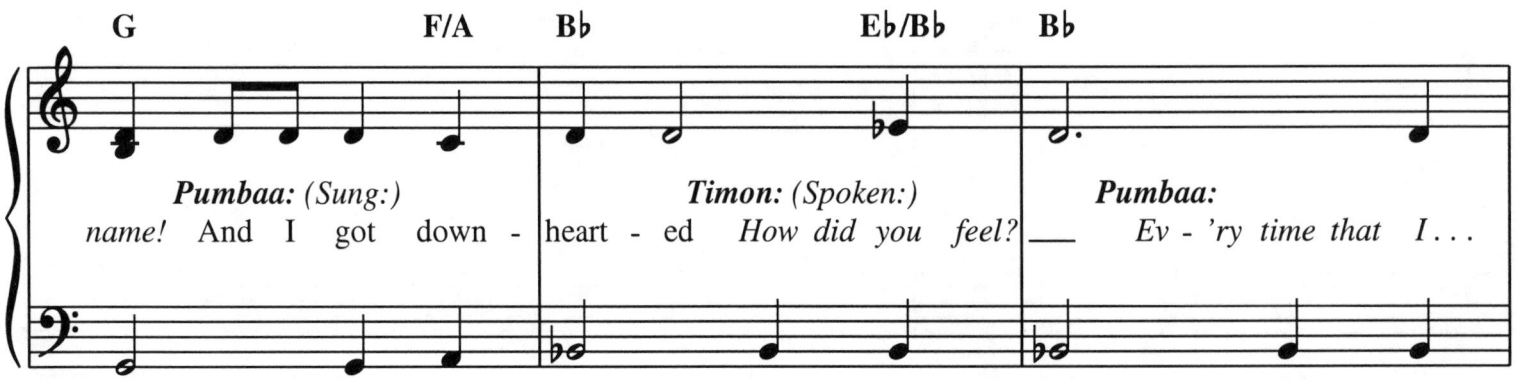

G   **F/A** **B♭**   **E♭/B♭** **B♭**

Pumbaa: *(Sung:)*   **Timon:** *(Spoken:)*   **Pumbaa:**

name! And I got down - heart - ed *How did you feel?* ___ *Ev - 'ry time that I . . .*

Timon:
Hey, Pumbaa, not in front | *of the kids.* *Oh, sorry.*

Pumbaa:

Timon Ana Pumbaa:
Ha - ku - na ma -

a tempo **f**

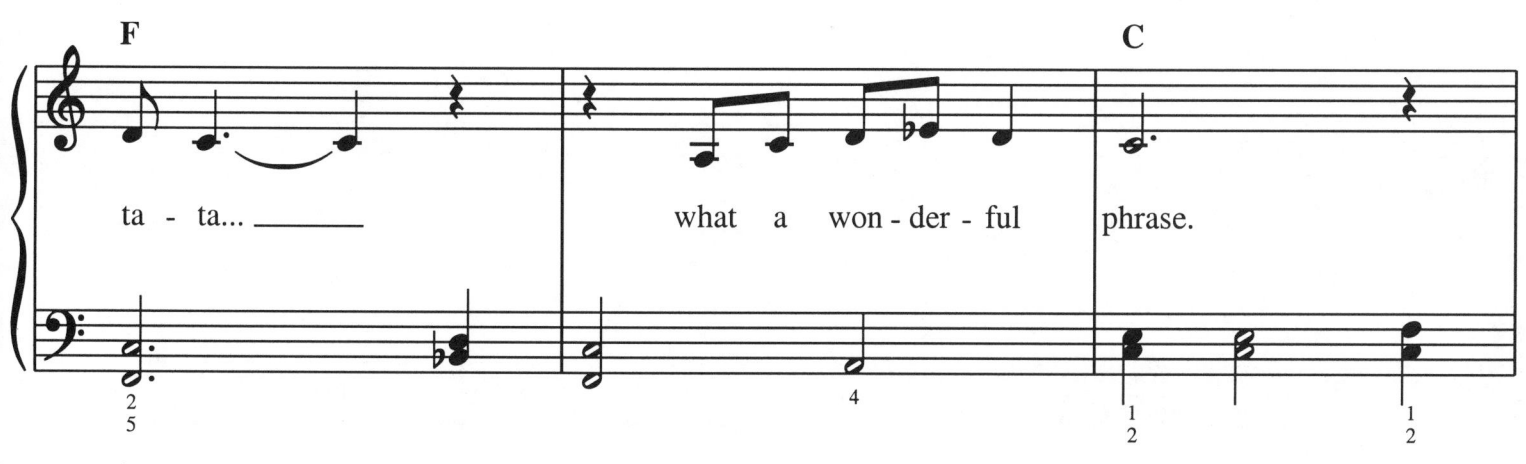

ta - ta... _____ what a won - der - ful phrase.

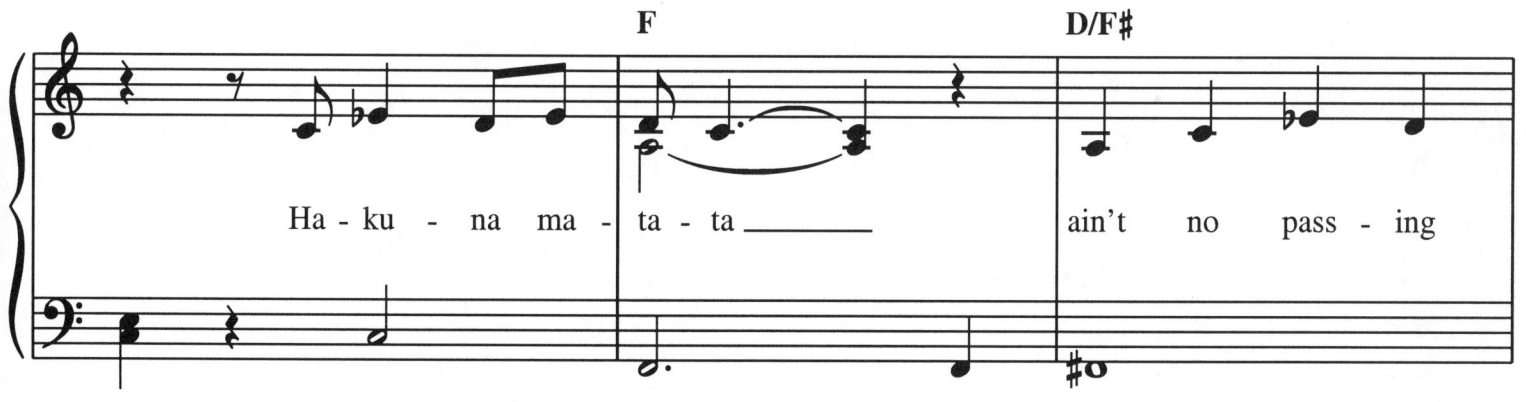

Ha - ku - na ma - ta - ta _____ ain't no pass - ing

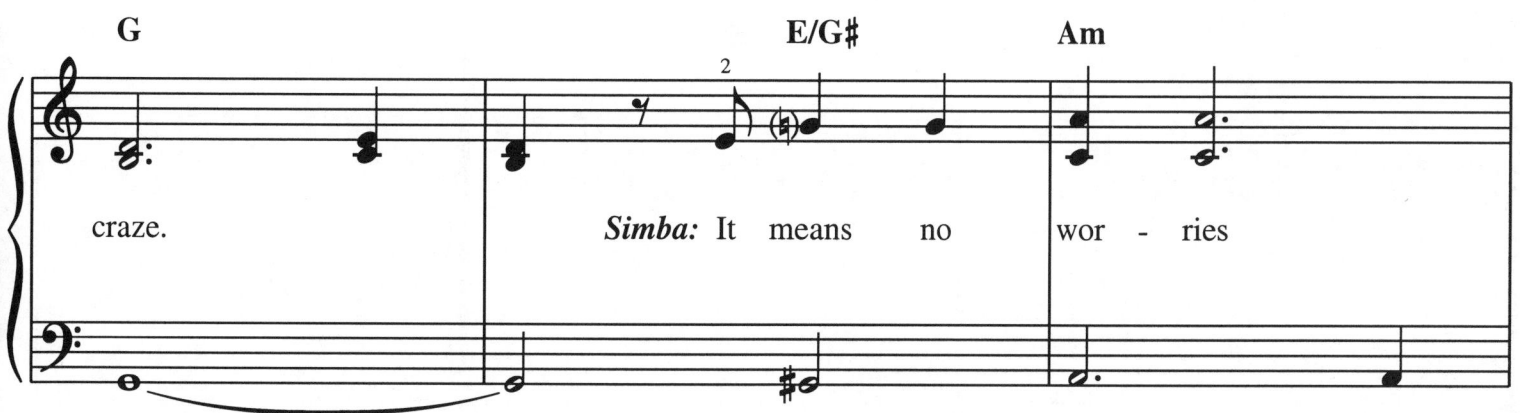

craze.

Simba: It means no wor - ries

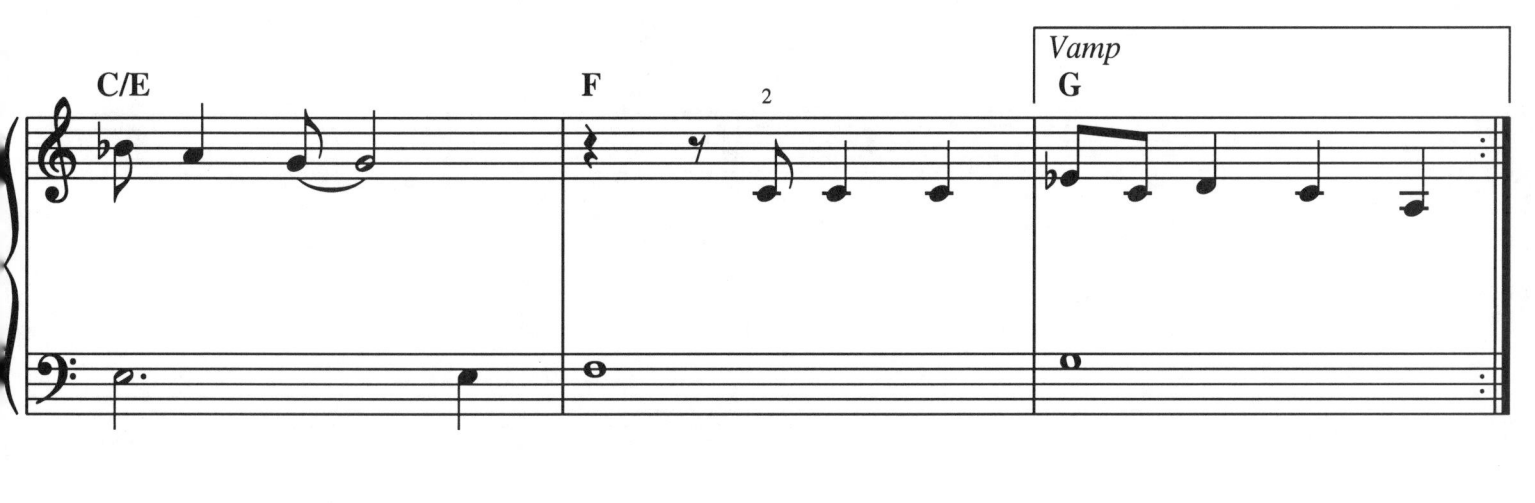

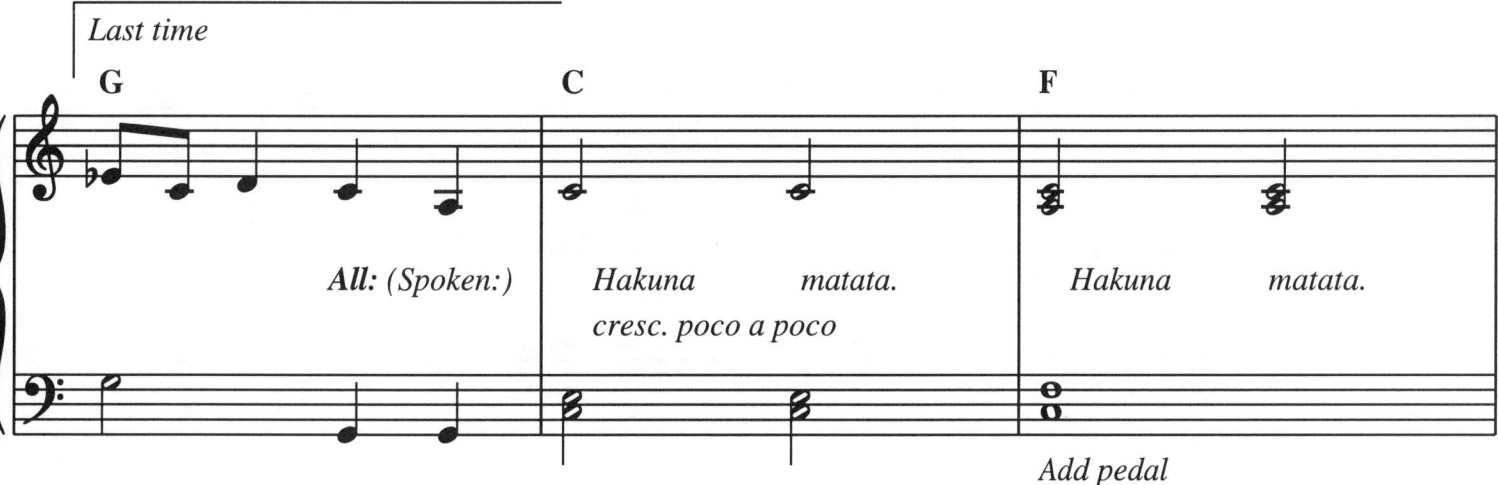

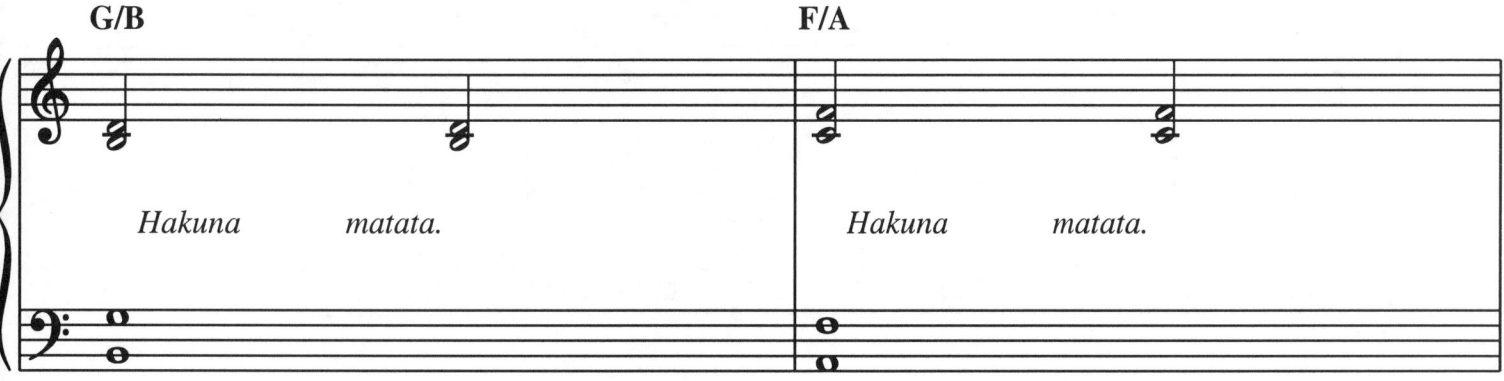

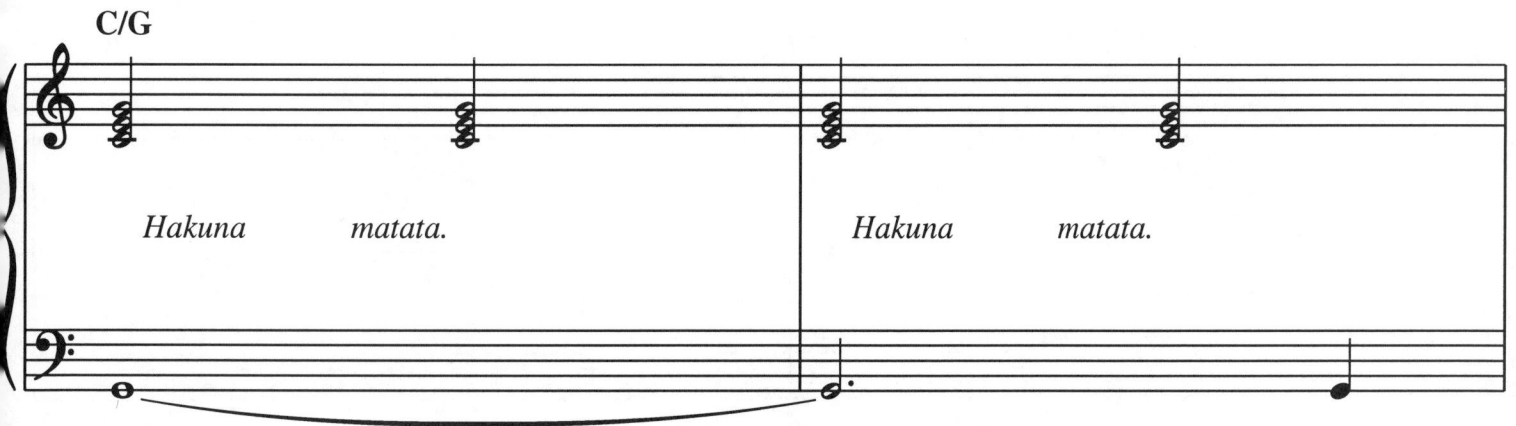

Repeat ad lib. and Fade

I WHISTLE A HAPPY TUNE

from THE KING AND I

Lyrics by OSCAR HAMMERSTEIN II
Music by RICHARD RODGERS

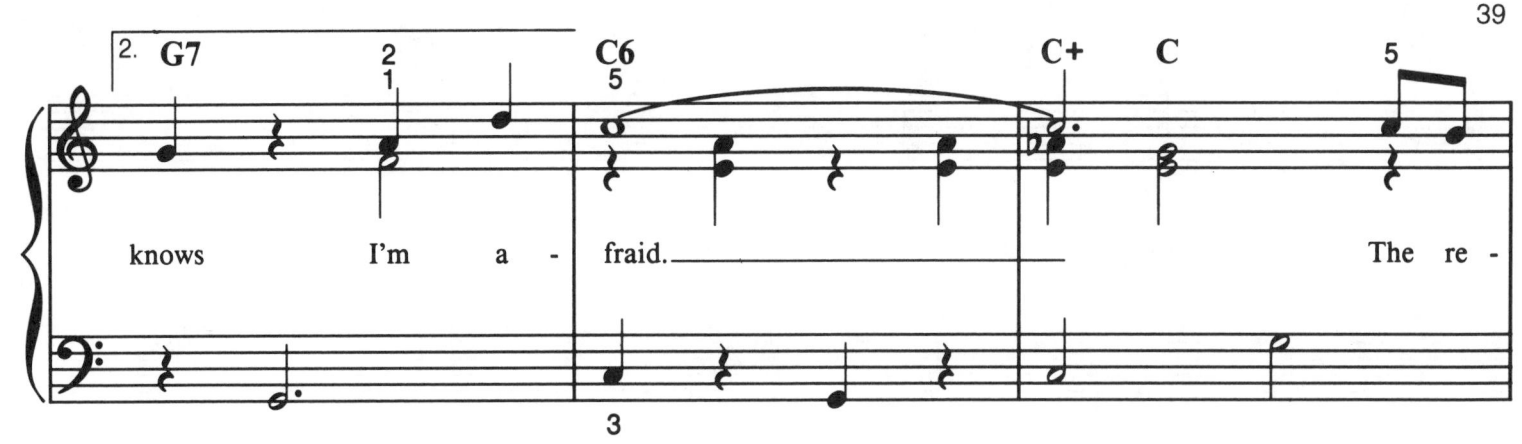

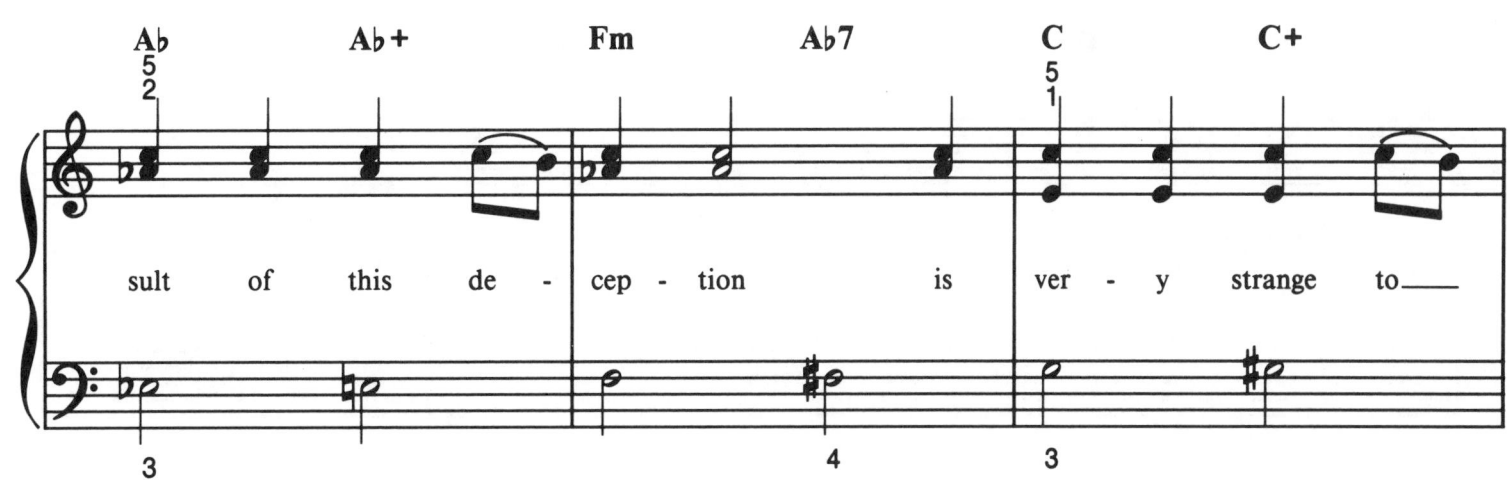

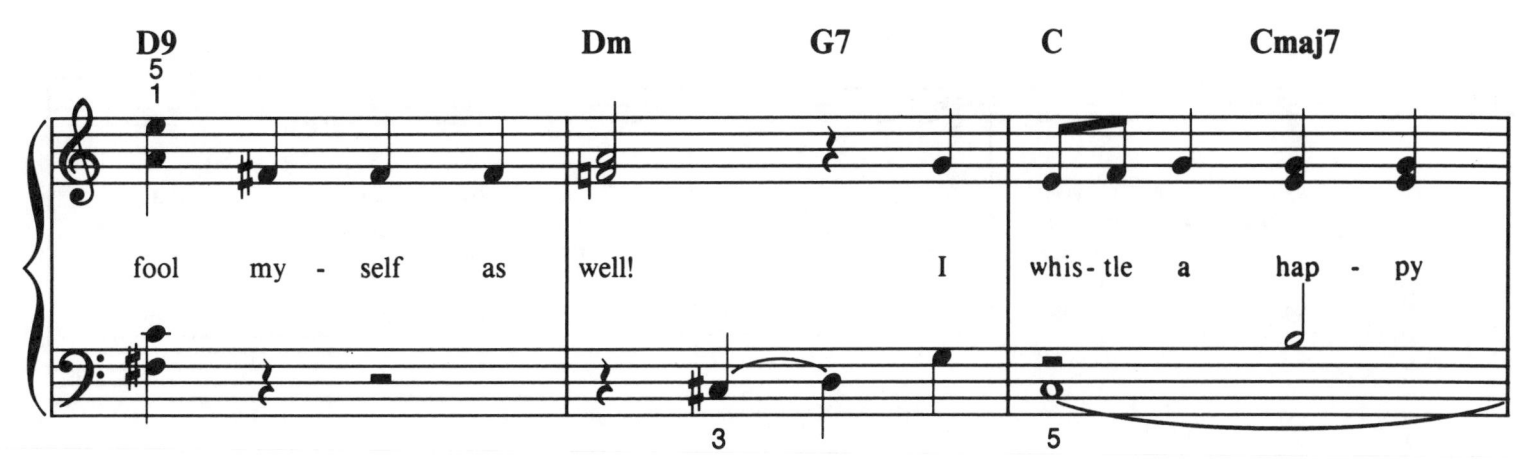

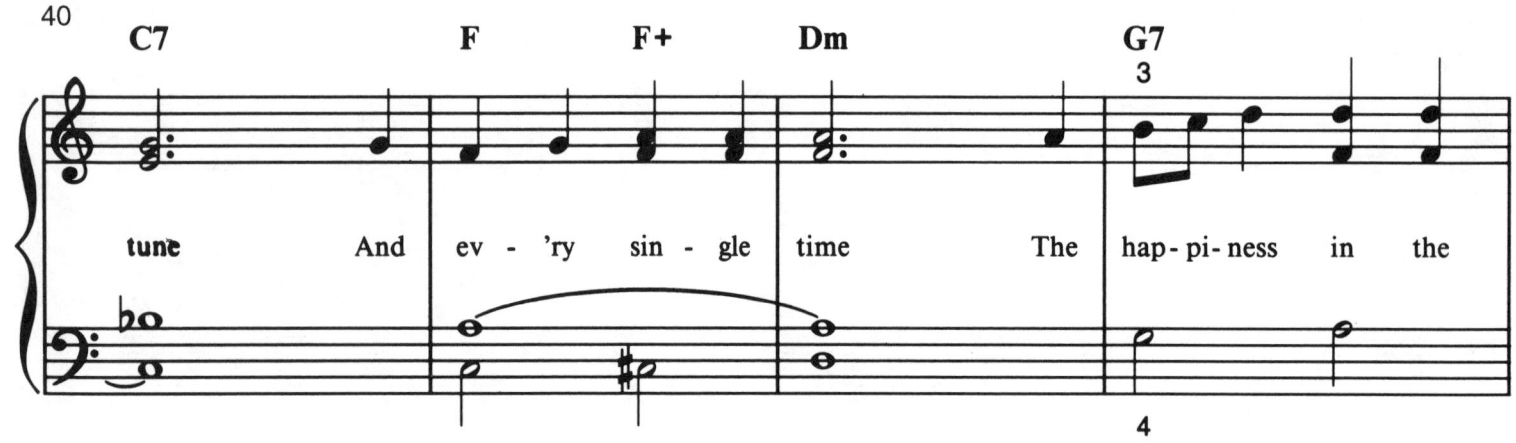

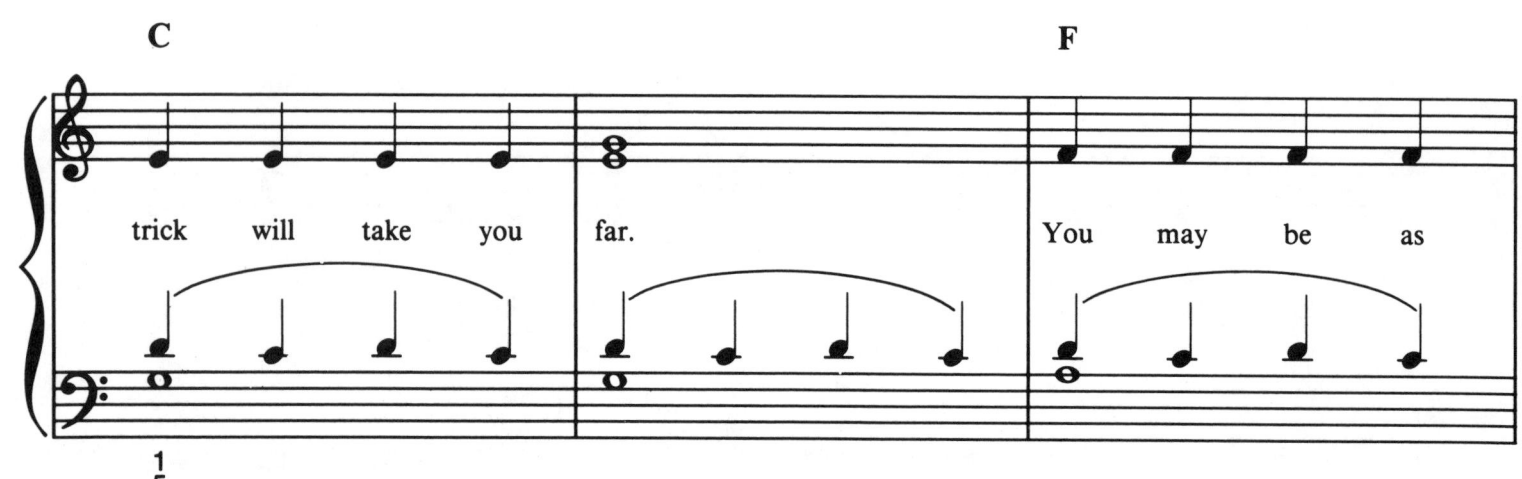

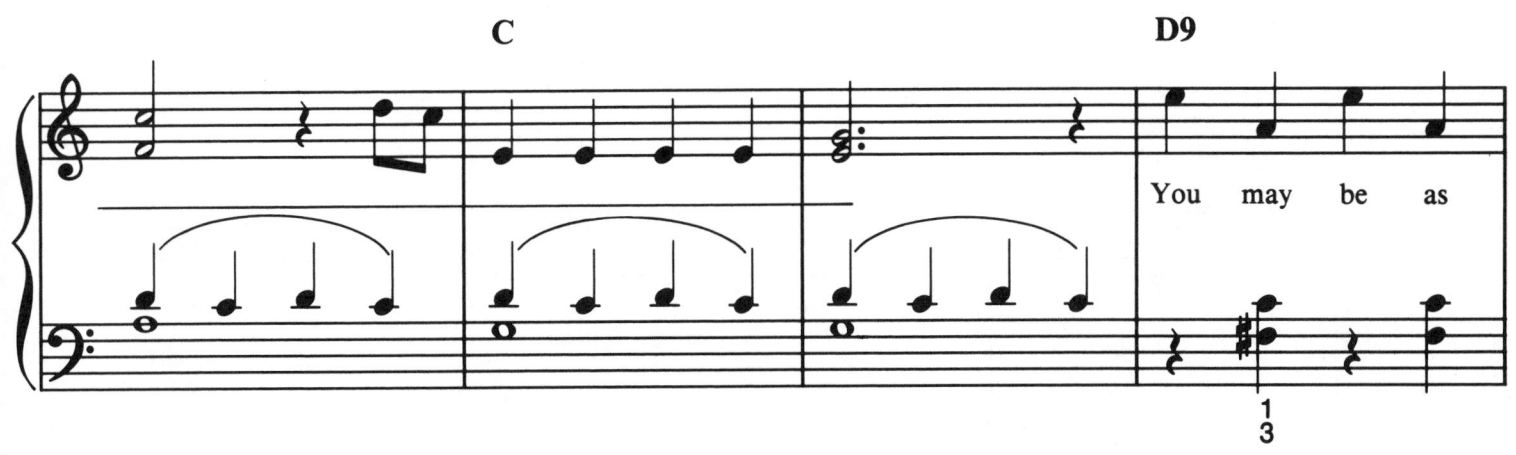

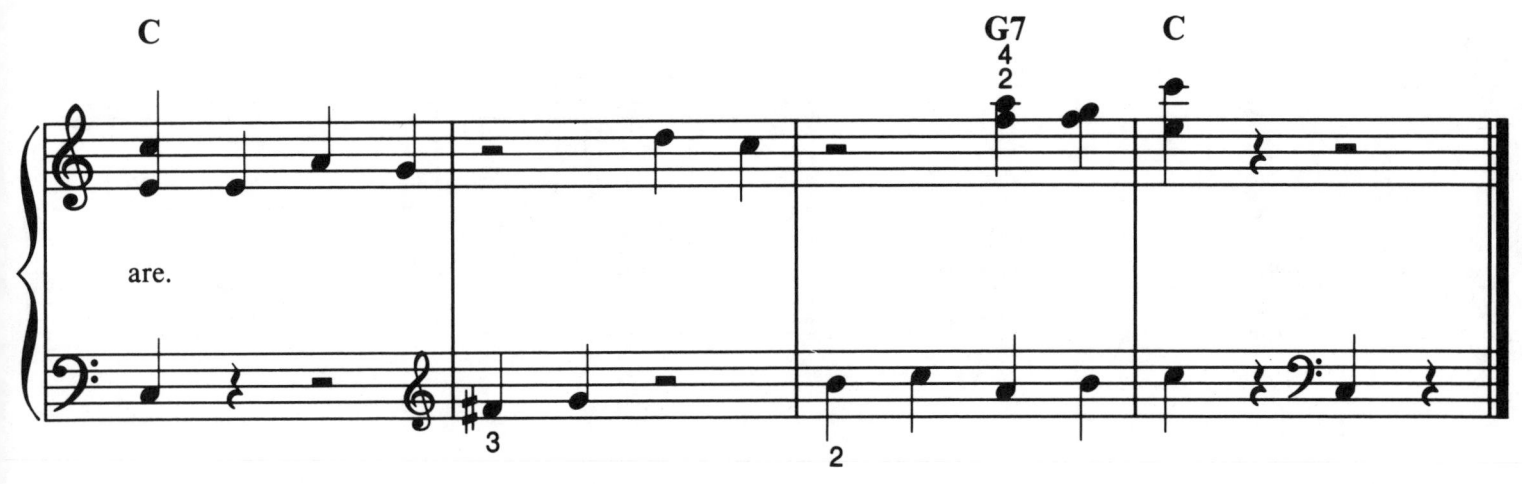

IF I HAD WORDS

featured in the Universal Motion Picture BABE

By JOHN HODGE

Bright Reggae

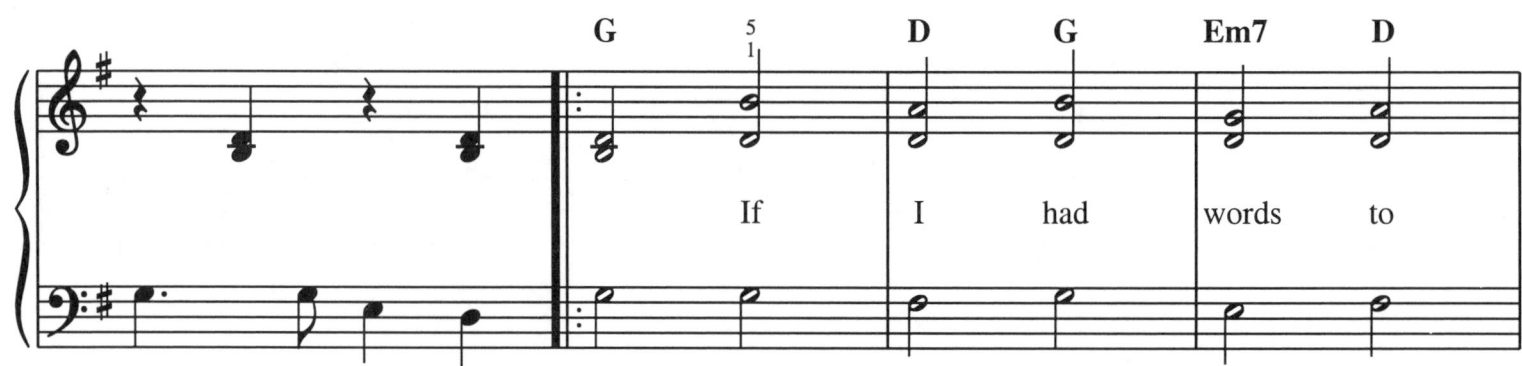

If   I   had   words   to

make   a   day   for   you,   I'd   sing

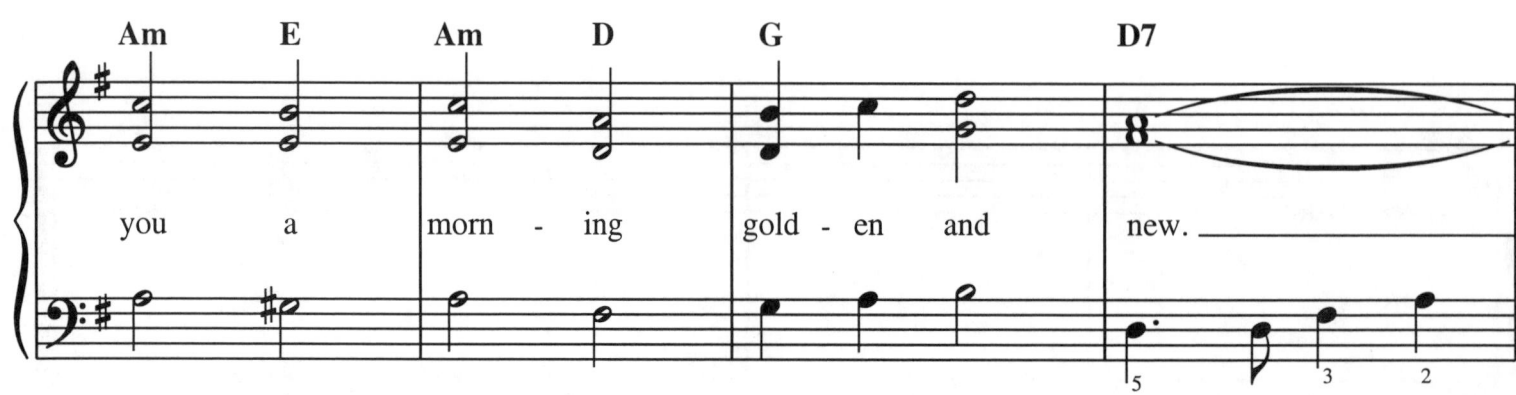

you   a   morn-   ing   gold-   en   and   new.

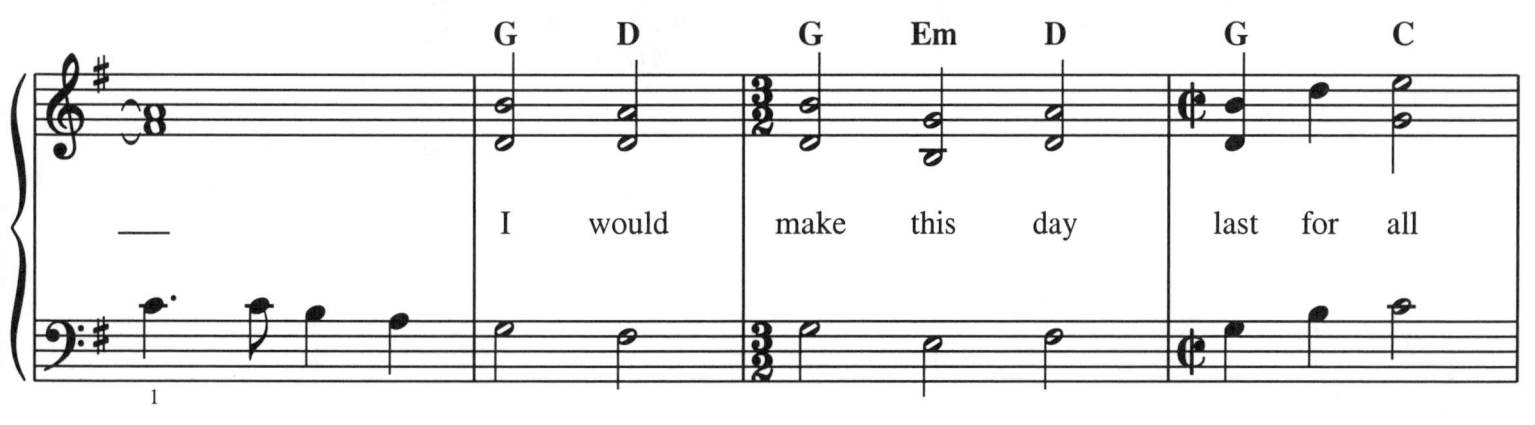

I would make this day last for all

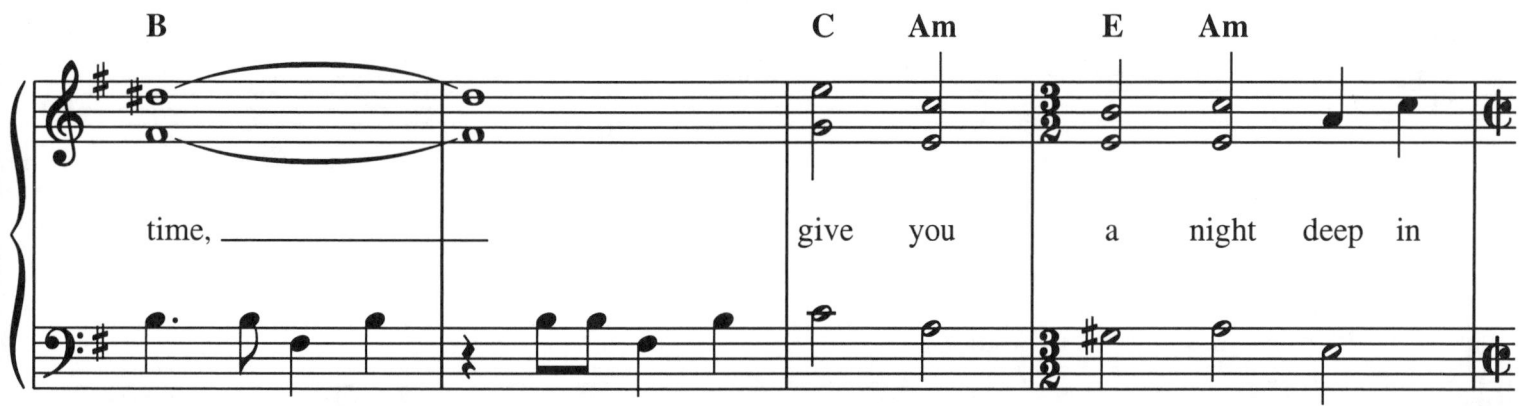

time, give you a night deep in

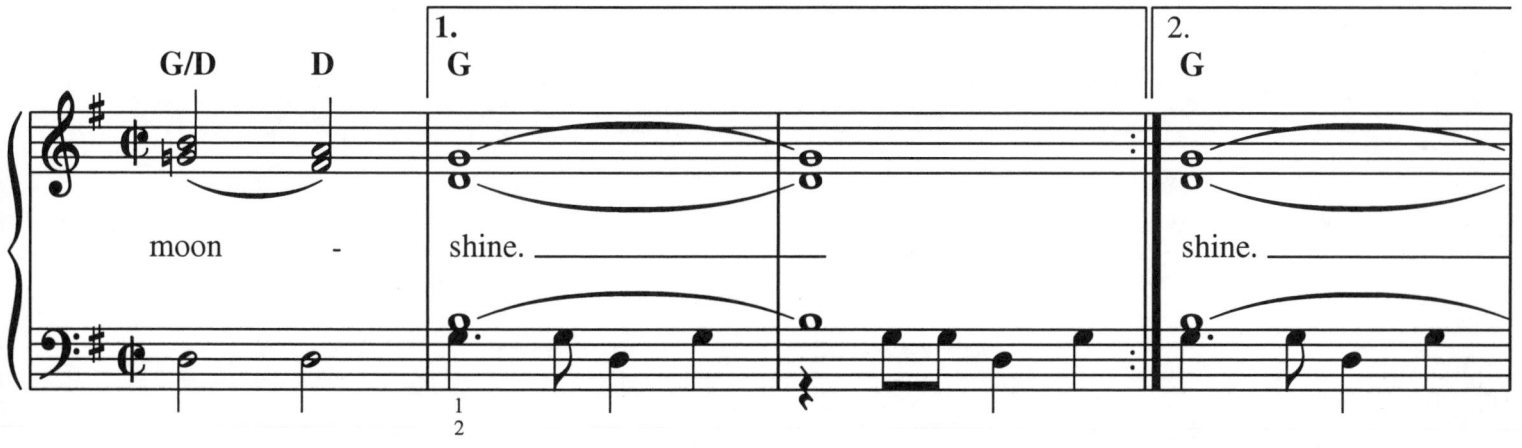

moon - shine.

shine.

THE LONELY GOATHERD
from THE SOUND OF MUSIC

Lyrics by OSCAR HAMMERSTEIN II
Music by RICHARD RODGERS

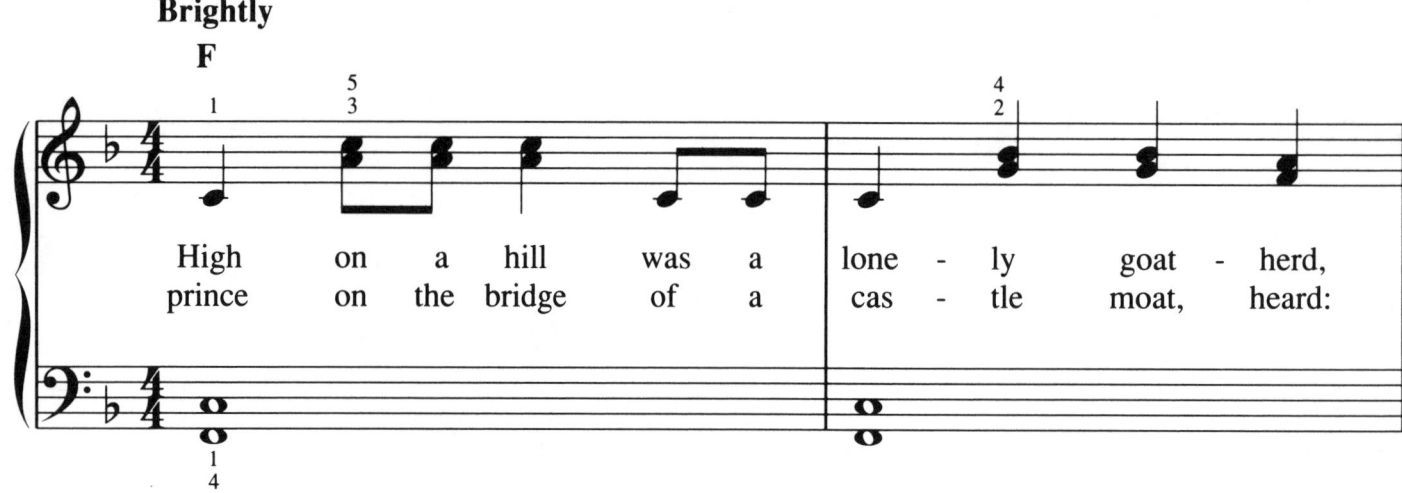

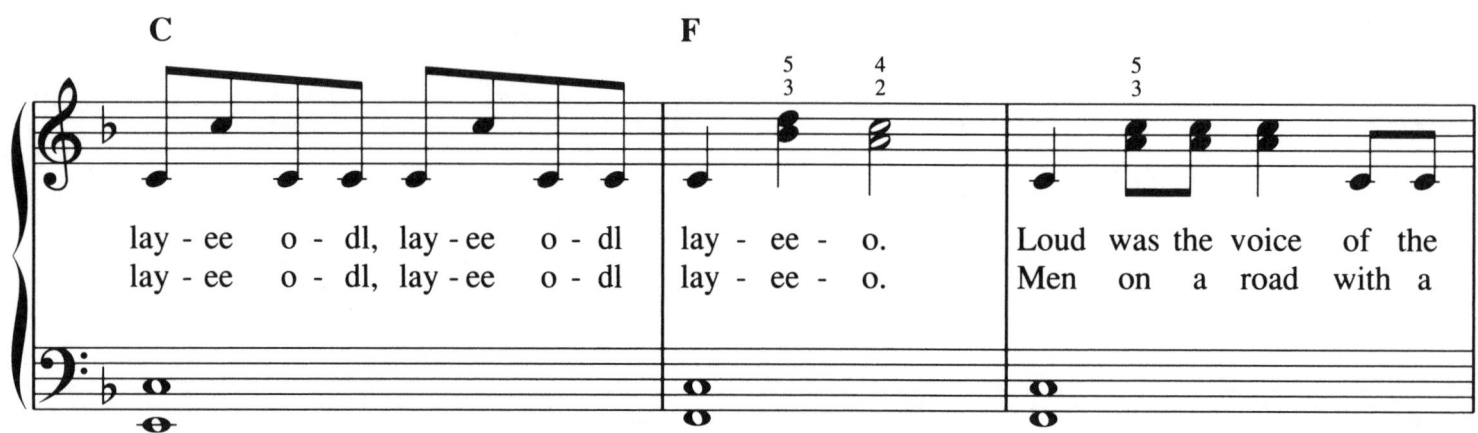

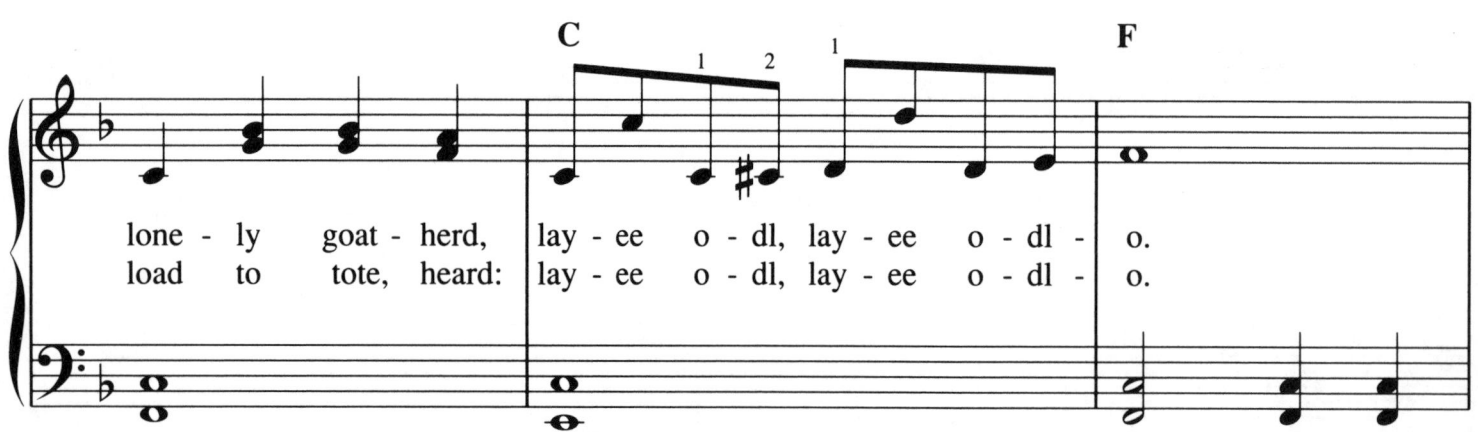

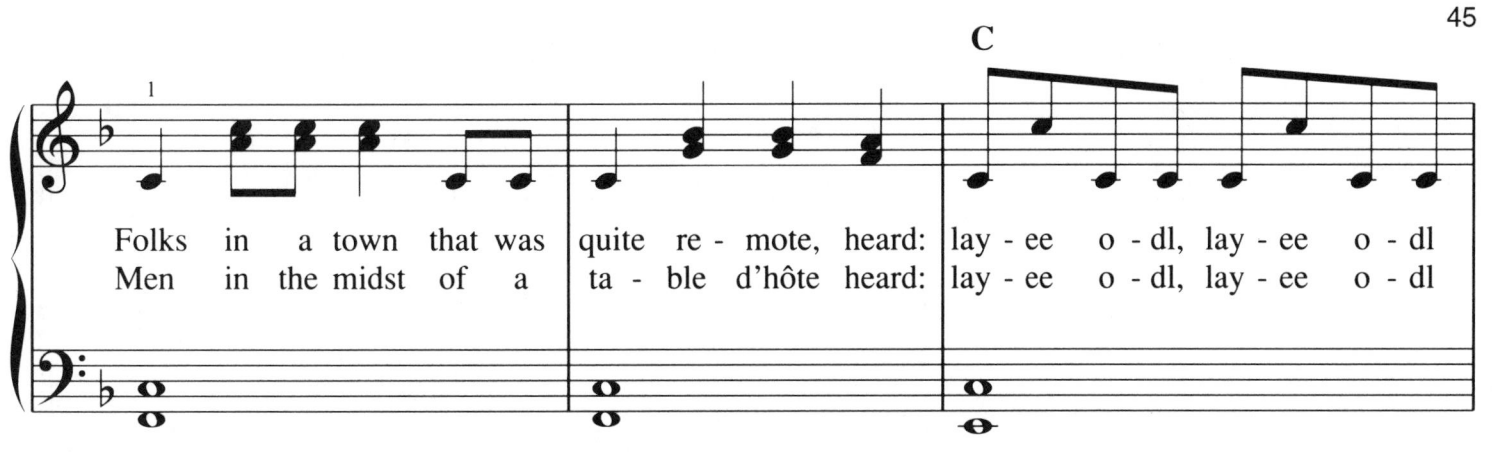

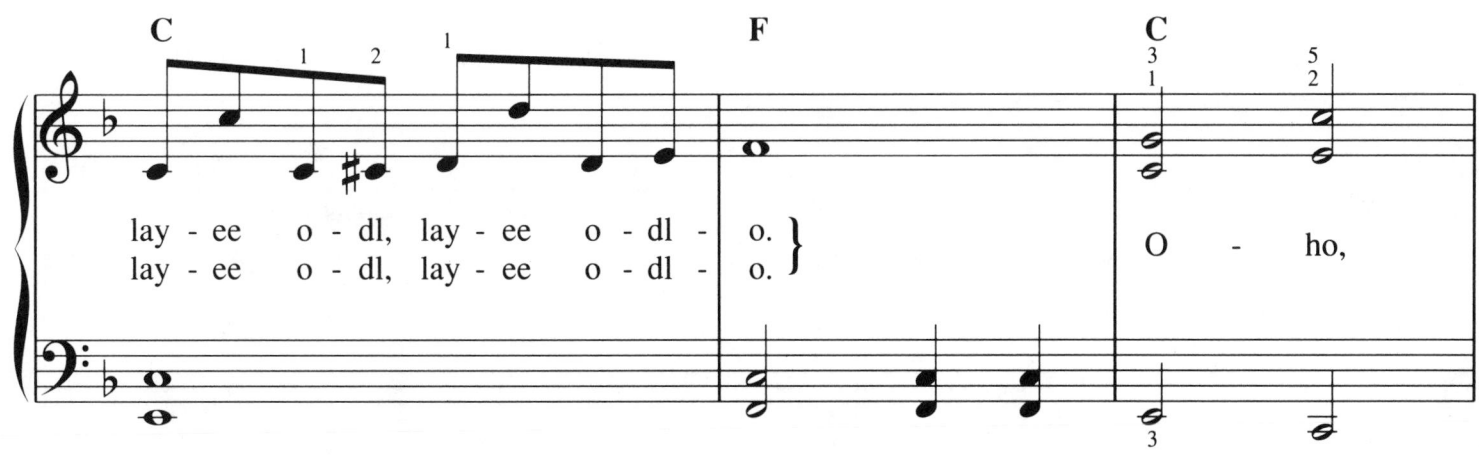

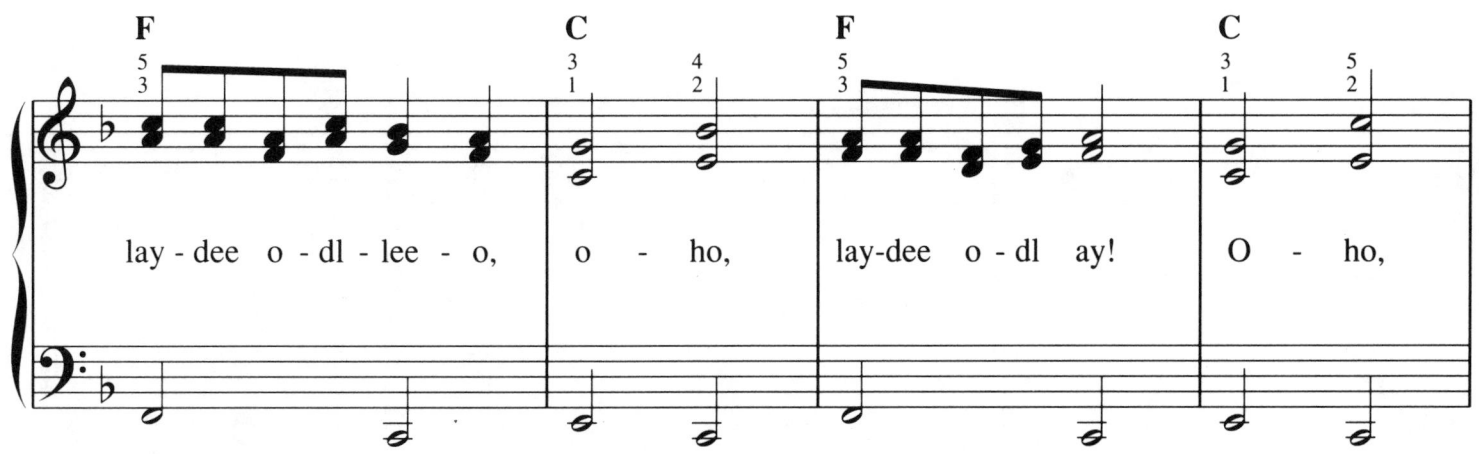

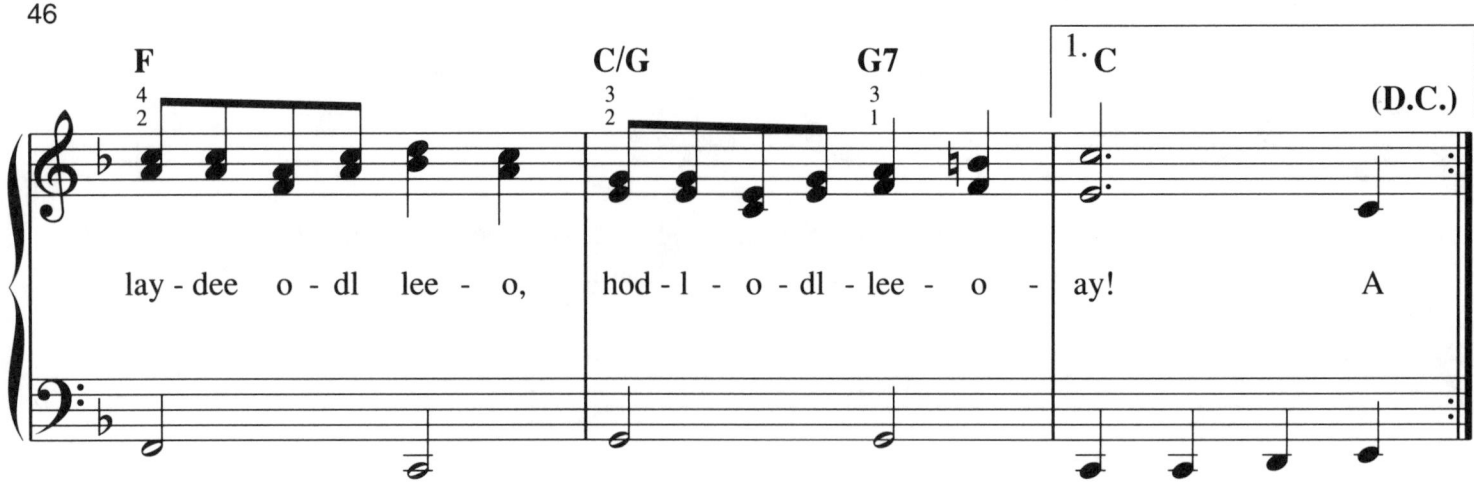

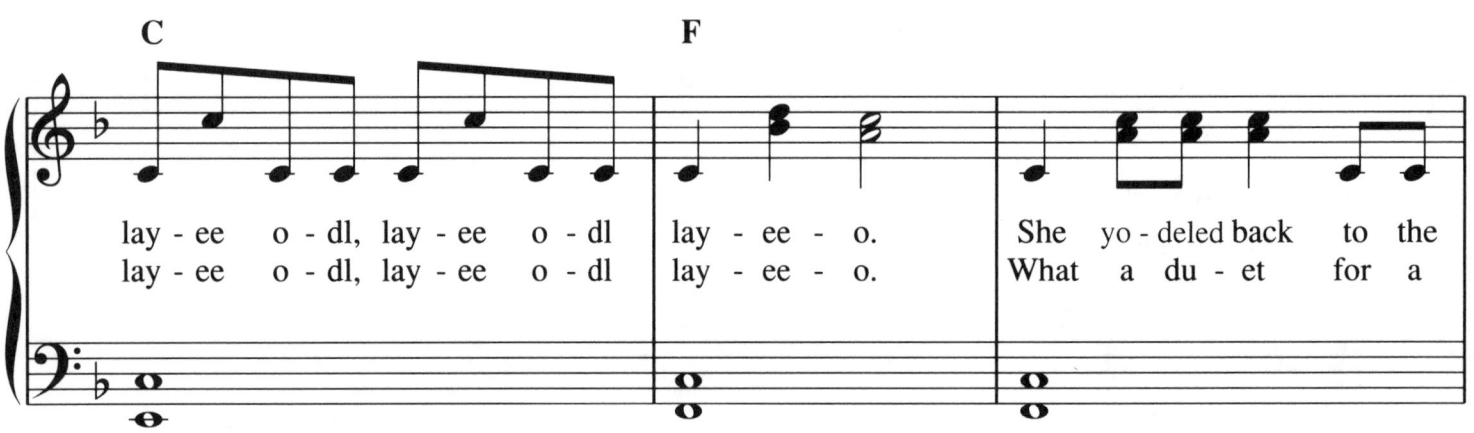

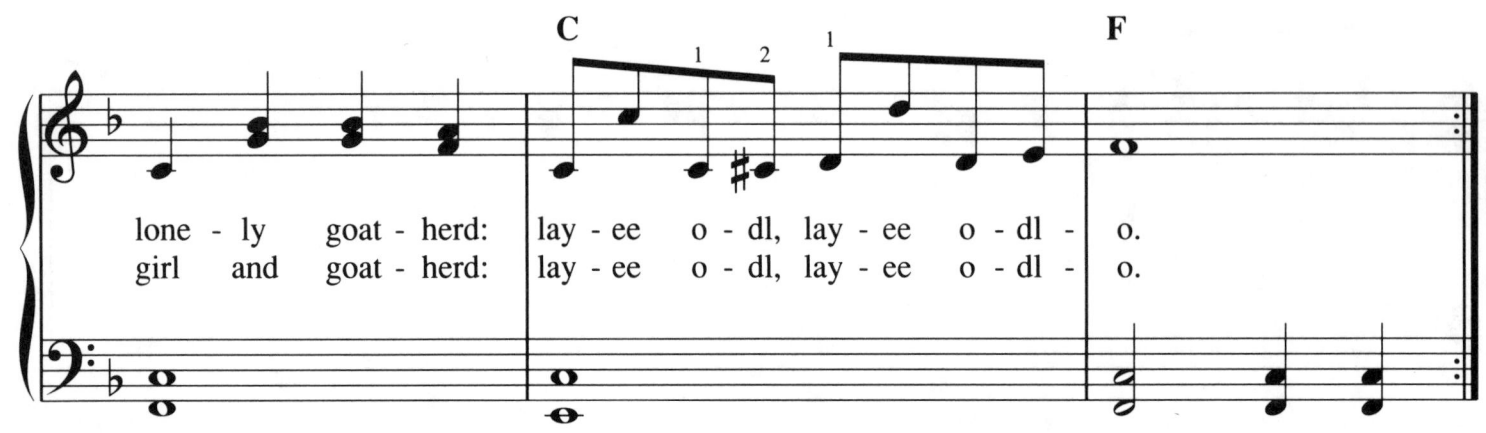

O - ho, lay-dee o - dl lee - o, o - ho, lay-dee o - dl ay!

O - ho, lay-dee o - dl lee - o hod - l - o - dl lee - o -

ay!   Hap - py are they, lay - ee o lay - ee lee - o!

O lay - lee o lay - lee lay - ee - o.   Soon the du - et will be -

come a tri - o, lay - ee o - dl, lay - ee o - dl - o. Ho - di

lay - ee _____ Ho - di lay - ee _____

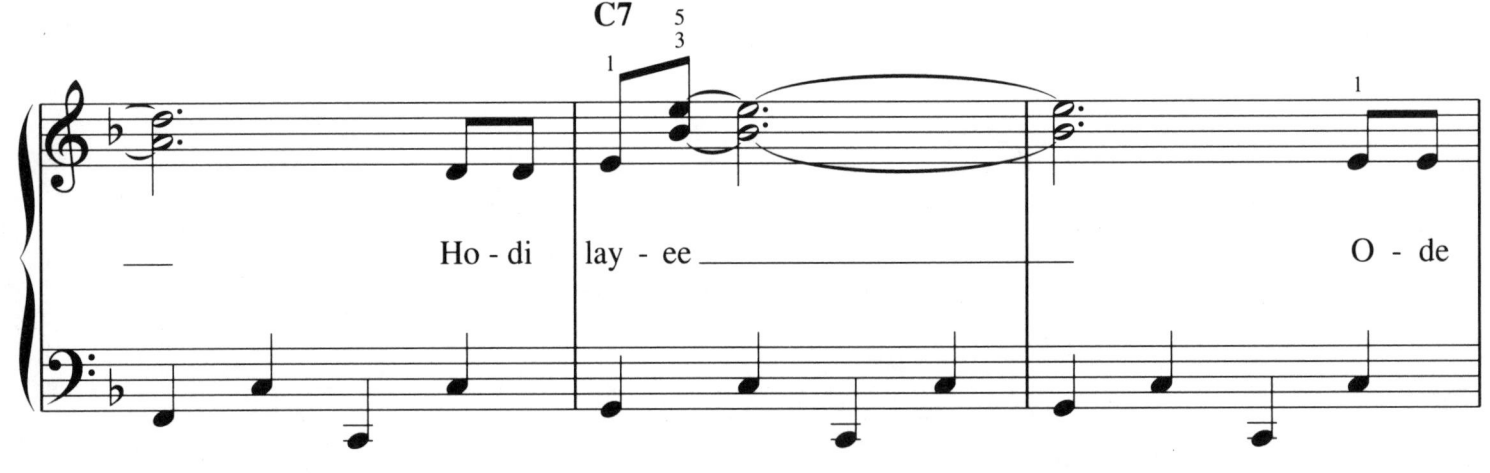

_____ Ho - di lay - ee _____ O - de

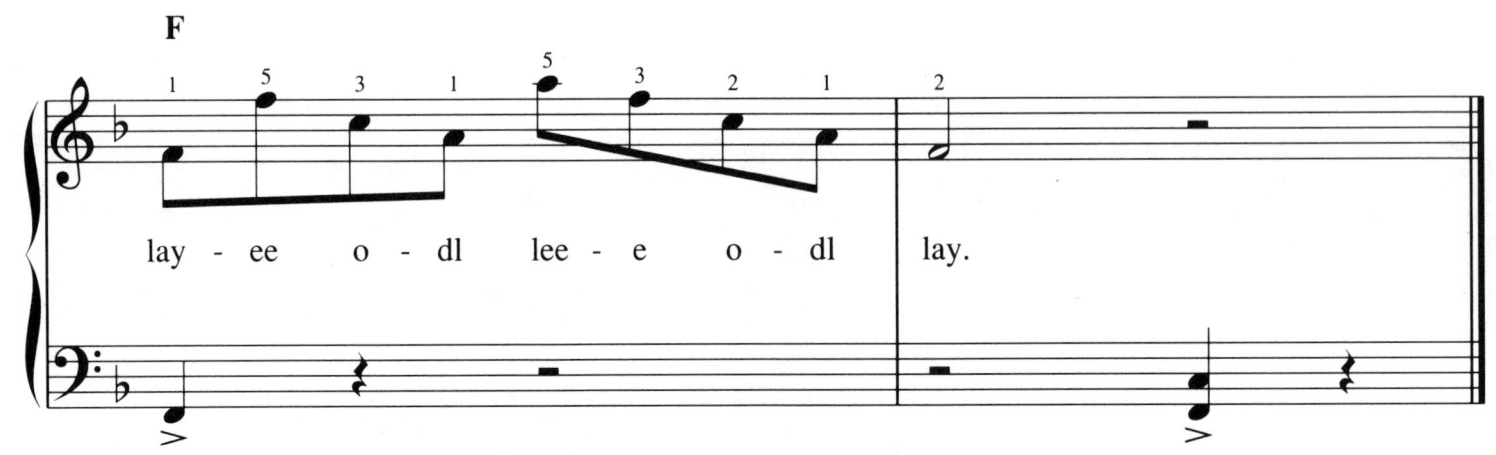

lay - ee o - dl lee - e o - dl lay.

RAIDERS MARCH

from the Paramount Motion Picture RAIDERS OF THE LOST ARK

Music by JOHN WILLIAMS

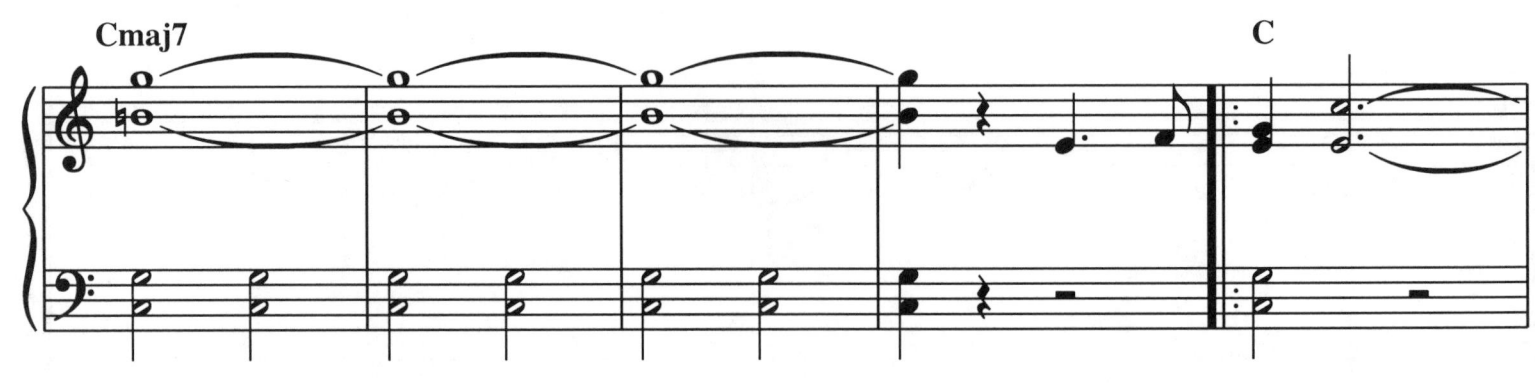

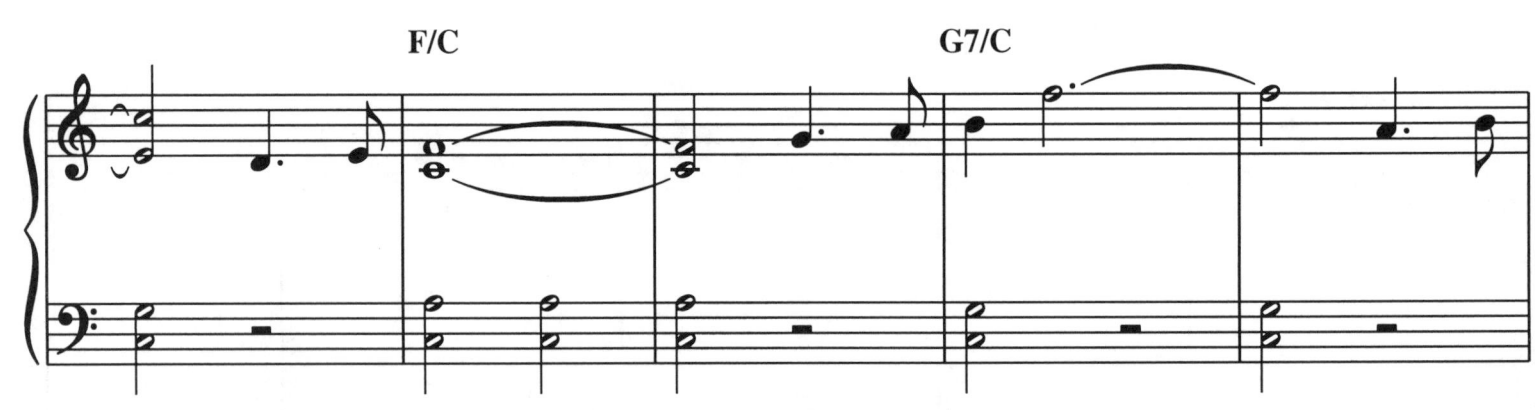

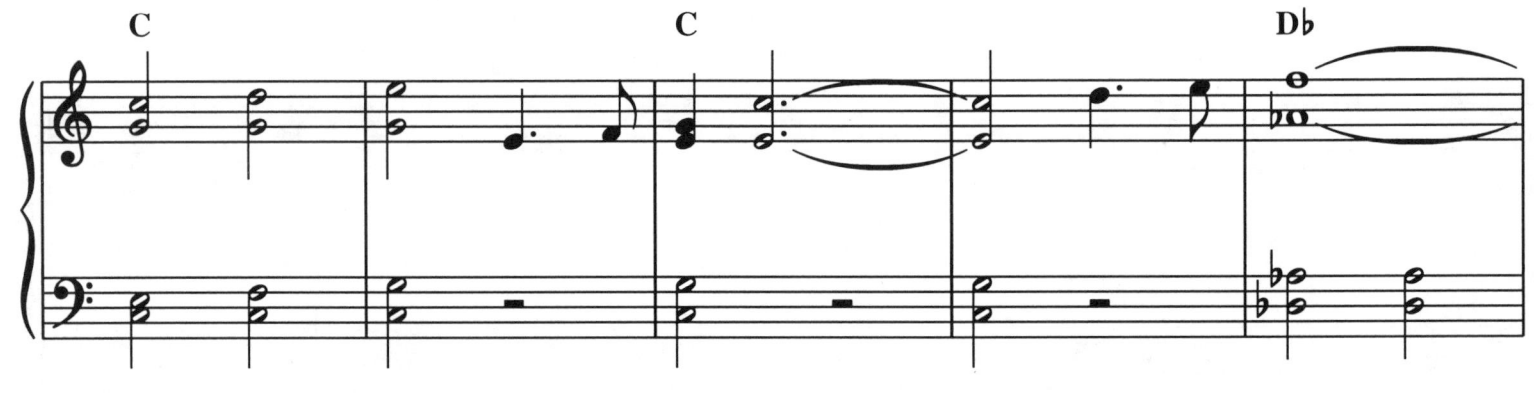

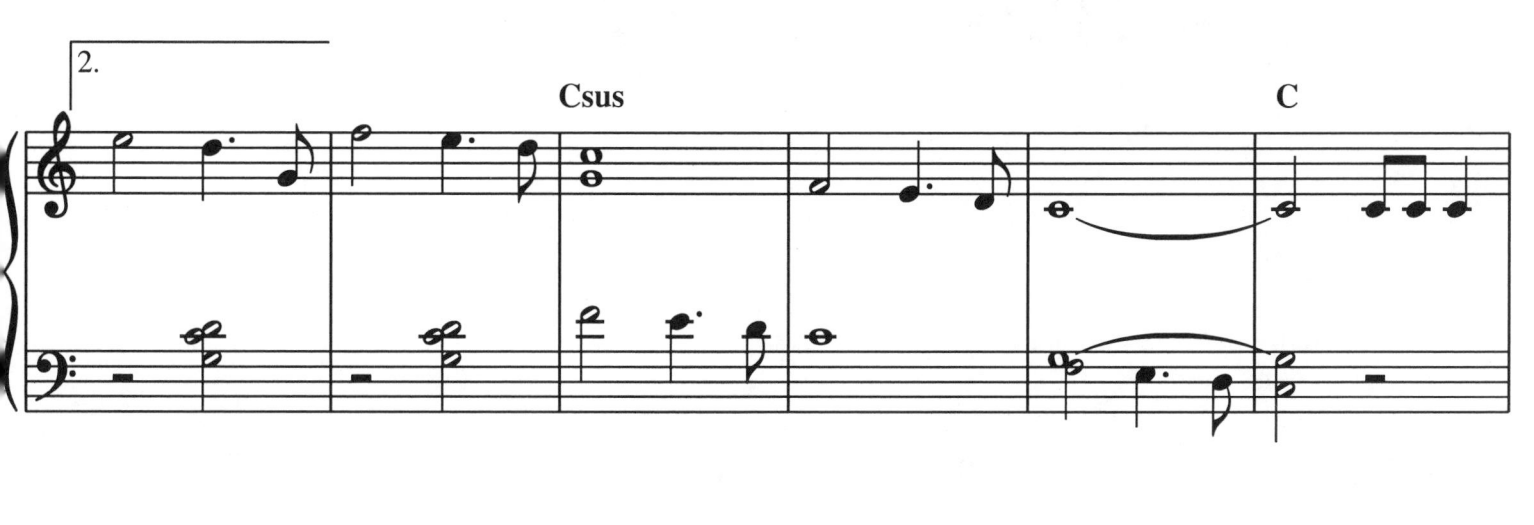

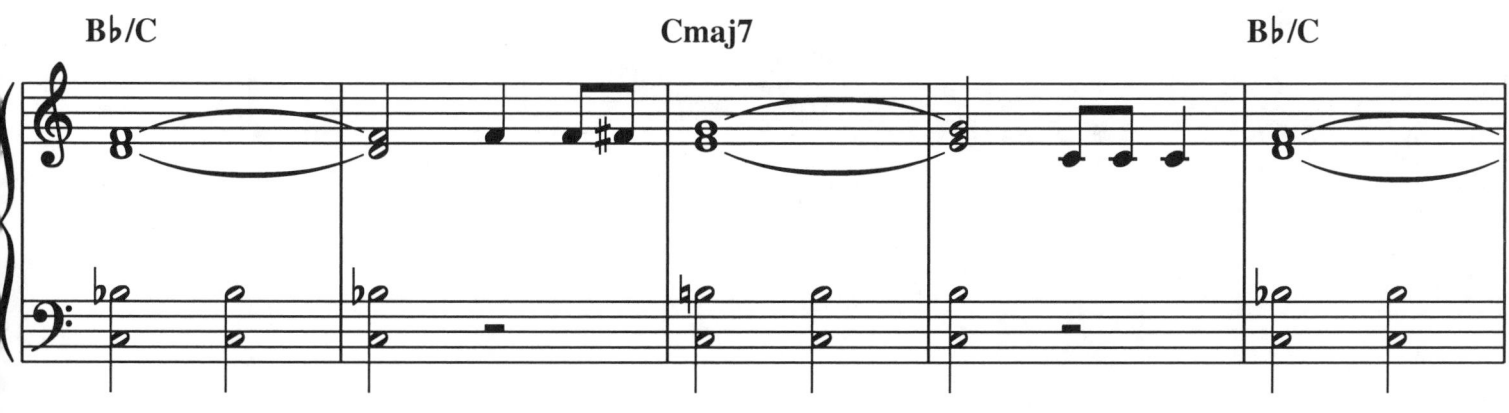

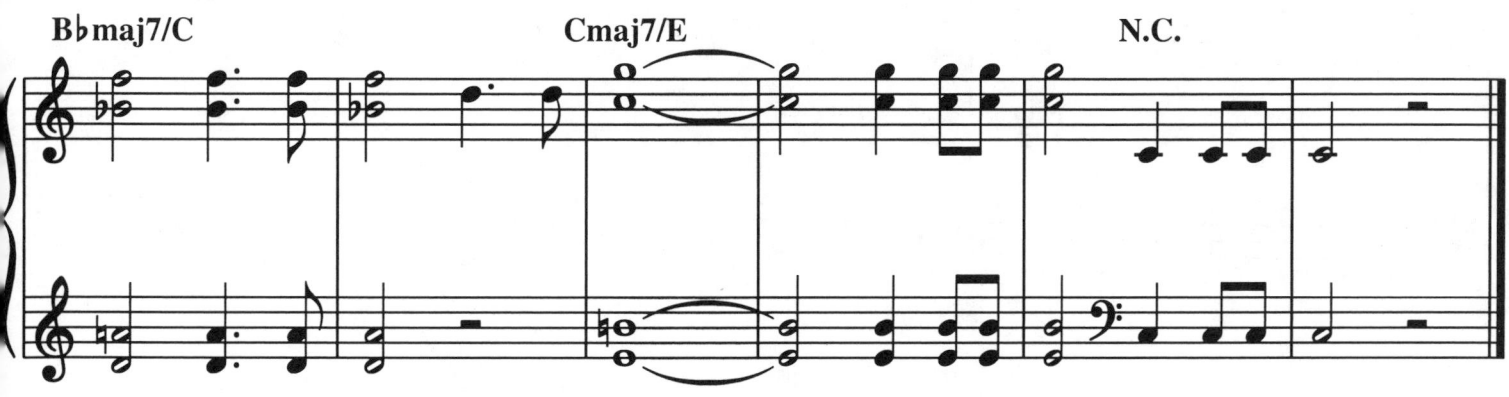

MOVIN' RIGHT ALONG

from THE MUPPET MOVIE

By PAUL WILLIAMS
and KENNETH L. ASCHER

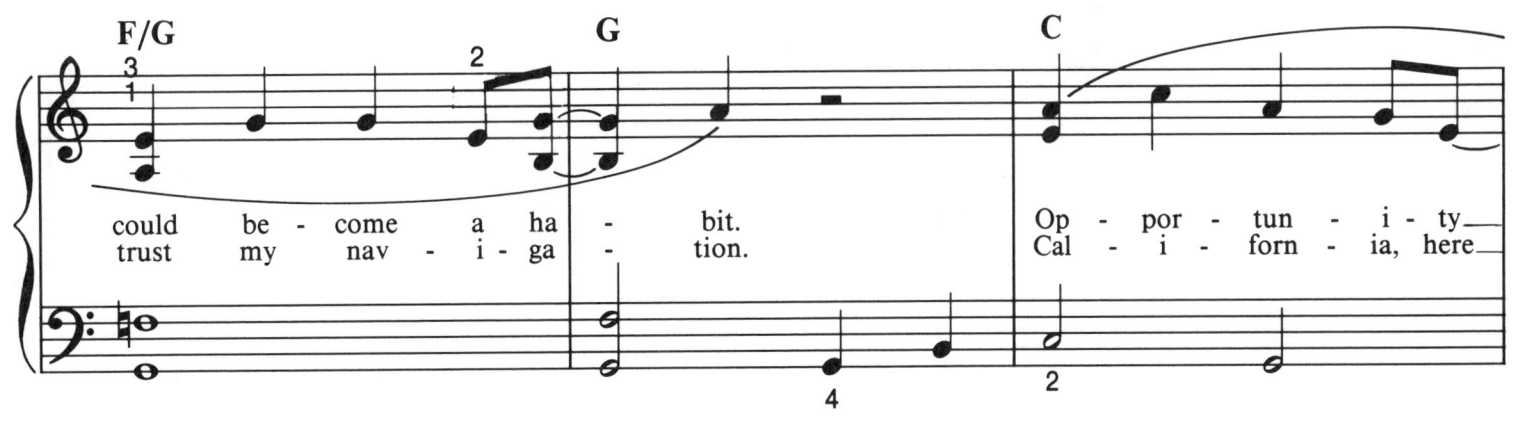

could be - come a ha - bit. | Op - por - tun - i - ty
trust my nav - i - ga - tion. | Cal - i - forn - ia, here

just knocked, let's | reach out and grab | it. To -
we come; that | pie in the sky | land.

geth - er we'll nab | it, we'll | hitch - hike, bus or
Palm trees and warm | sand, though | sad - ly we just

yel - low cab it. | | | Mov - in' right a - | long,
left Rhode Is - land. | | | Mov - in' right a - | long.

foot - loose and fan - cy free.
hey L. A., where've you gone?

Get - tin' there is half the fun; come share it with me.
Send some - one to fetch us, we're in Sas - katch - e - wan.

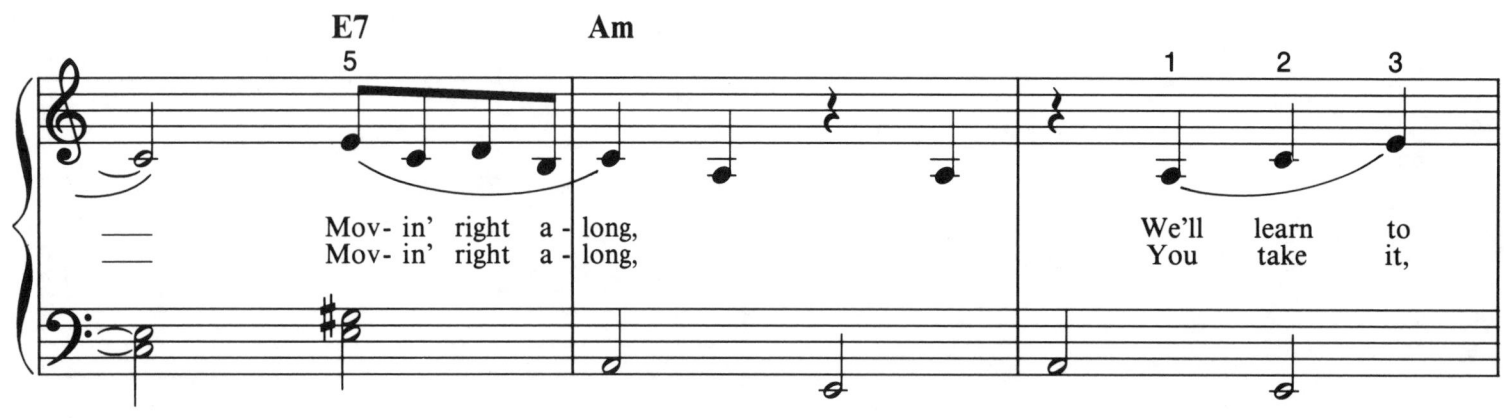

Mov- in' right a - long,   We'll learn to
Mov- in' right a - long,   You take it,

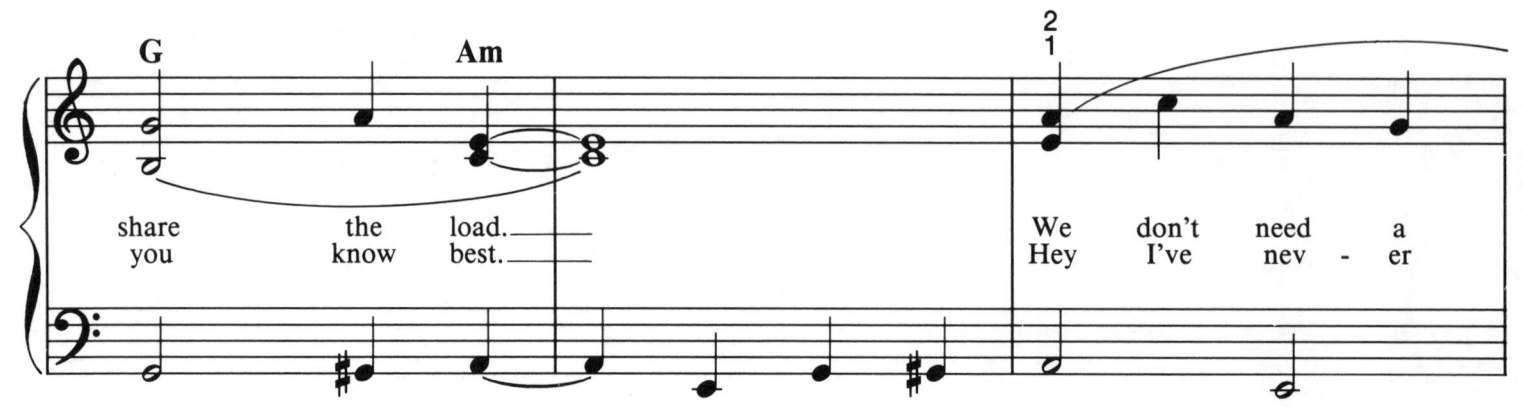

share the load.   We don't need a
you know best.   Hey I've nev - er

map to keep this show on the road.
seen the sun come

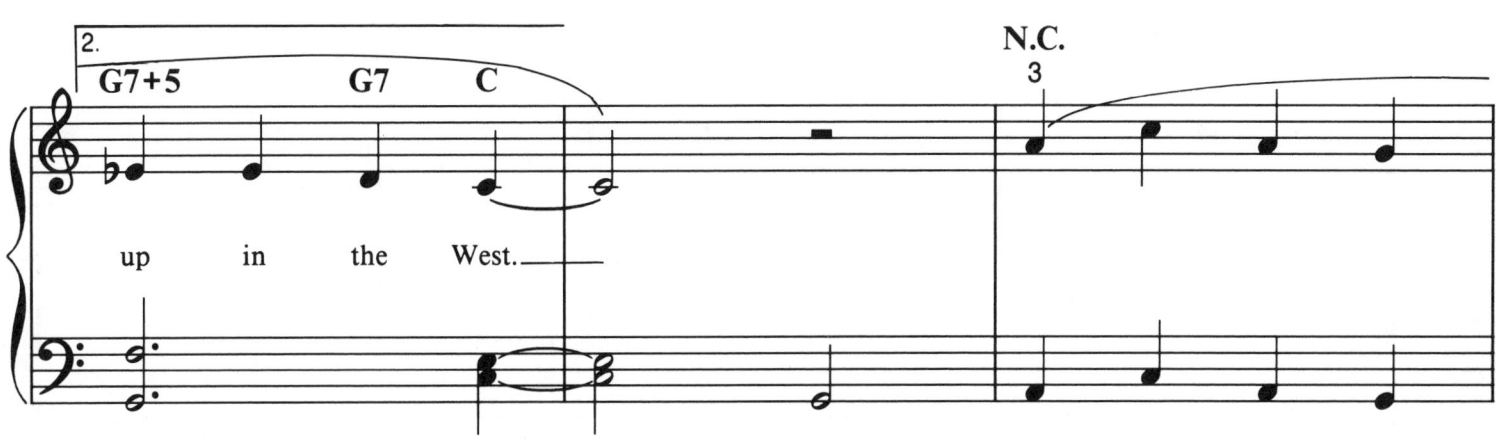

up in the West.

Verse 3: Movin' right along, we're truly birds of a feather,
We're in this together and you know where you're goin'.
Movie stars with flashy cars and life with the top down.
We're stormin' the big town.
Yeah! Storm is right, should it be snowin'?

Movin' right along, do I see signs of men?
Yeah, "welcome" on the same post that says "come back again".
Movin' right along, foot-loose and fance free.
You're ready for the big time, is it ready for me?

MY FAVORITE THINGS
from THE SOUND OF MUSIC

Lyrics by OSCAR HAMMERSTEIN II
Music by RICHARD RODGERS

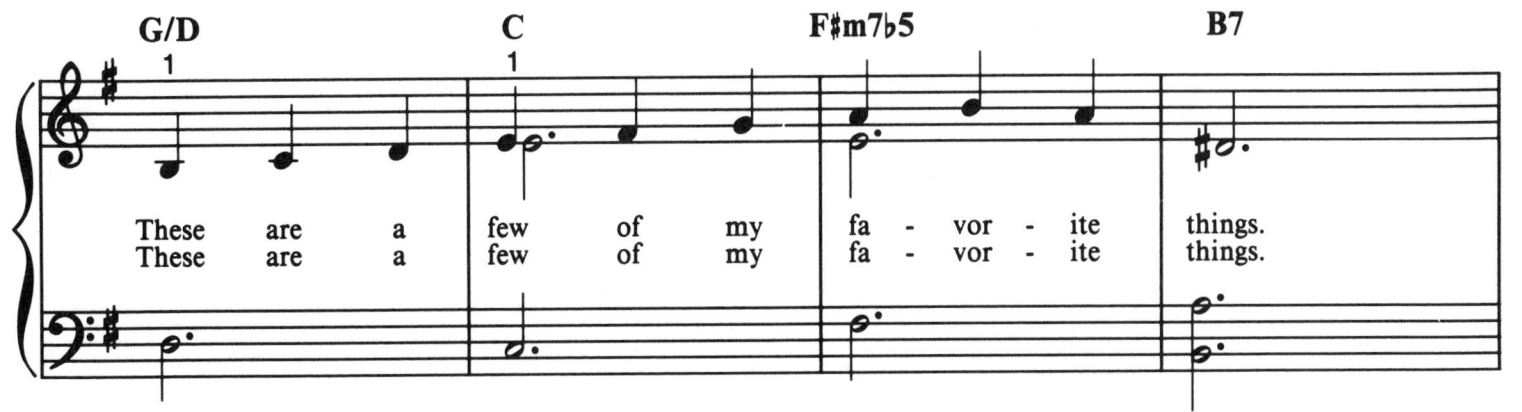

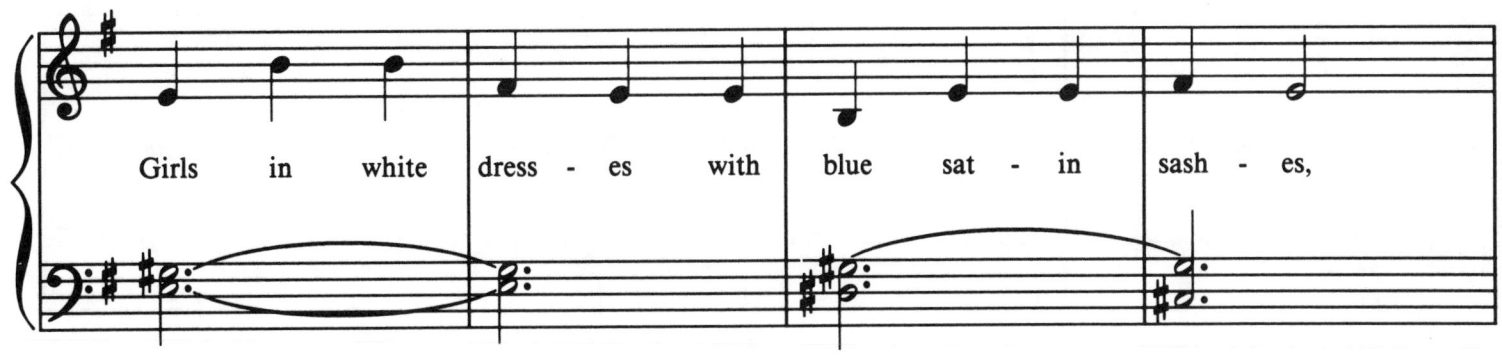

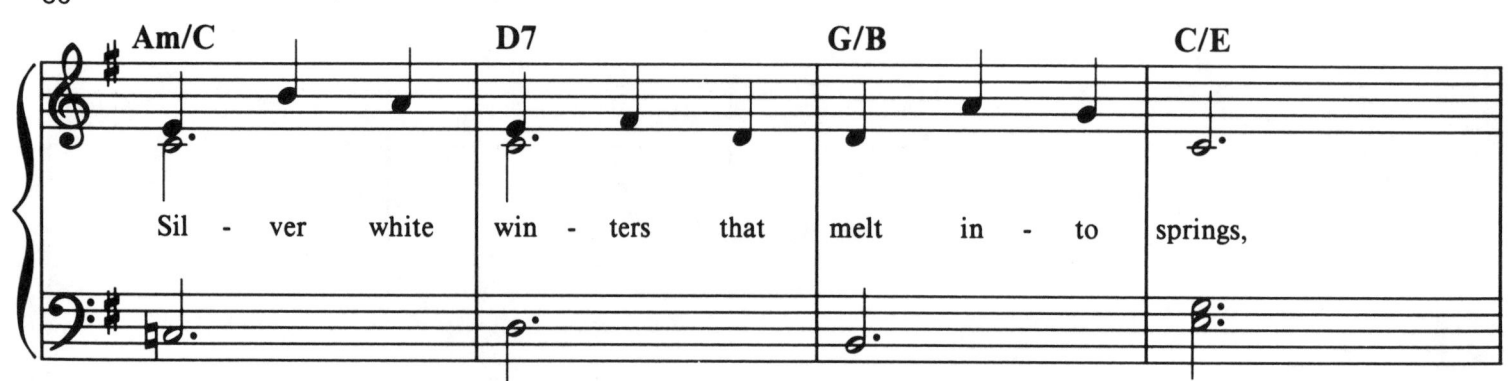

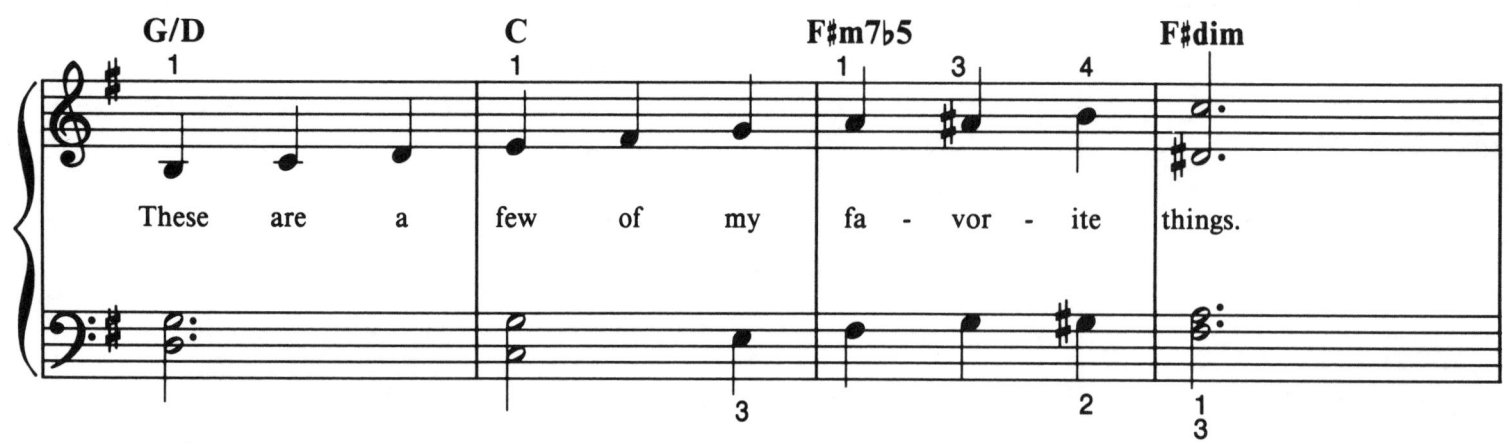

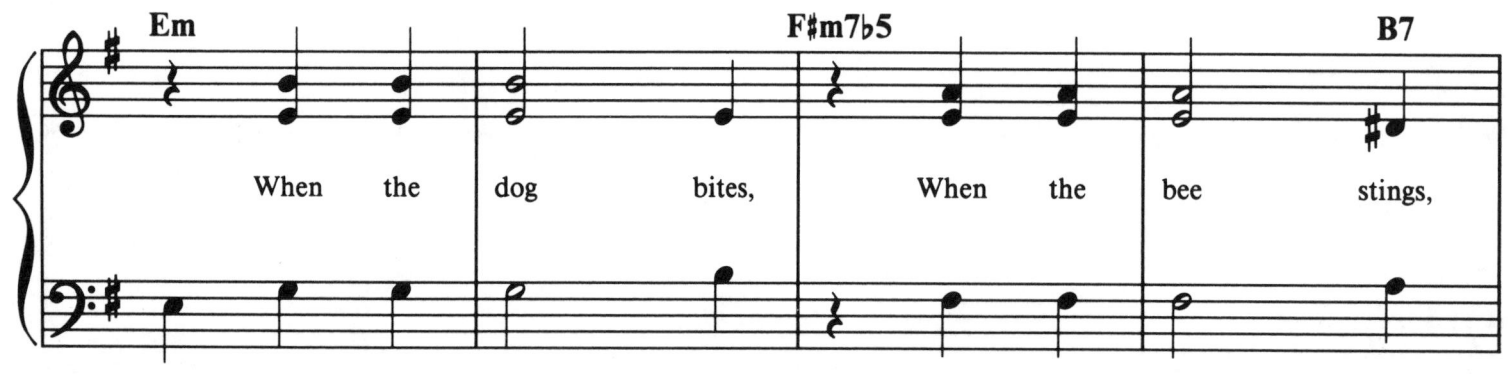

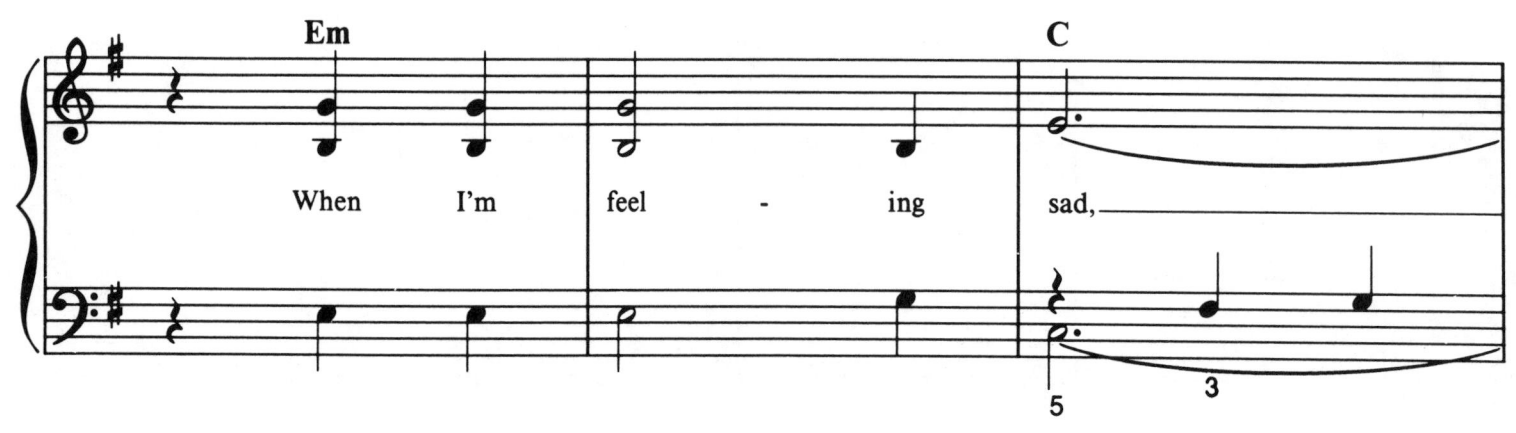

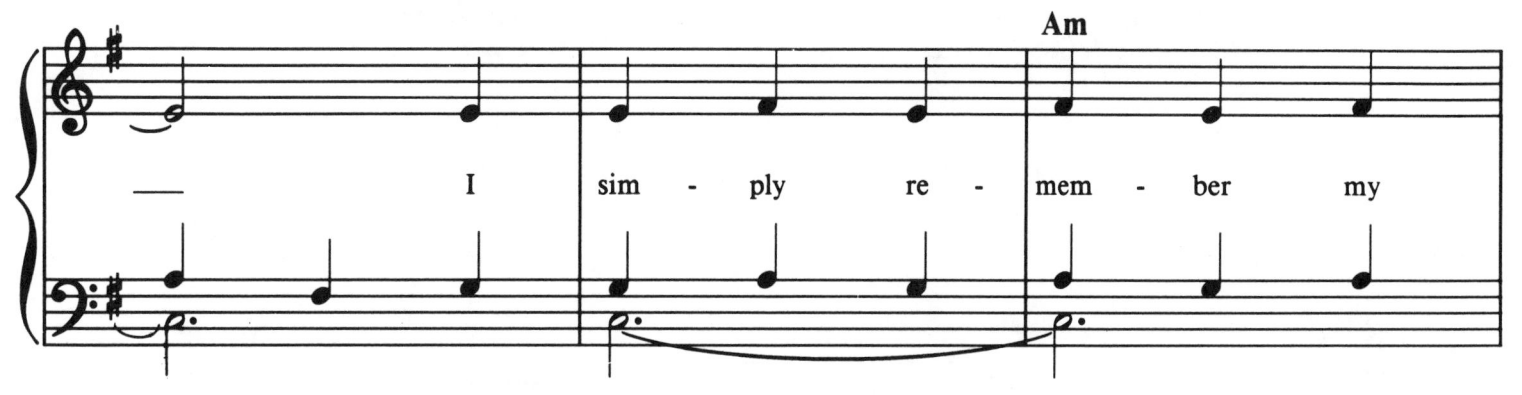

I sim - ply re - mem - ber my

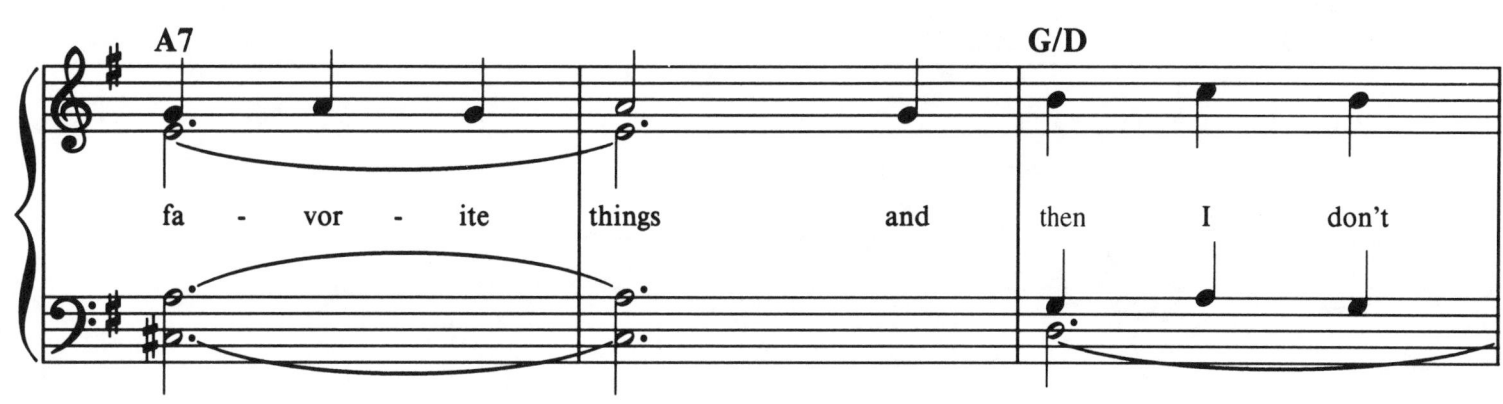

fa - vor - ite things and then I don't

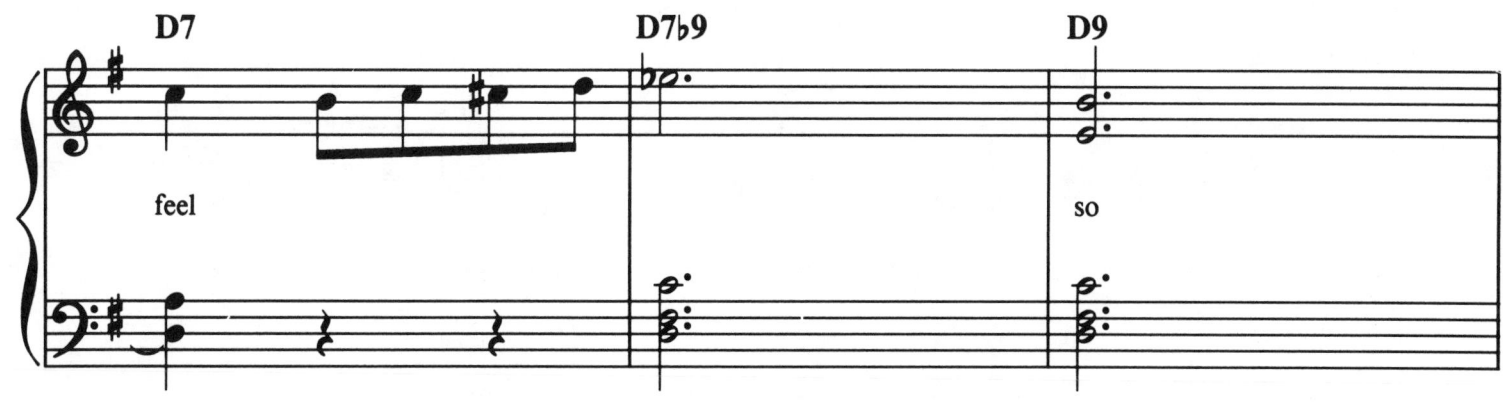

feel so

bad.

PART OF YOUR WORLD
from Walt Disney's THE LITTLE MERMAID

Lyrics by HOWARD ASHMAN
Music by ALAN MENKEN

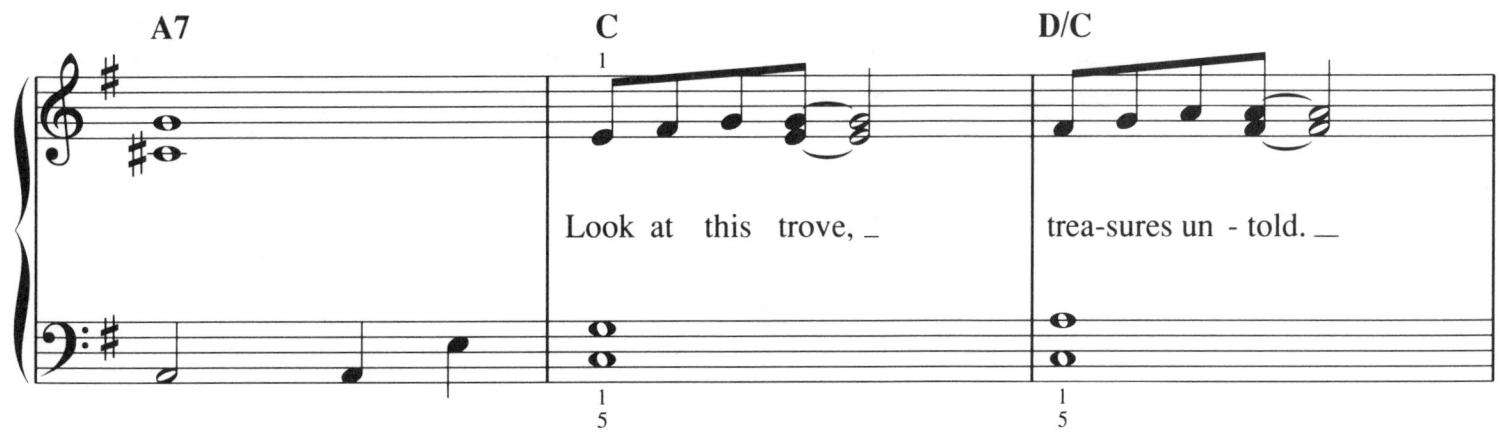

Look at this trove, _ trea-sures un - told. _

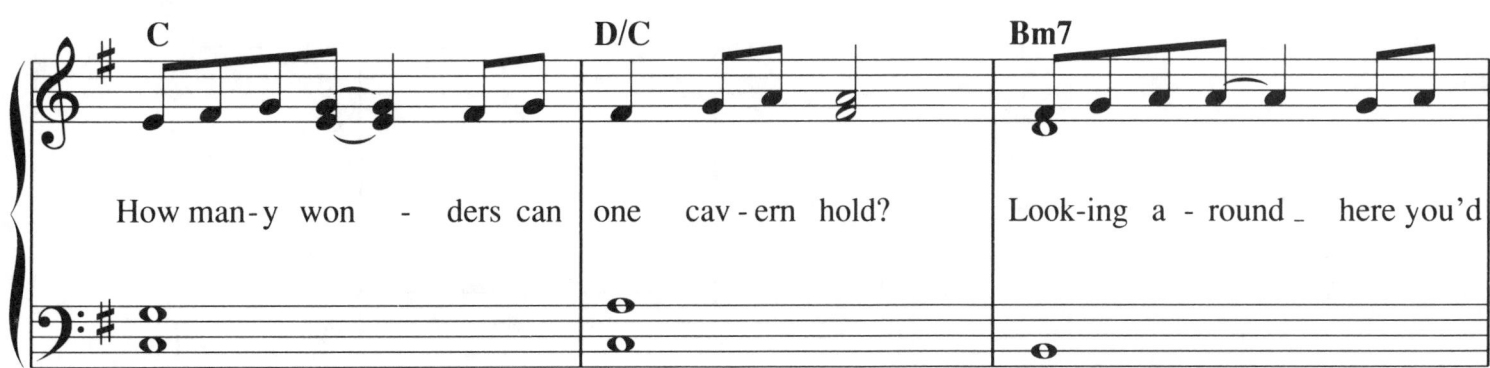

How man-y won - ders can one cav-ern hold? Look-ing a - round _ here you'd

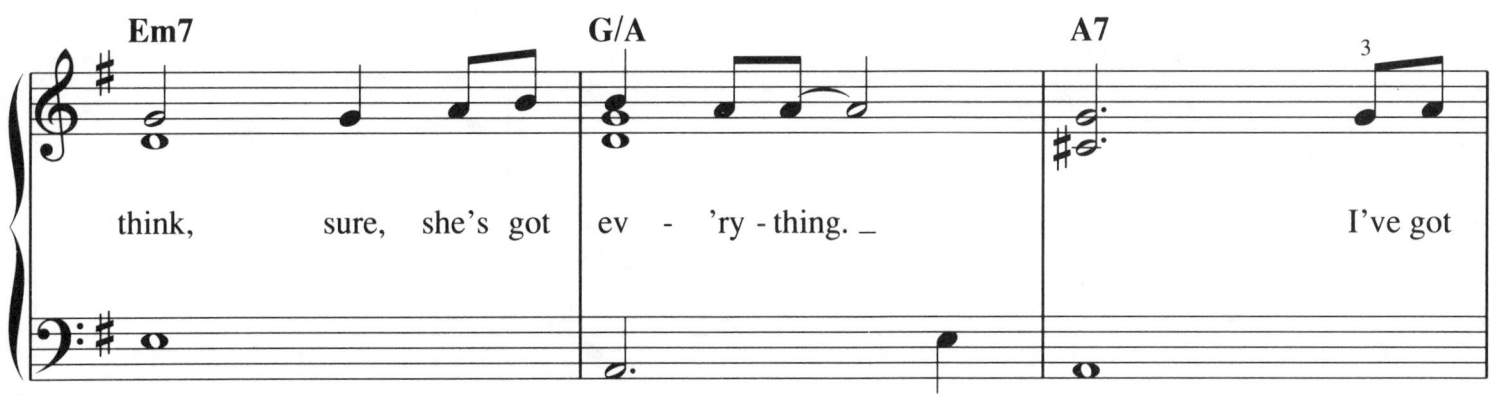

think, sure, she's got ev - 'ry - thing. _ I've got

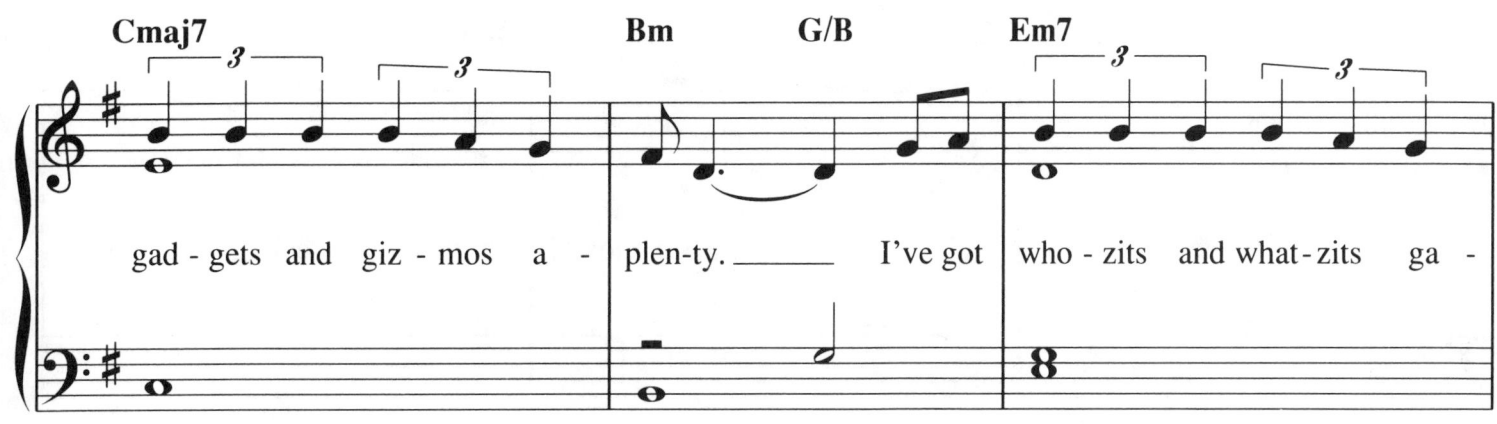

gad - gets and giz - mos a - plen-ty. _____ I've got who - zits and what-zits ga -

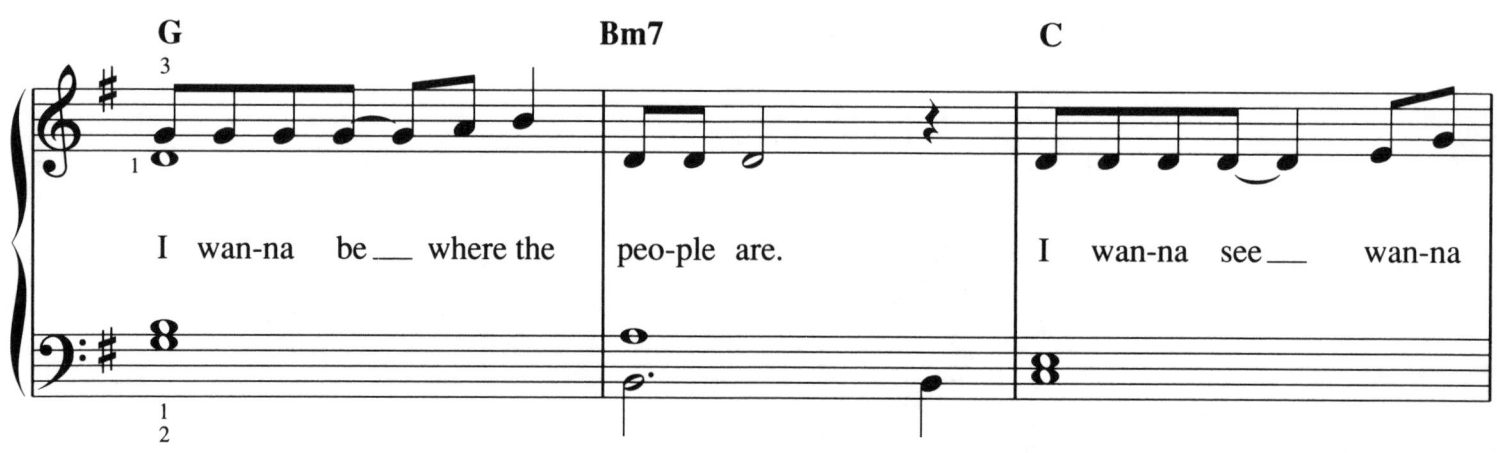

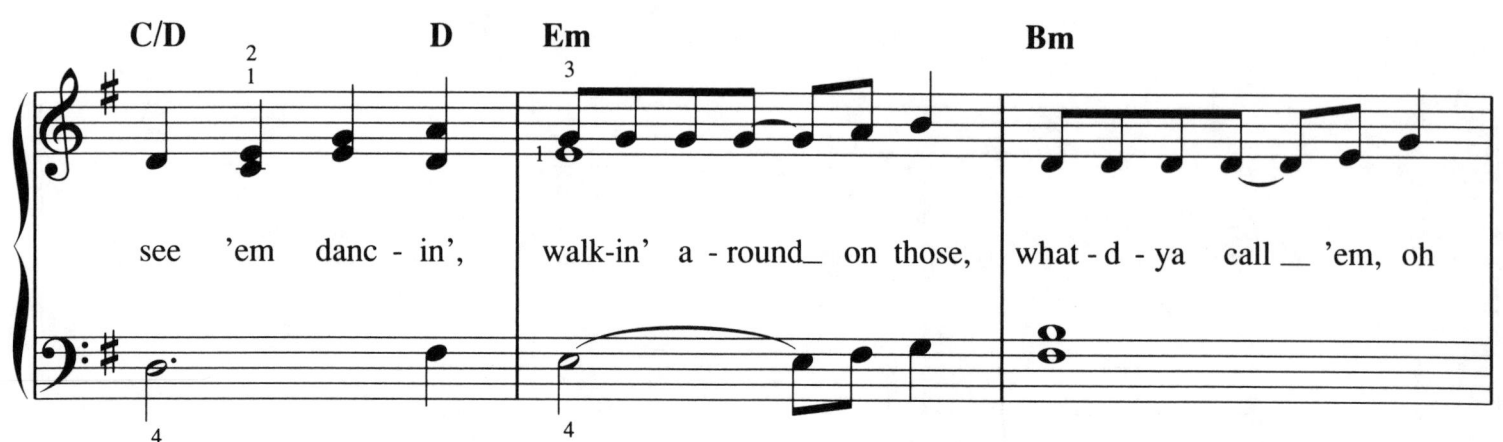

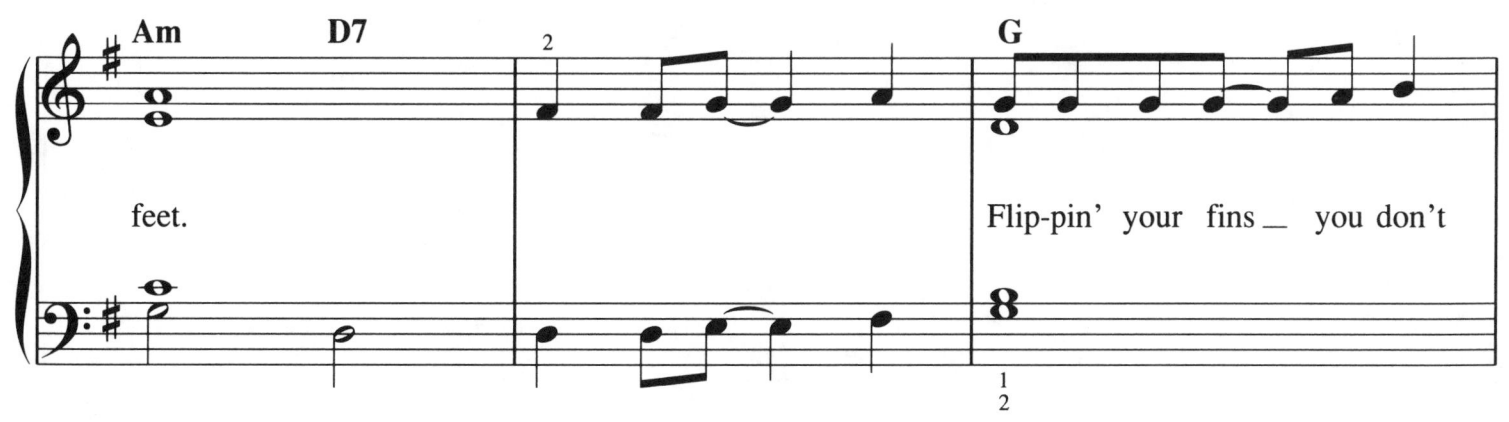

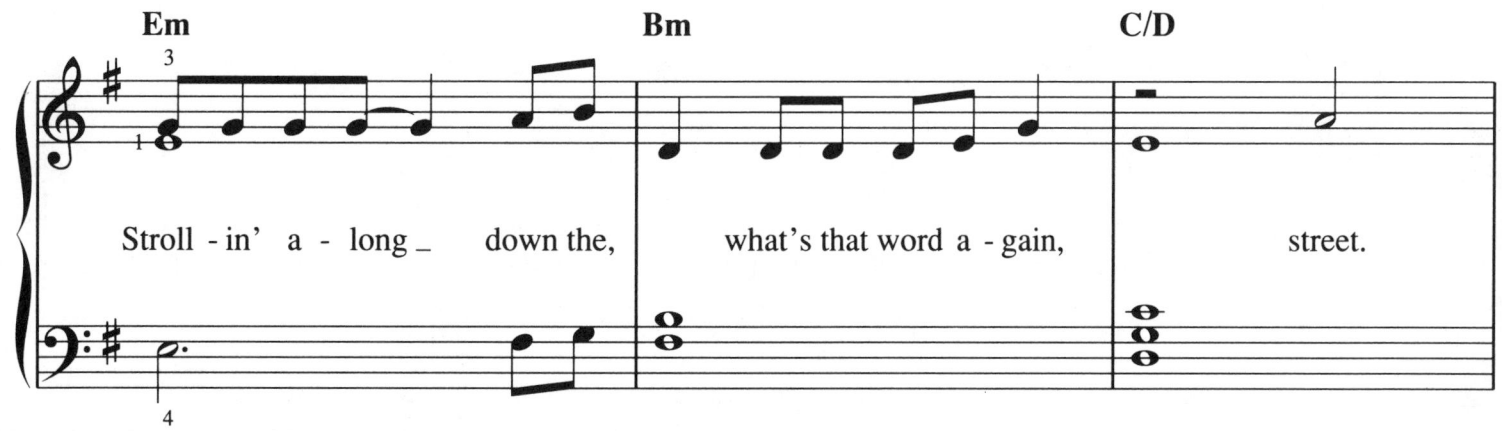

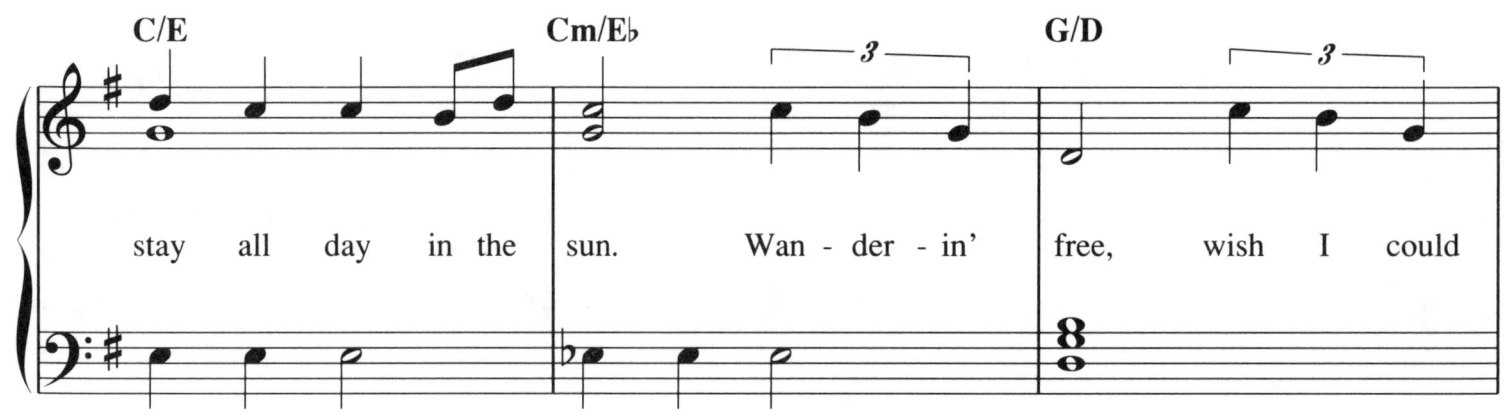

stay all day in the sun. Wan - der - in' free, wish I could

be part of that world. _____ What would I

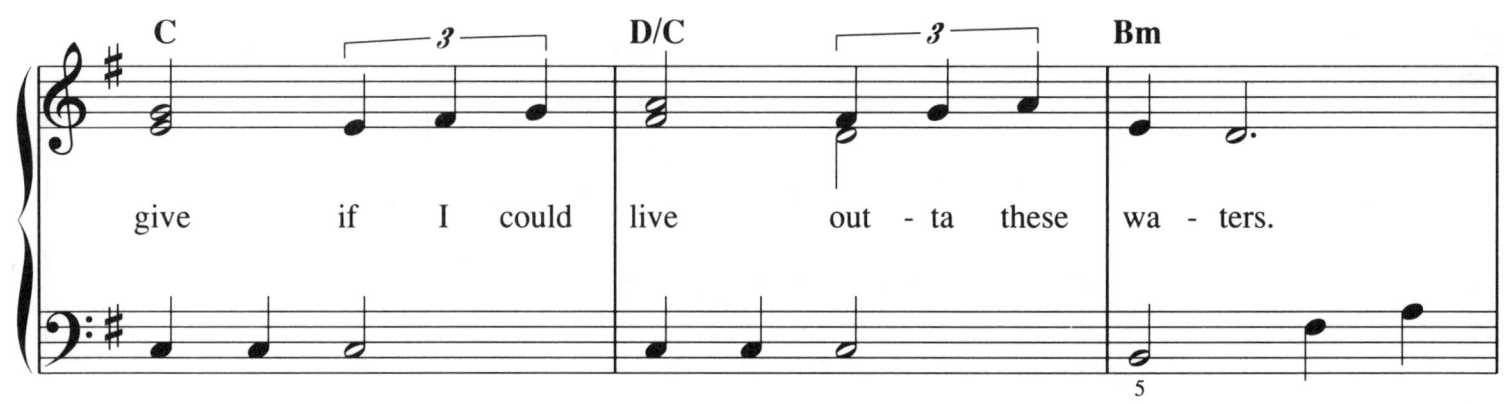

give if I could live out - ta these wa - ters.

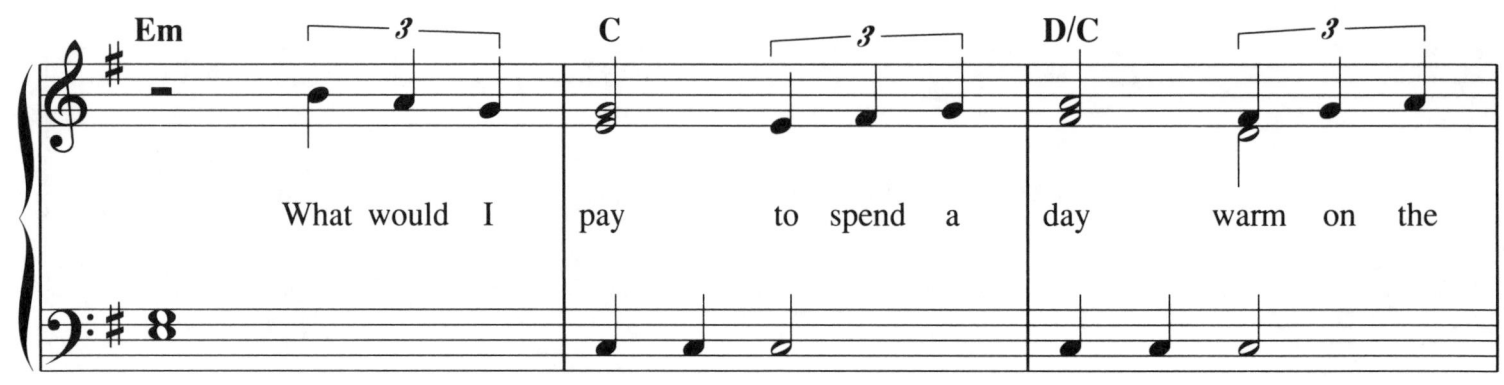

What would I pay to spend a day warm on the

sand. Bet - cha on land they un - der -

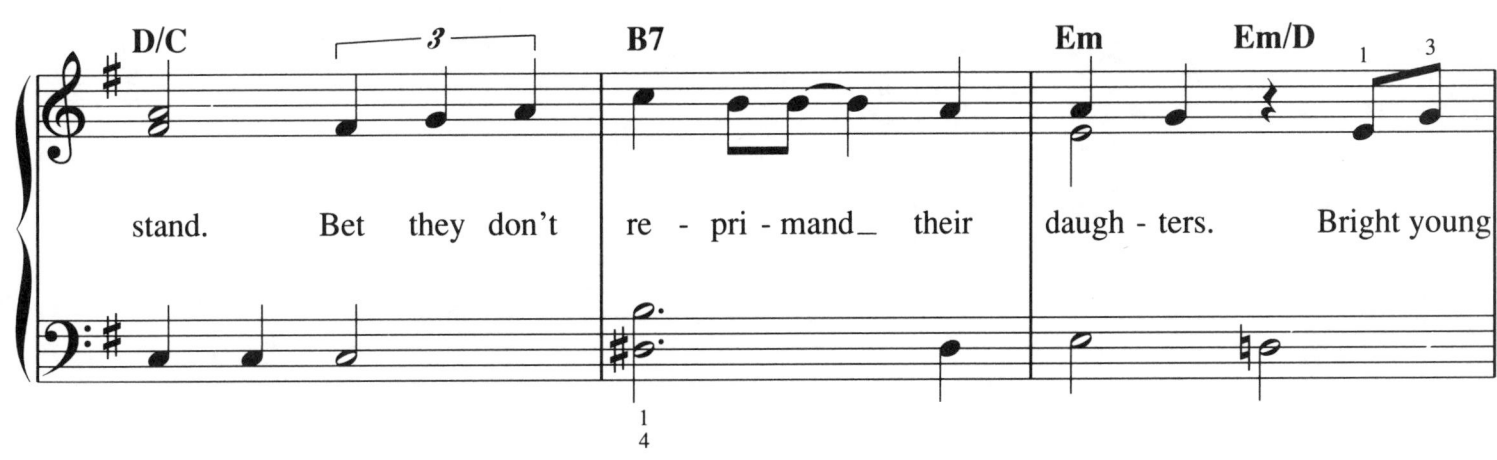

stand. Bet they don't re - pri - mand_ their daugh - ters. Bright young

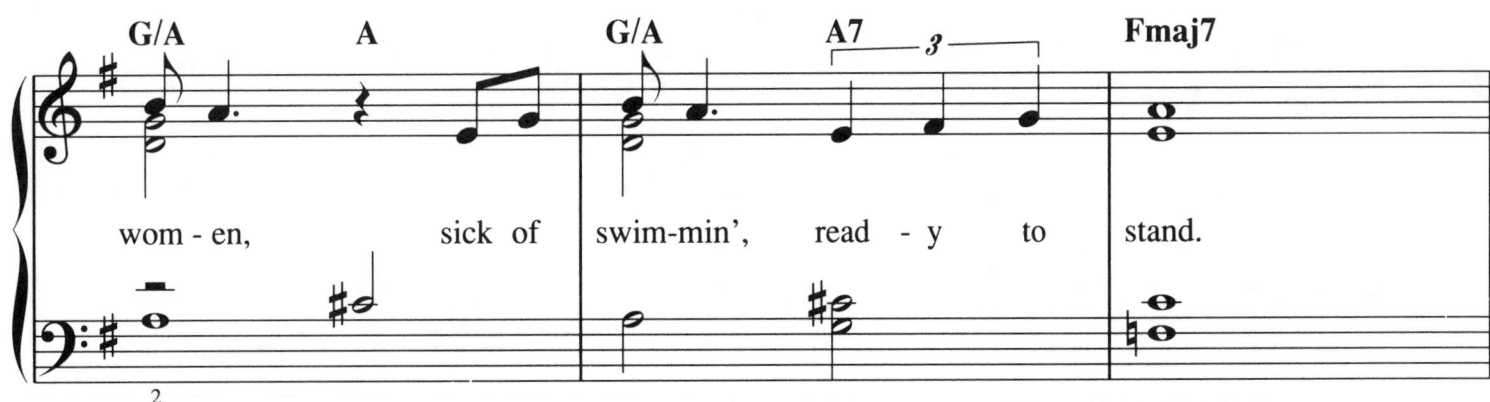

wom - en, sick of swim - min', read - y to stand.

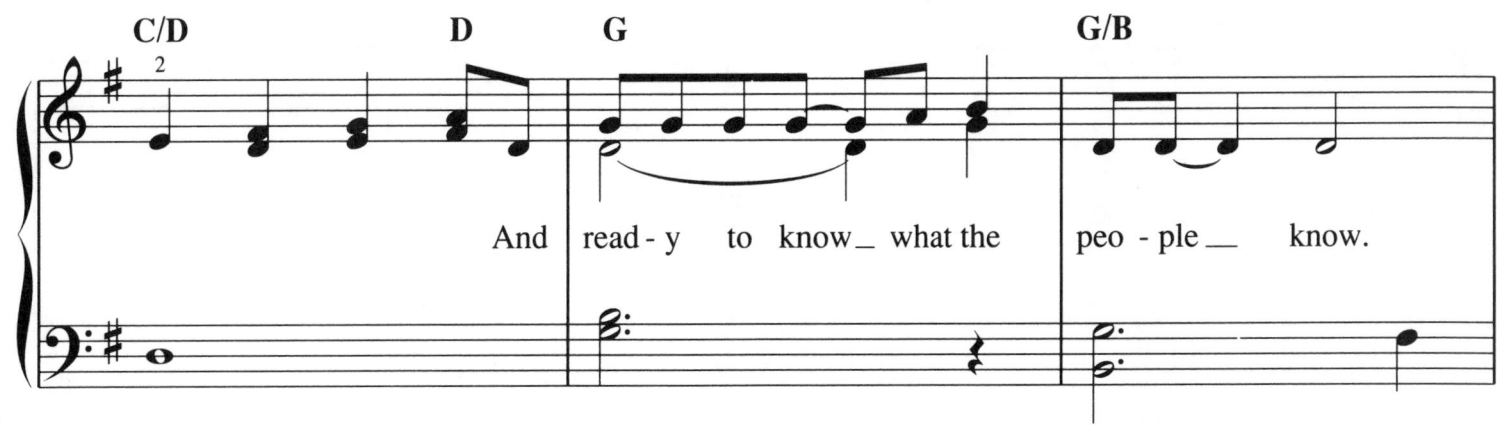

And read - y to know_ what the peo - ple _ know.

68

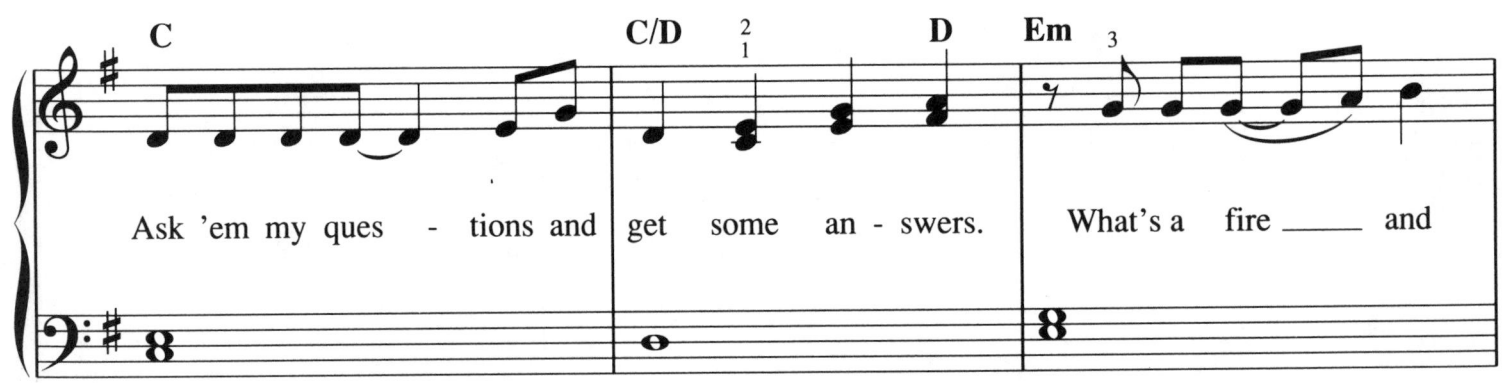

Ask 'em my ques - tions and get some an - swers. What's a fire _____ and

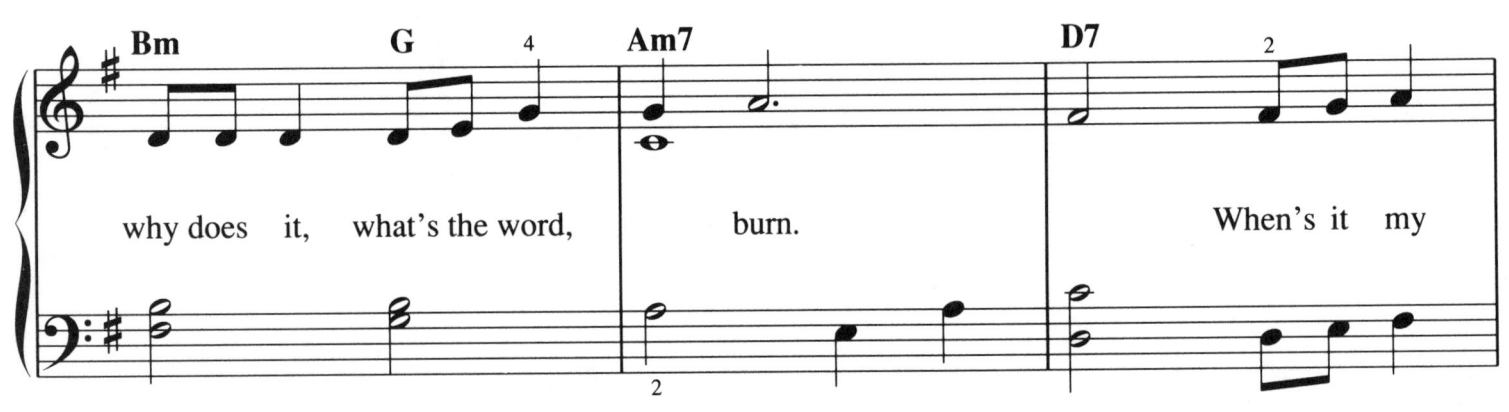

why does it, what's the word, burn. When's it my

turn? Would-n't I love, love to ex - plore that shore up a -

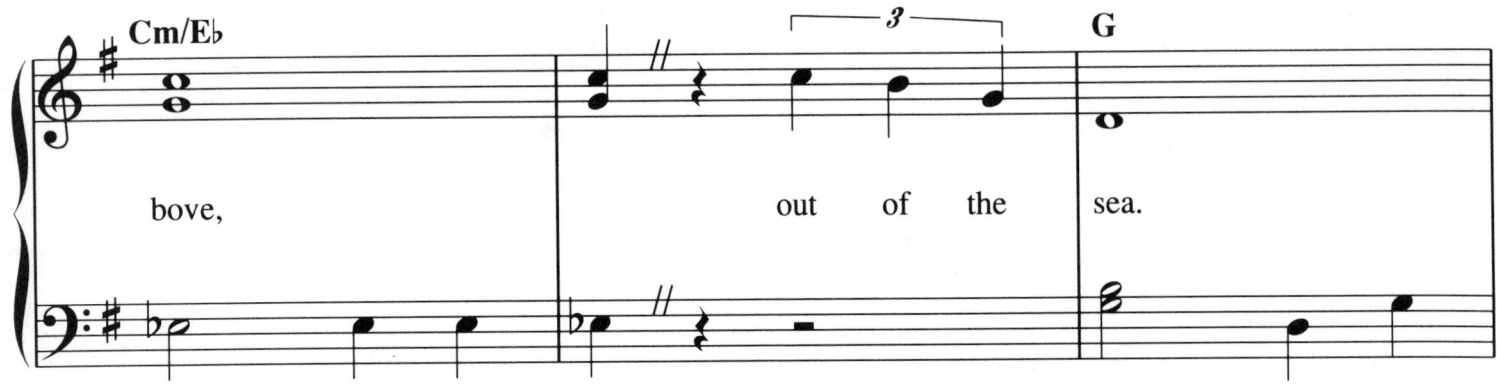

bove, out of the sea.

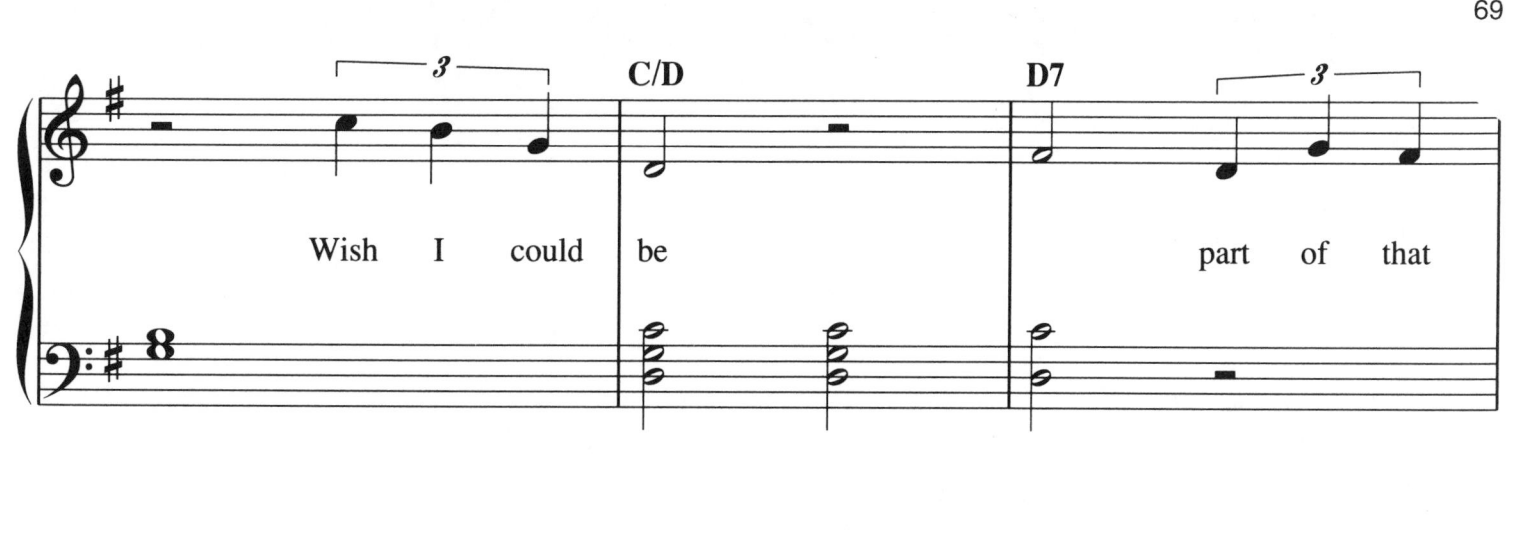

Wish I could be part of that

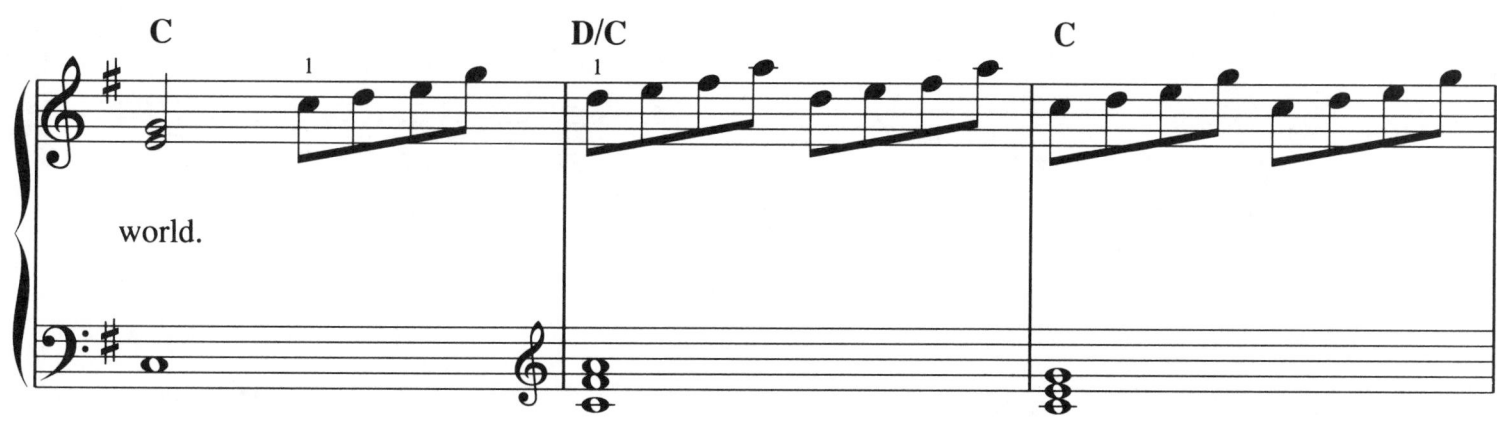

world.

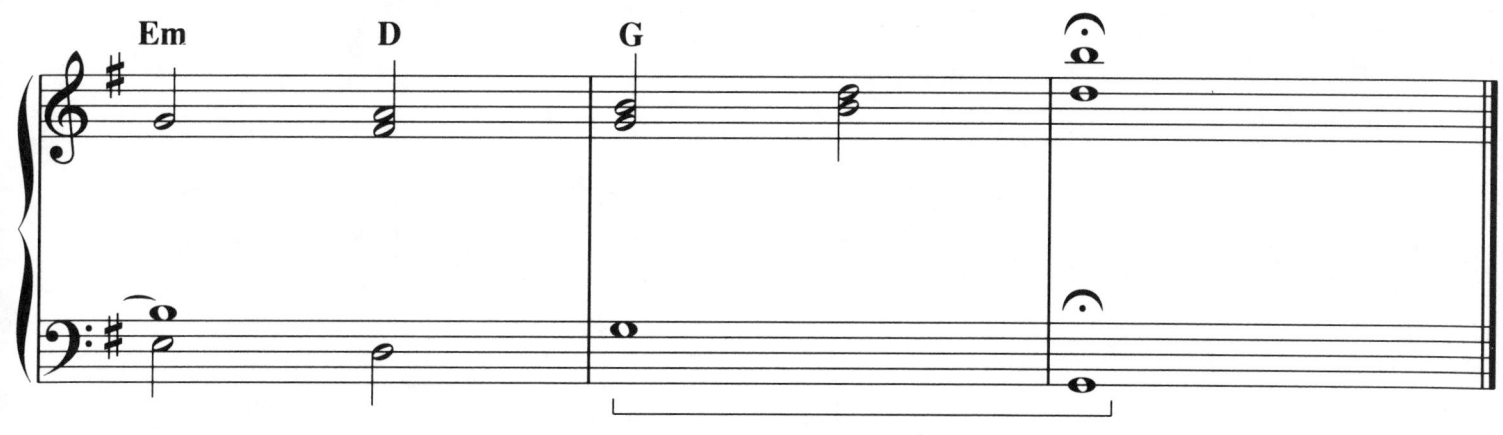

THE RAINBOW CONNECTION
from THE MUPPET MOVIE

Words and Music by PAUL WILLIAMS
and KENNETH L. ASCHER

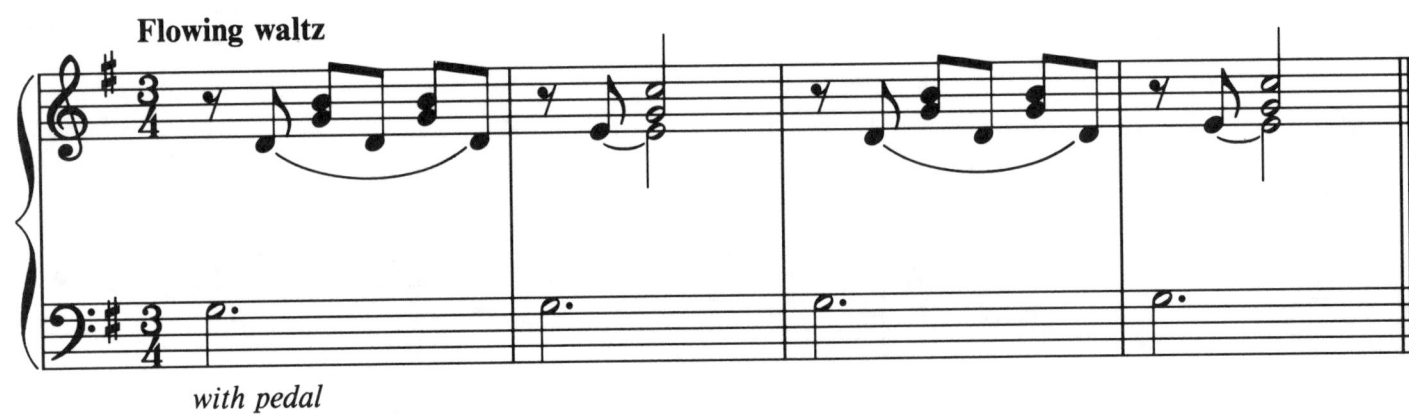

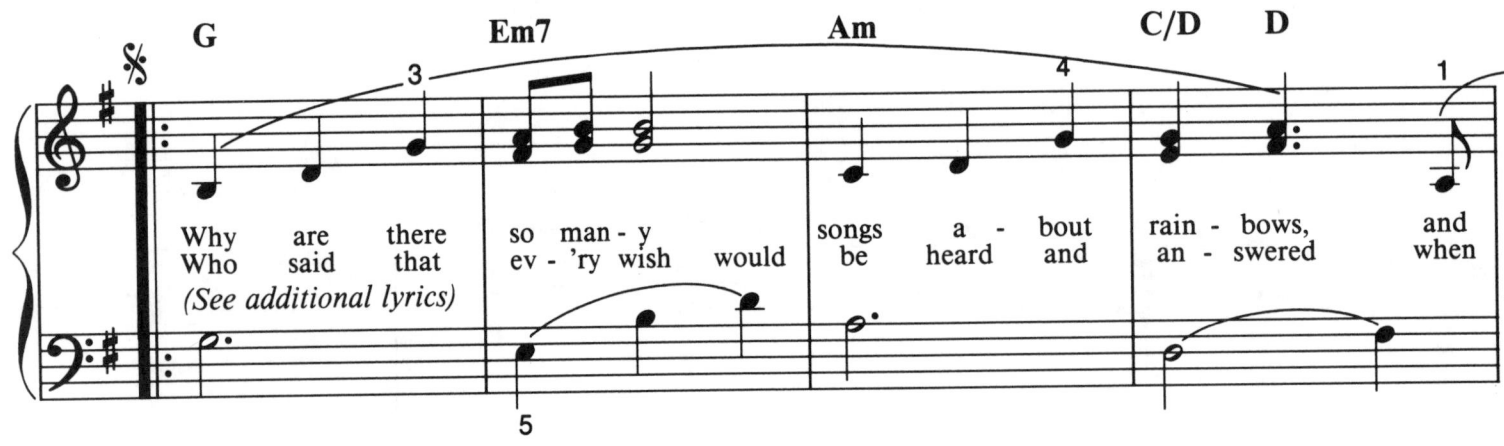

Why are there so man-y songs a-bout rain-bows, and
Who said that ev-'ry wish would be heard and an-swered when
(See additional lyrics)

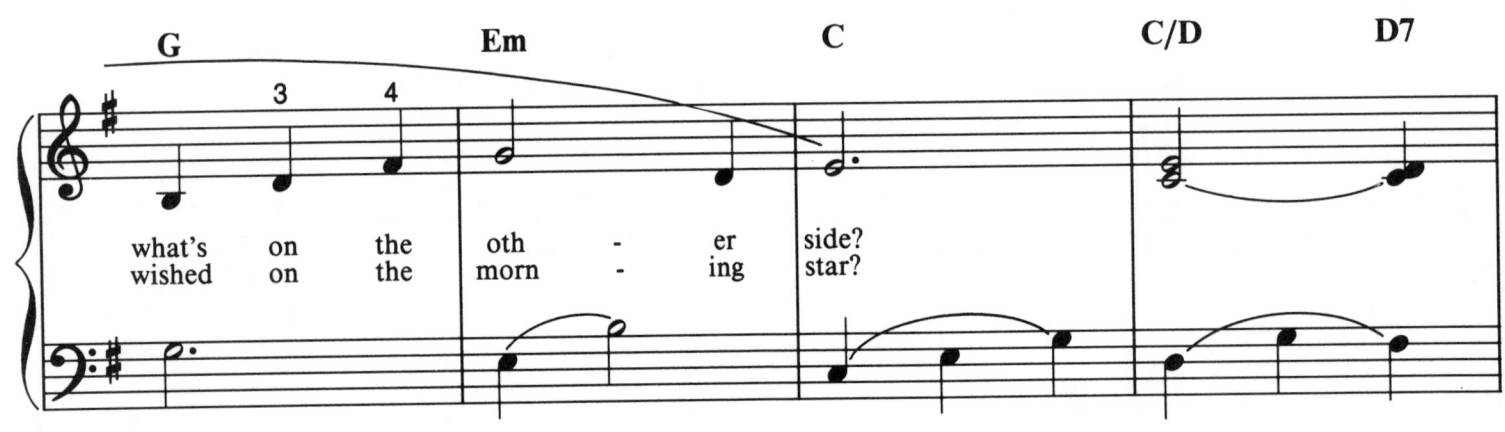

what's on the oth - er side?
wished on the morn - ing star?

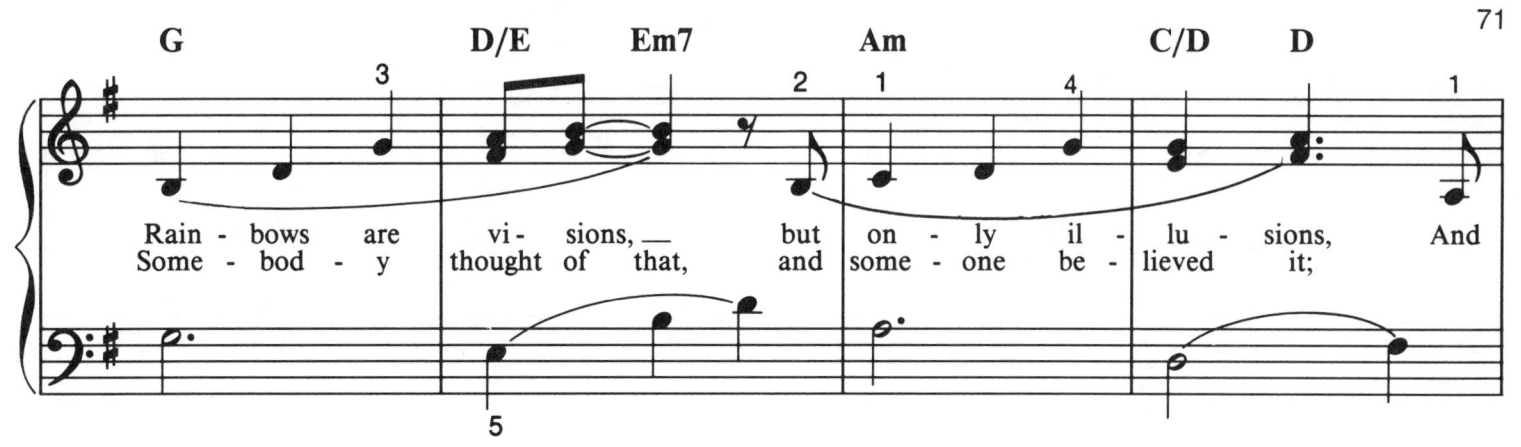

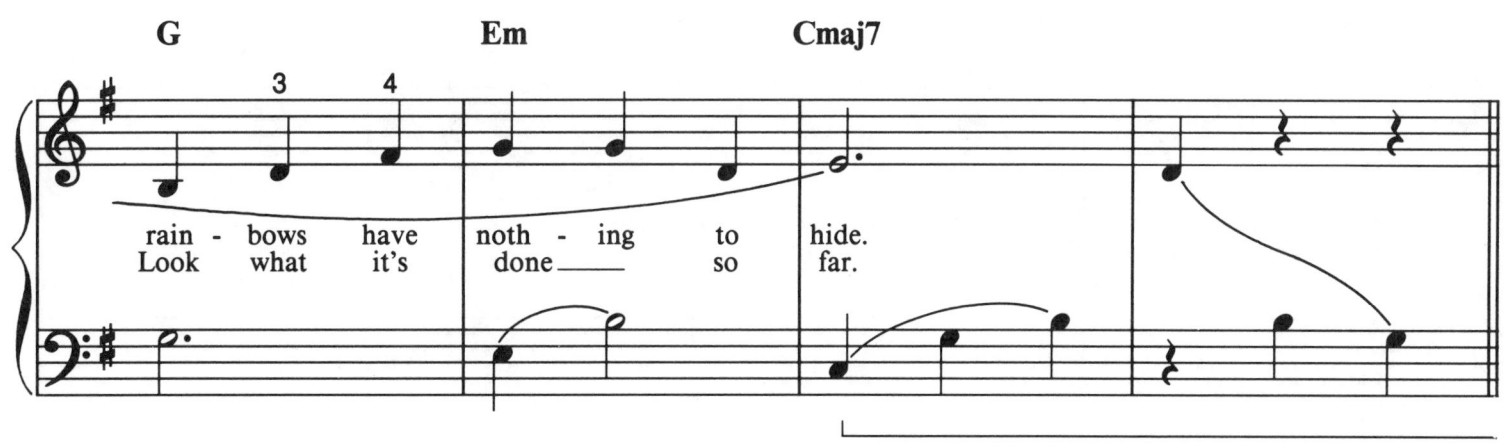

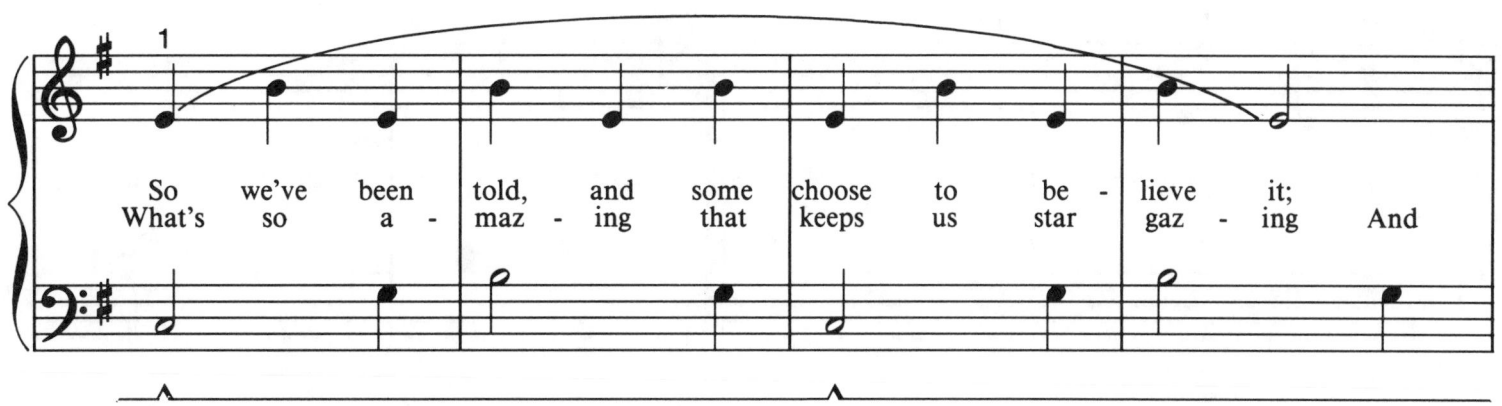

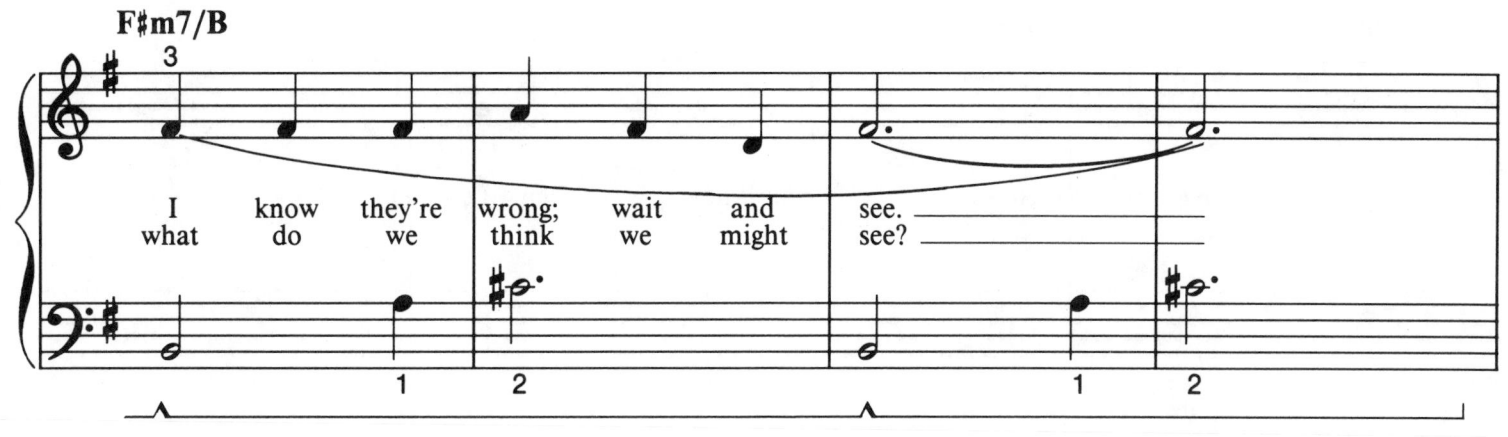

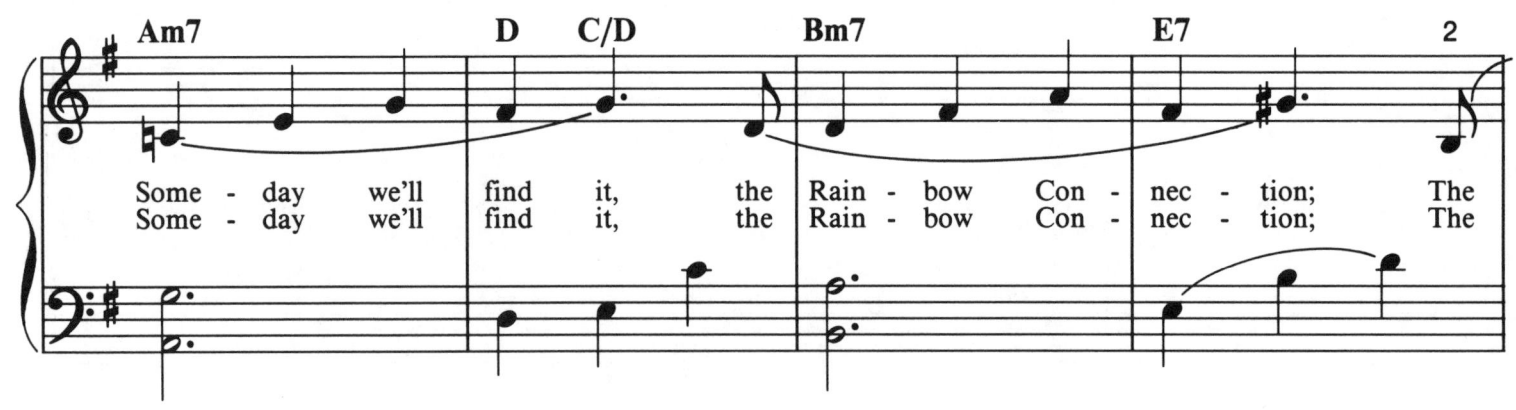

Some - day we'll find it, the Rain - bow Con - nec - tion; The
Some - day we'll find it, the Rain - bow Con - nec - tion; The

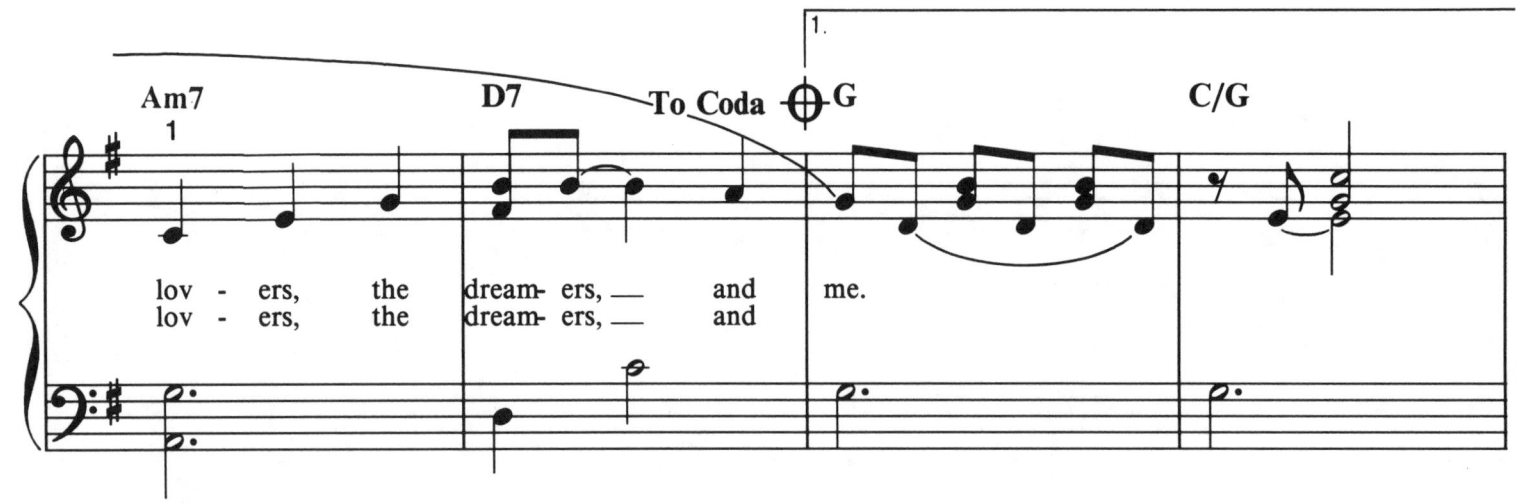

lov - ers, the dream- ers, ___ and me.
lov - ers, the dream- ers, ___ and

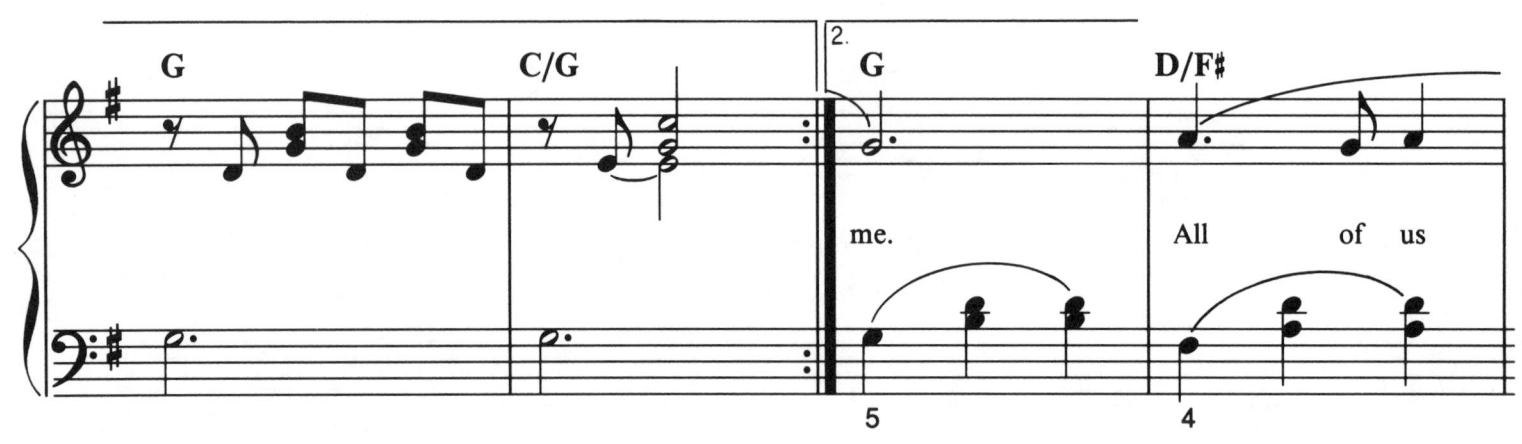

me. All of us

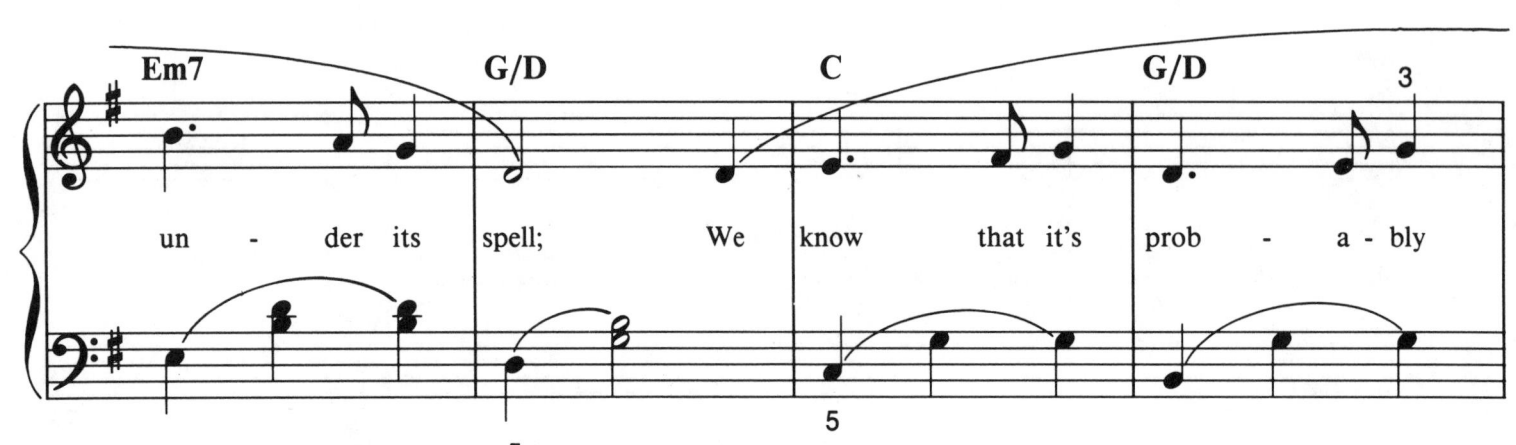

un - der its spell; We know that it's prob - a - bly

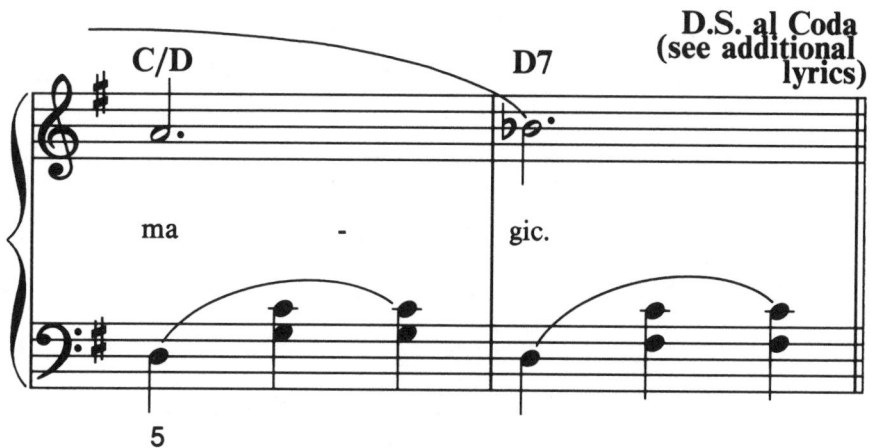

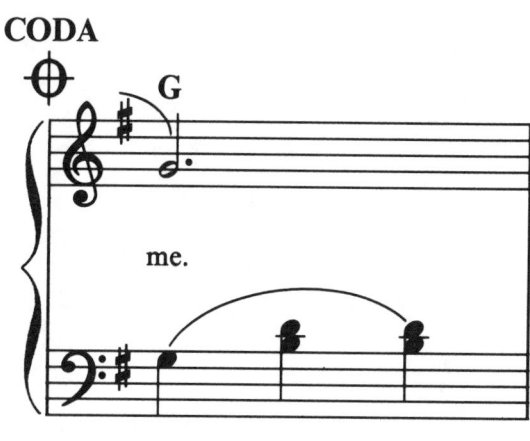

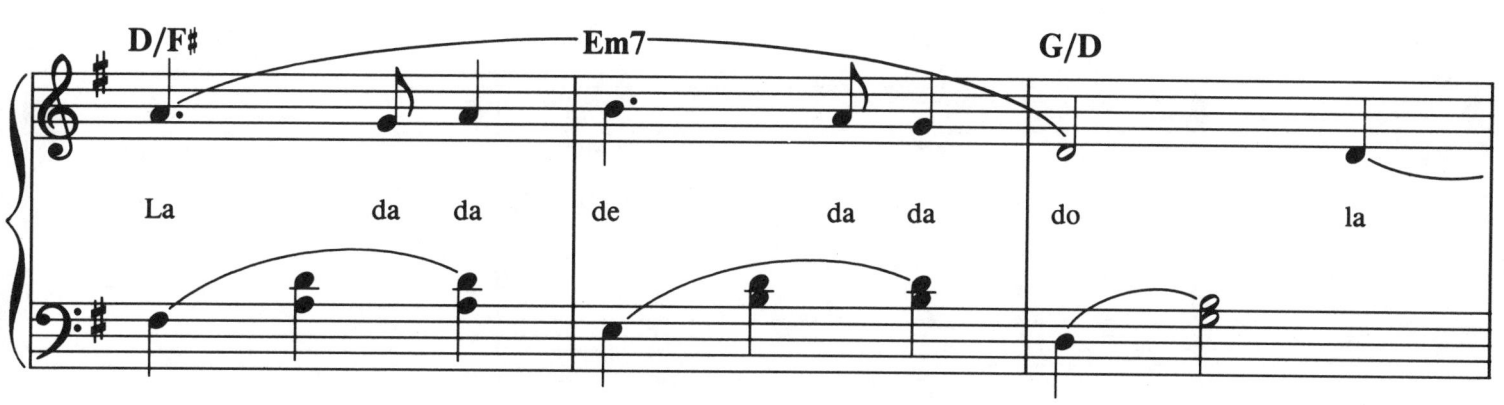

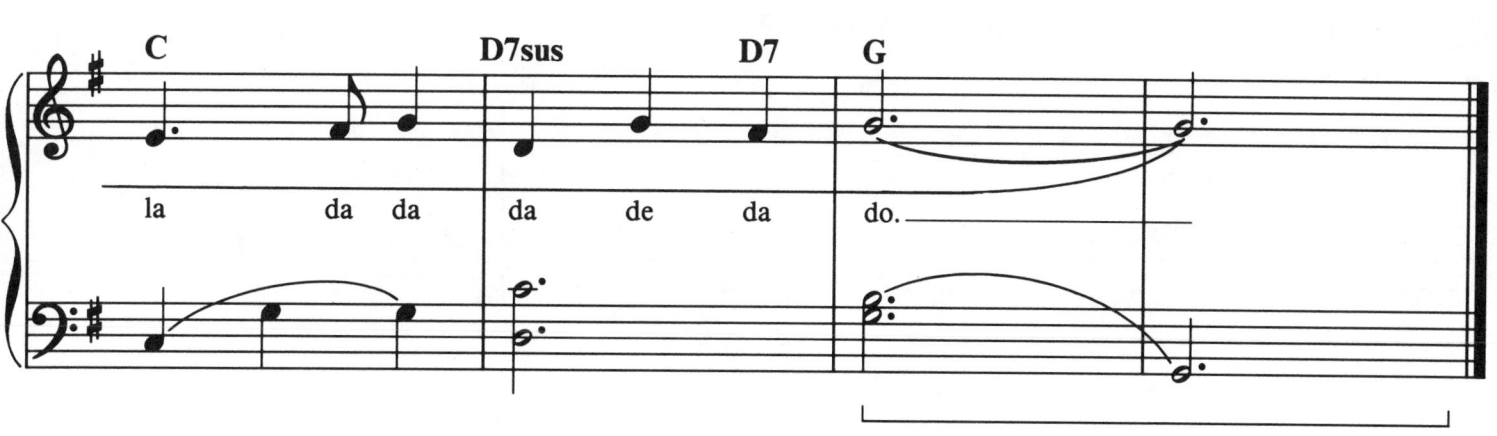

Additional Lyrics
Verse 3: Have you been half asleep and have you heard voices?
I've heard them calling my name.
Is this the sweet sound that calls the young sailors?
The voice might be one and the same.
I've heard it too many times to ignore it.
It's something that I'm s'posed to be.
Someday we'll find it,
The Rainbow Connection;
The lovers, the dreamers and (me.)
(To Coda)

REFLECTION
from Walt Disney Pictures' MULAN

Music by MATTHEW WILDER
Lyrics by DAVID ZIPPEL

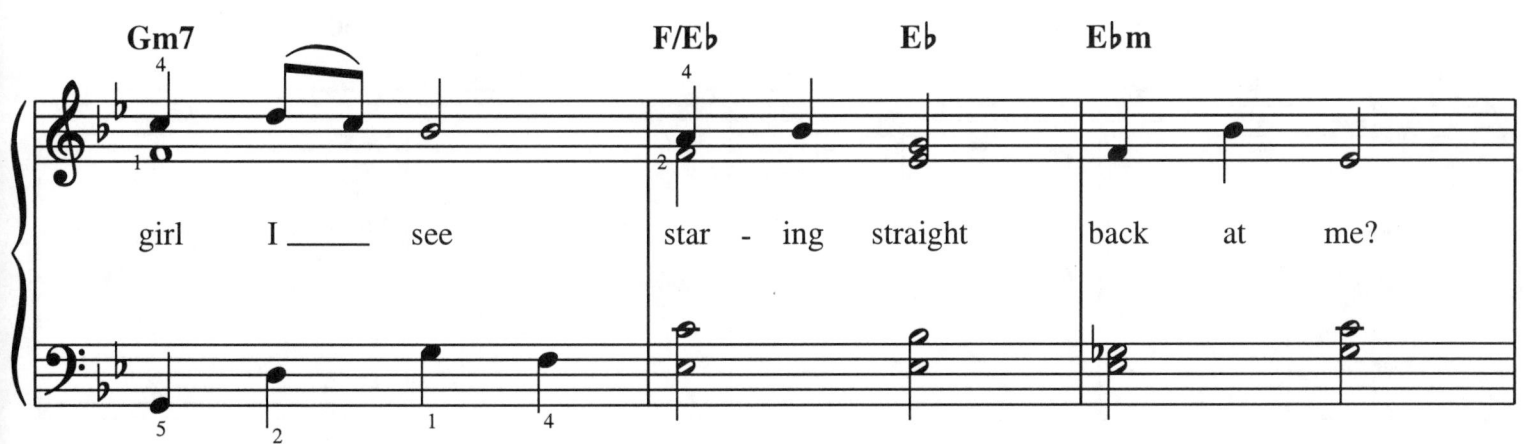

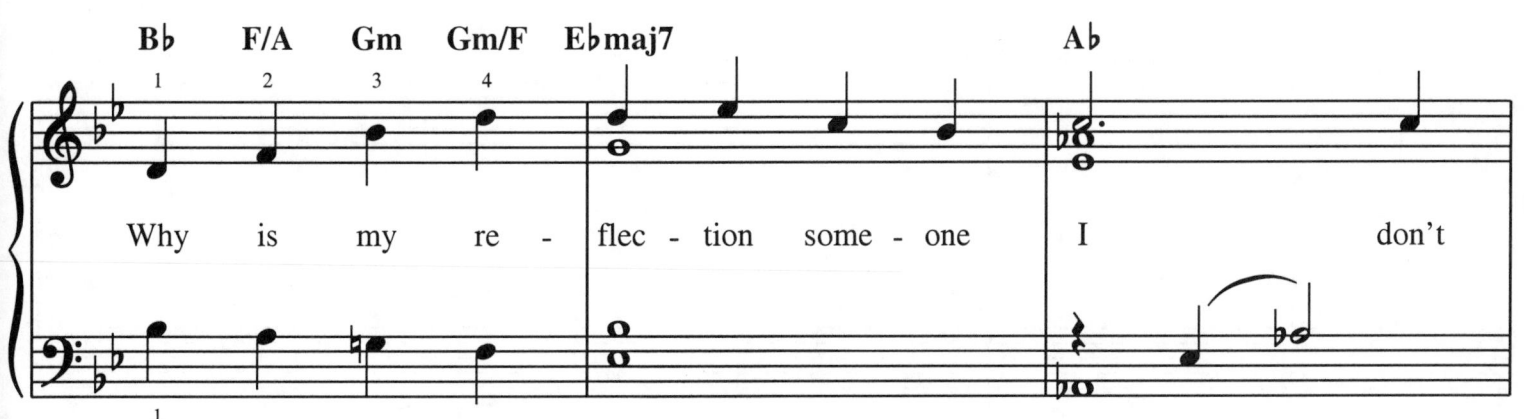

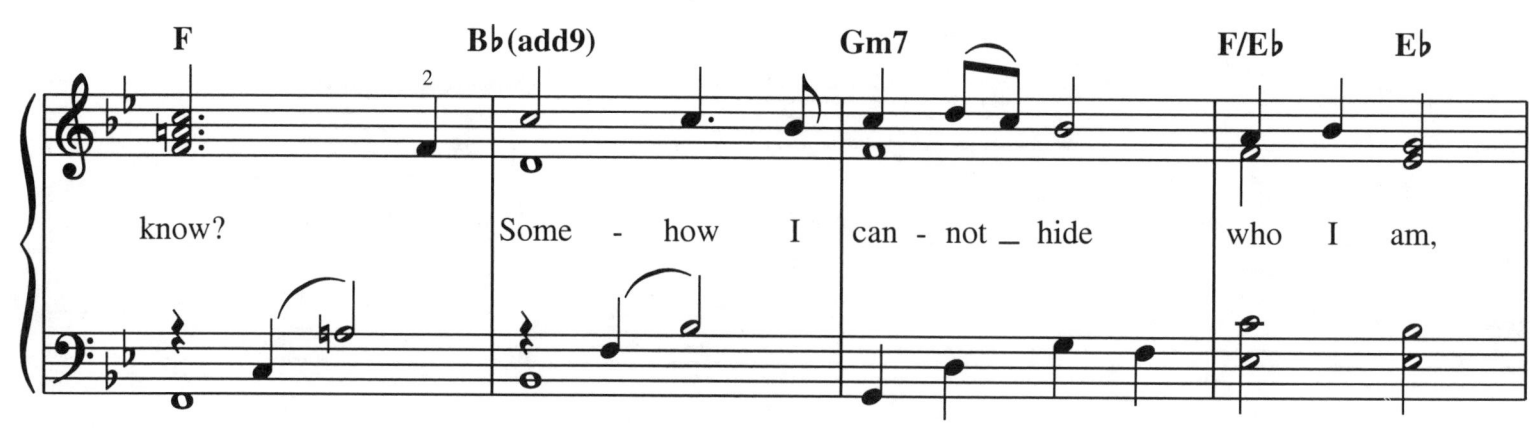

know? Some - how I can - not _ hide who I am,

though I've tried. When will my re - flec - tion show who I am in -

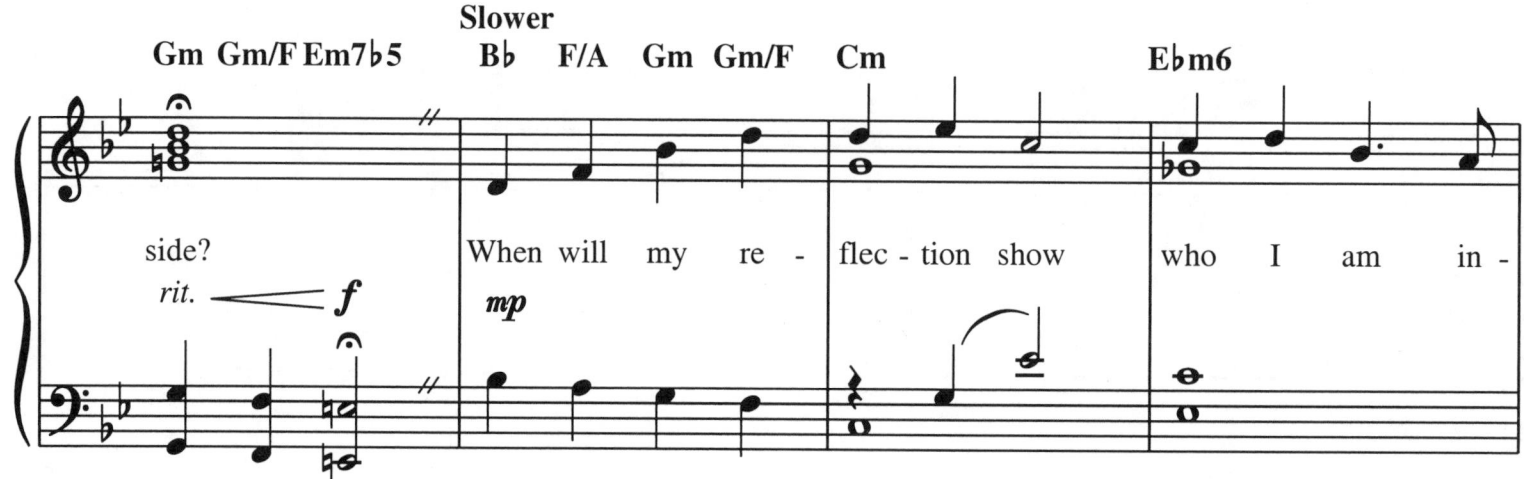

side? When will my re - flec - tion show who I am in -

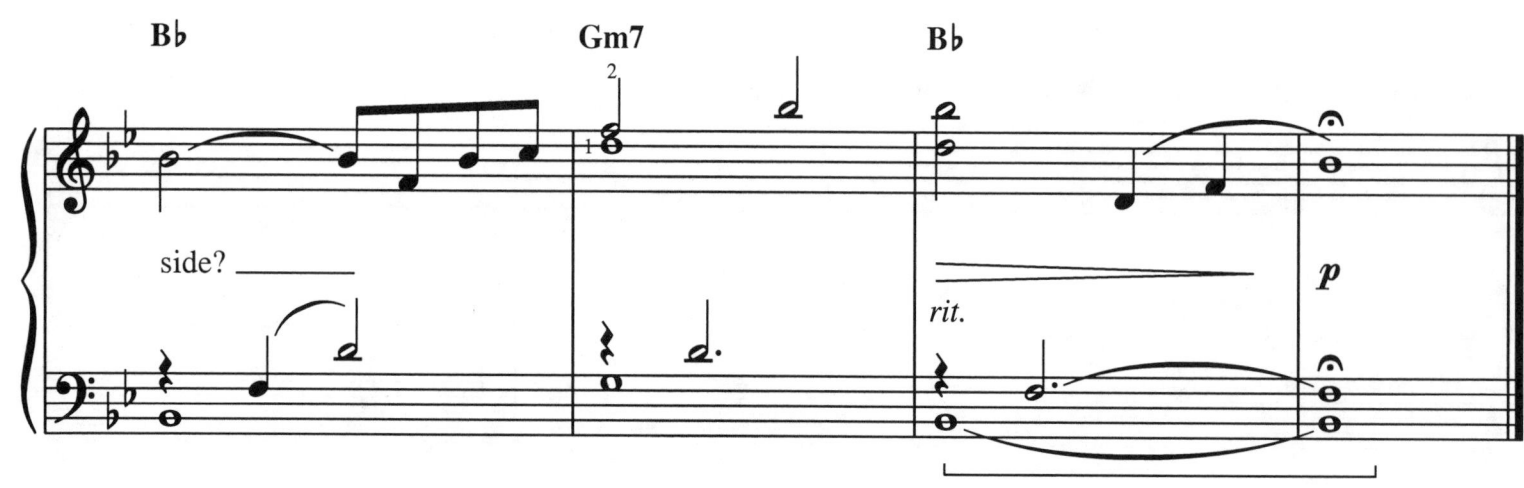

side? _____

SAYING GOODBYE
from THE MUPPETS TAKE MANHATTAN

By JEFF MOSS

Don't want to leave;

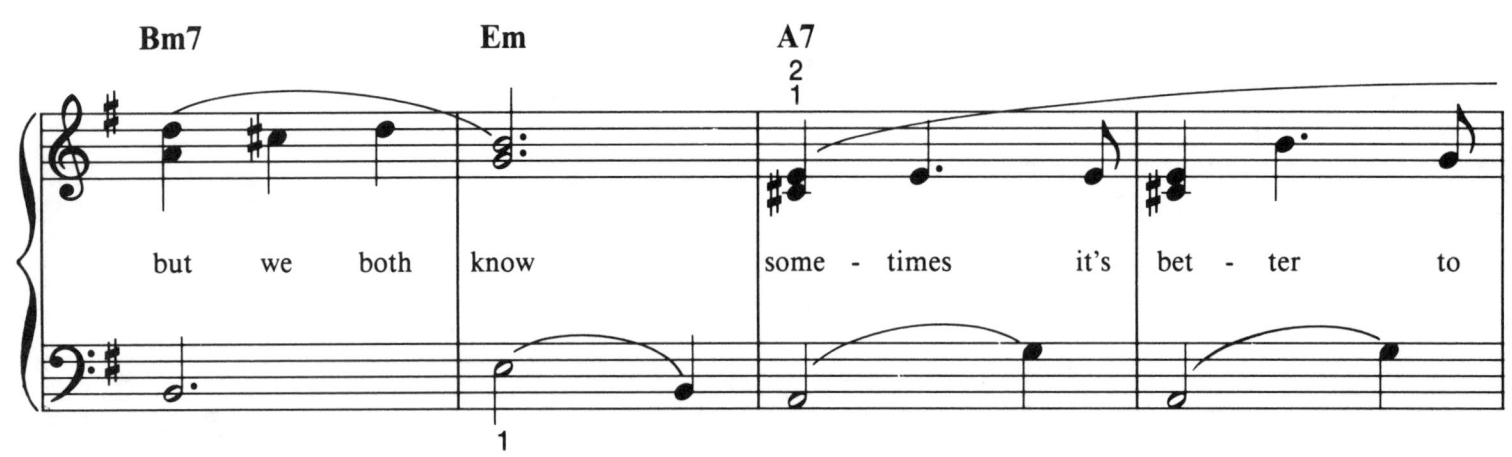

but we both know some - times it's bet - ter to

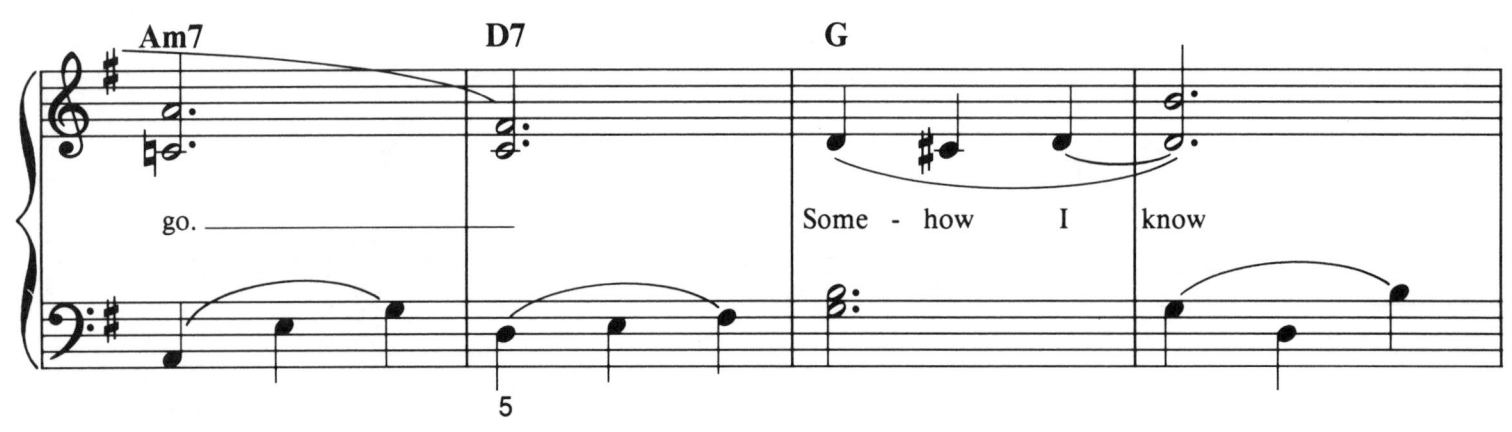

go. _____ Some - how I know

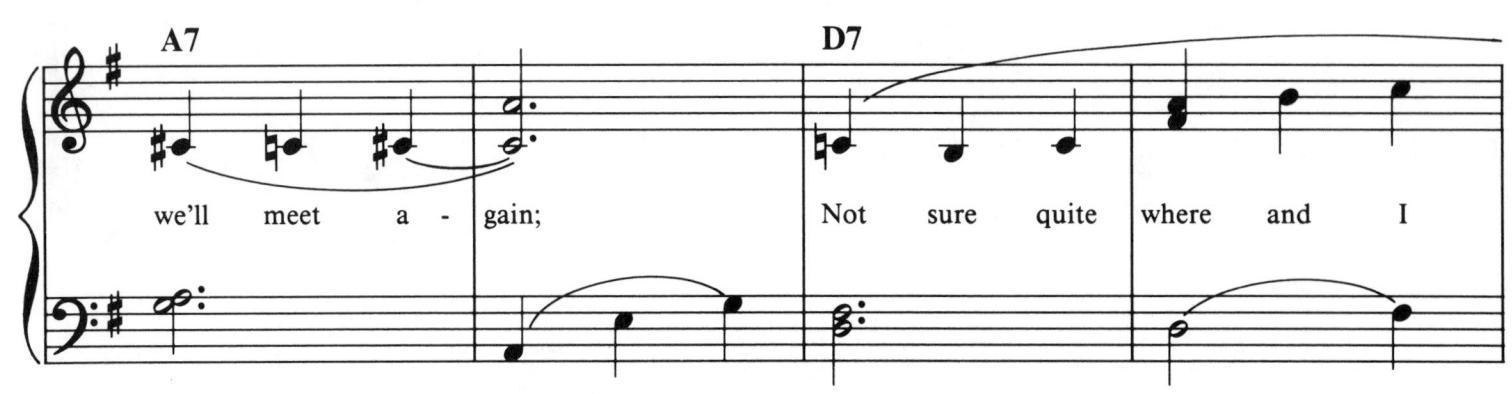

we'll meet a - gain; Not sure quite where and I

don't know just when. You're in my heart,

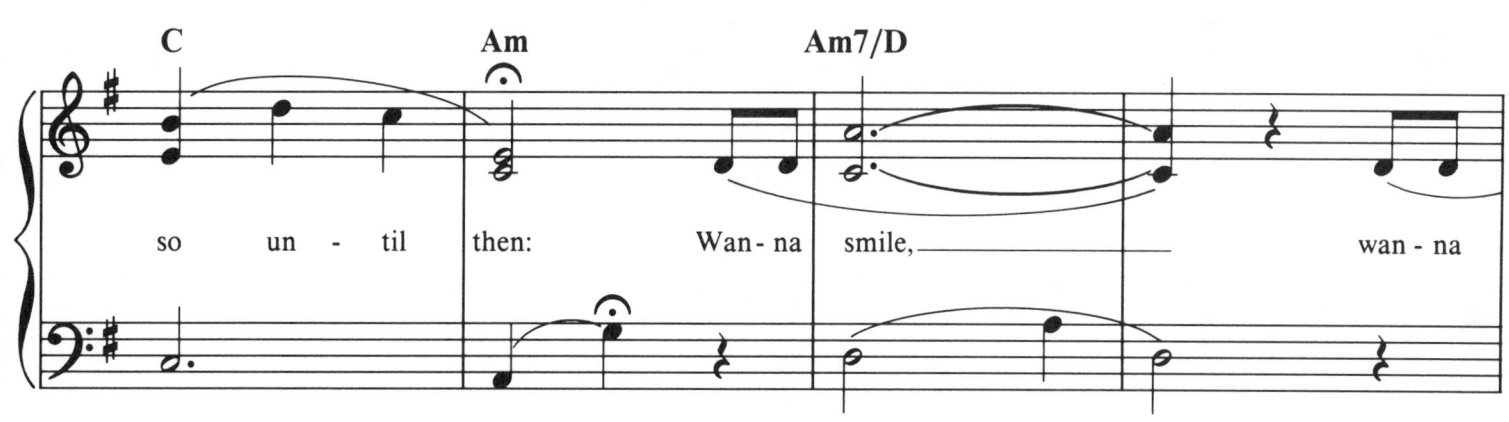

so un - til then: Wan - na smile, _____ wan - na

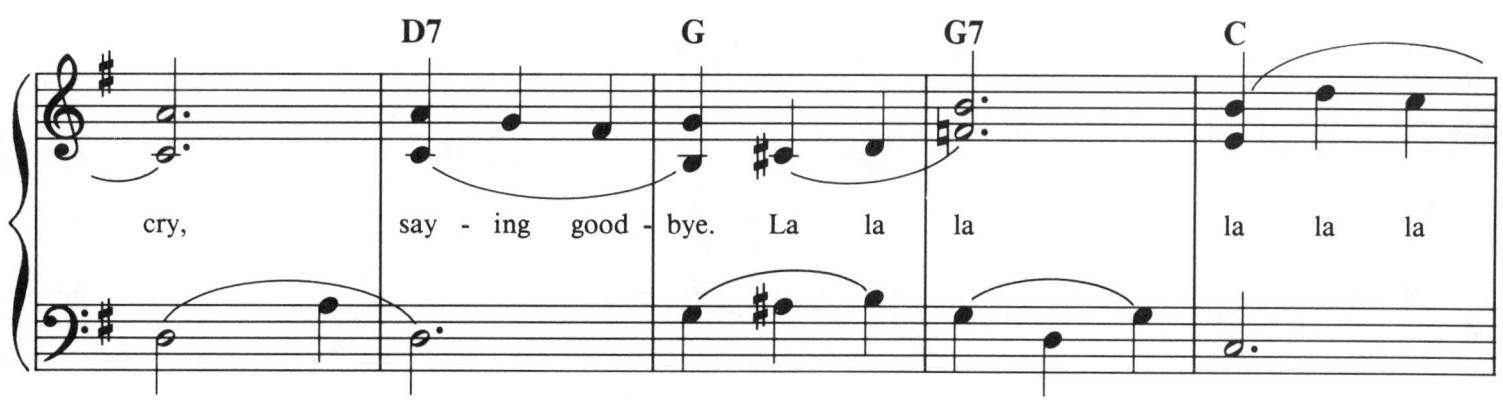

cry, say - ing good - bye. La la la la la la

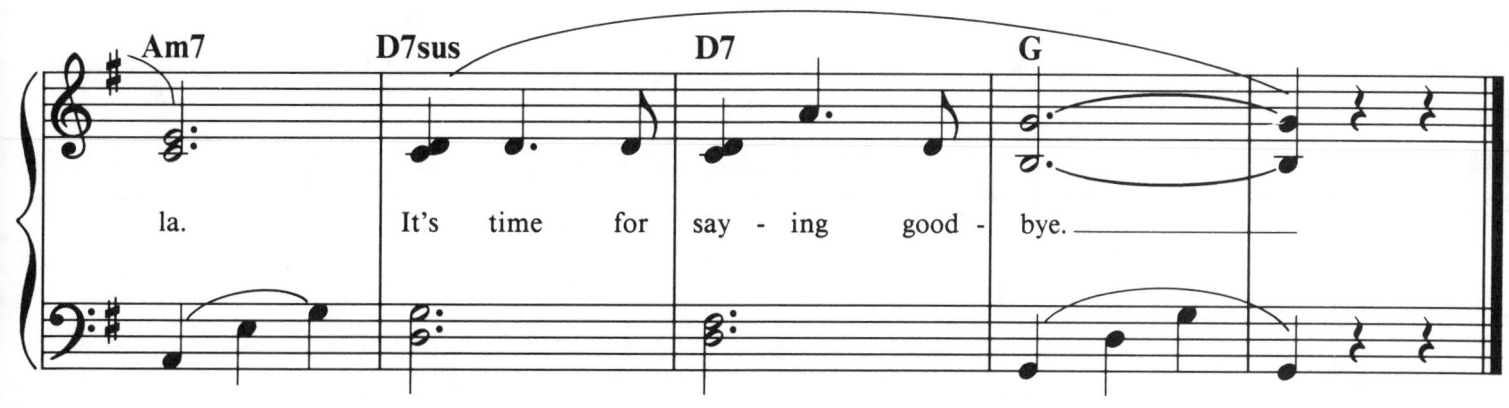

la. It's time for say - ing good - bye. _____

SOMEDAY OUT OF THE BLUE

(Theme from El Dorado)
from THE ROAD TO EL DORADO

Music by ELTON JOHN
and PATRICK LEONARD
Lyrics by TIM RICE

STAR TREK® THE MOTION PICTURE

Theme from the Paramount Picture STAR TREK: THE MOTION PICTURE

Music by JERRY GOLDSMITH

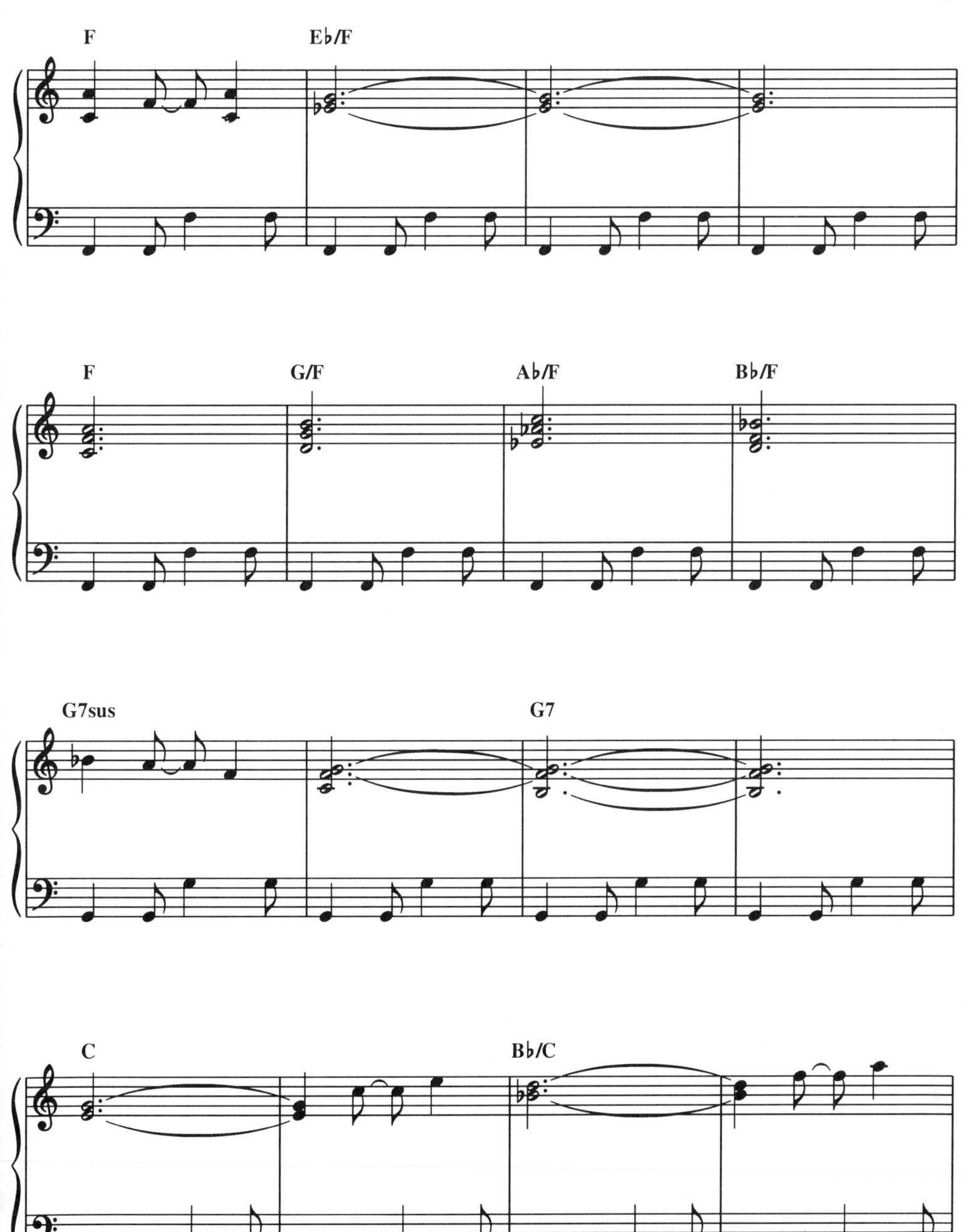

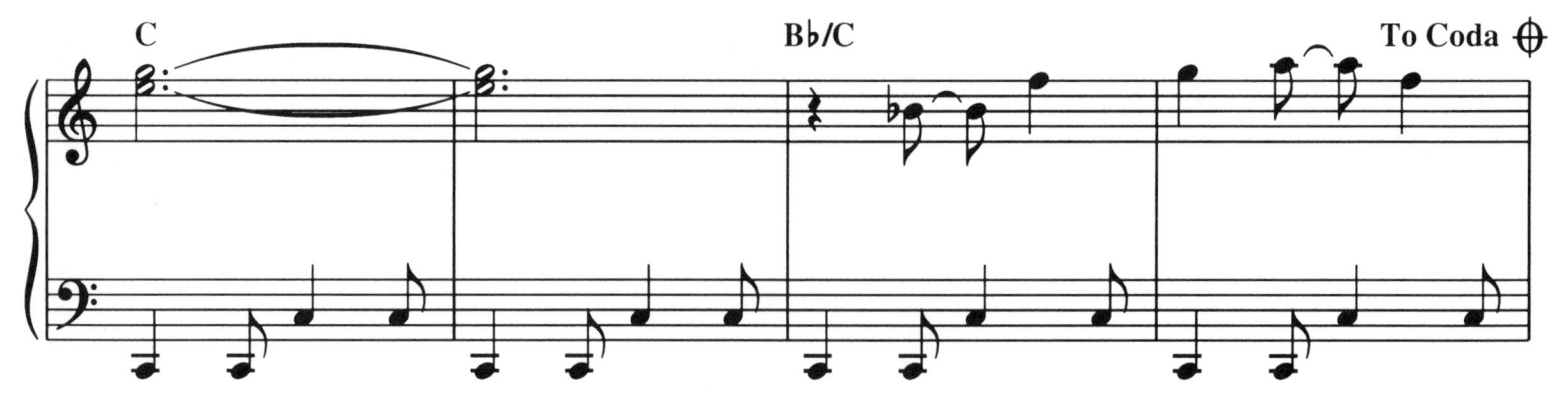

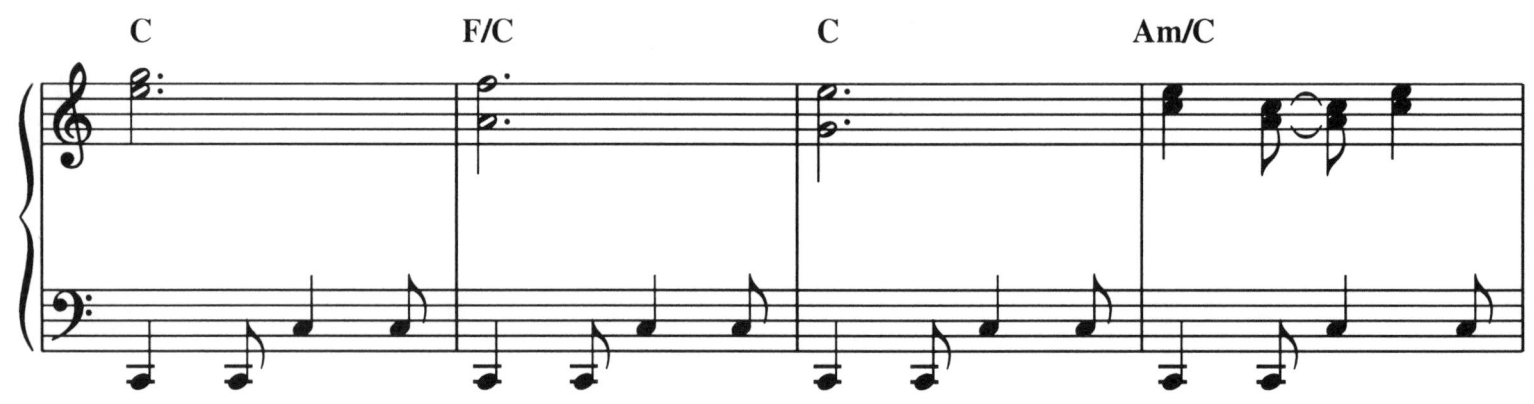

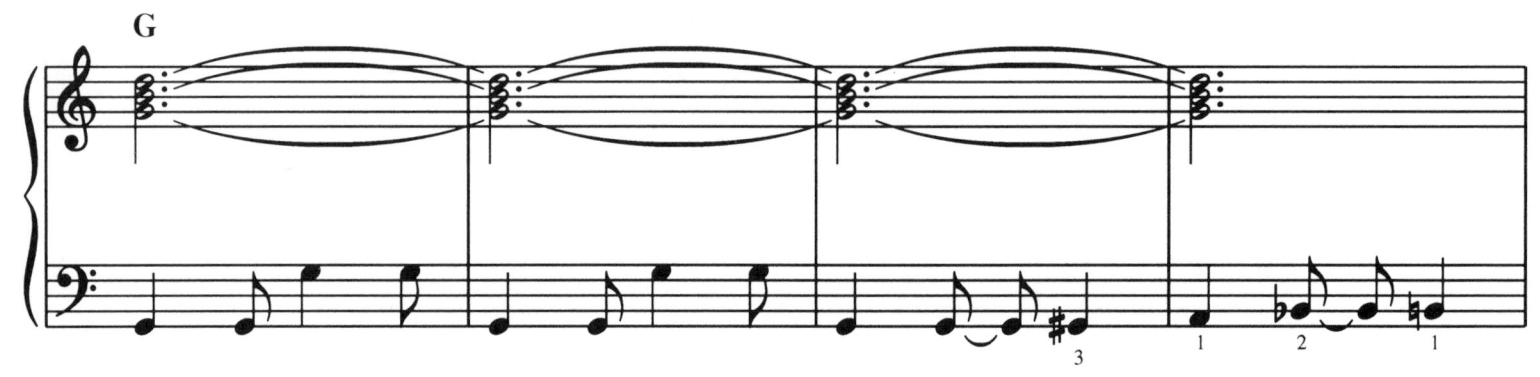

D.S. al Coda

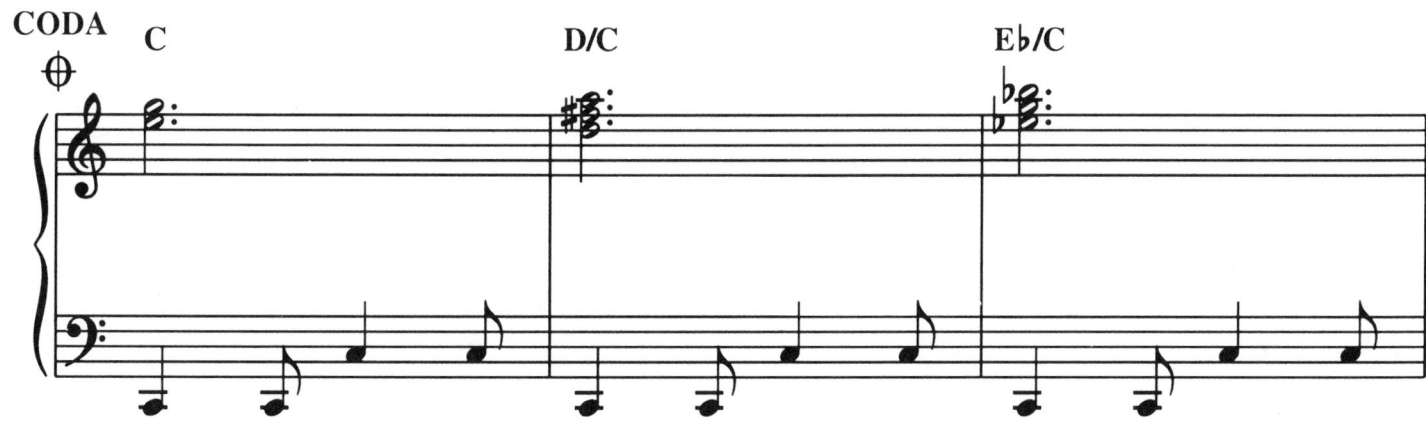

CODA

C   D/C   Eb/C

Db/C   Ab/Eb

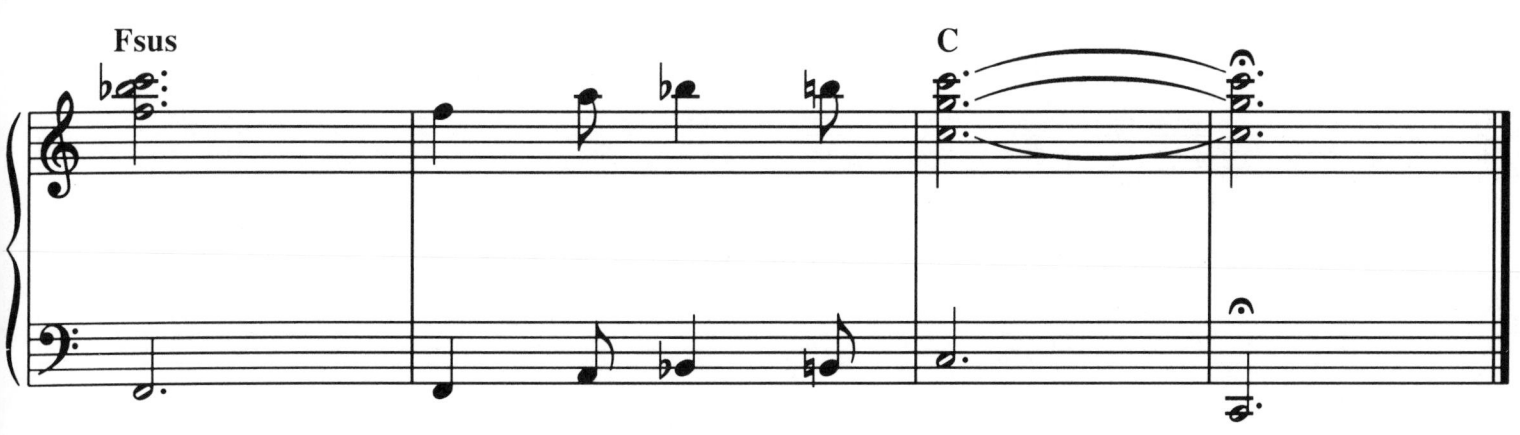

Fsus   C

SUPERCALIFRAGILISTIC-EXPIALIDOCIOUS

from Walt Disney's MARY POPPINS

Words and Music by RICHARD M. SHERMAN
and ROBERT B. SHERMAN

Um did - dle did - dle did - dle um did - dle ay!

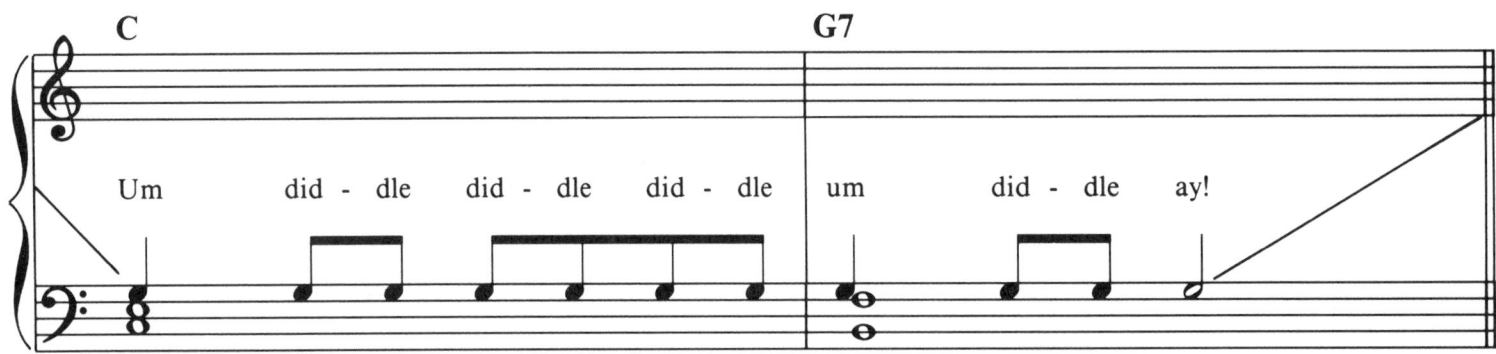

Um did - dle did - dle did - dle um did - dle ay!

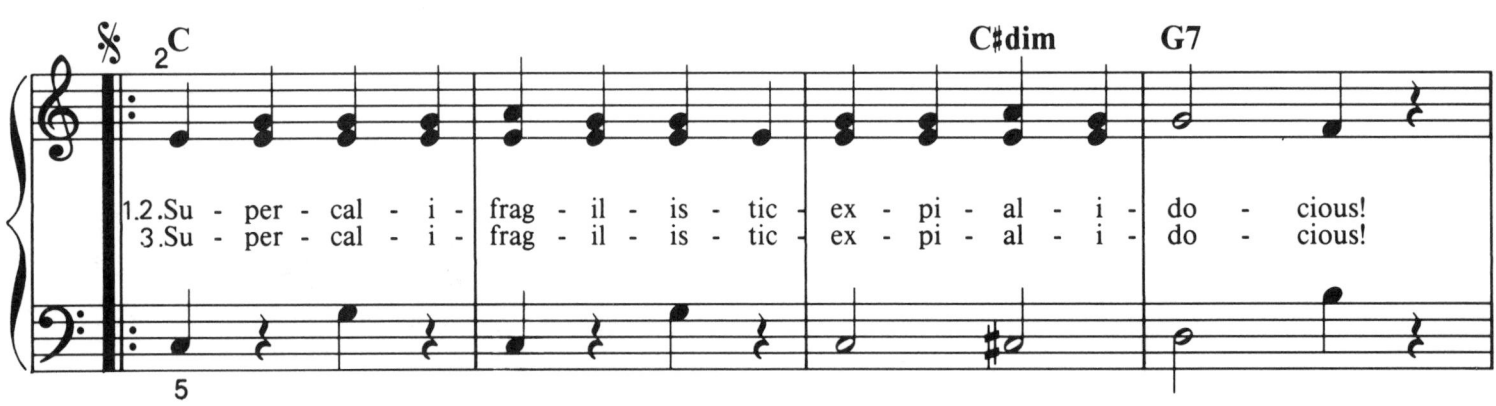

1.2.Su - per - cal - i - frag - il - is - tic - ex - pi - al - i - do - cious!
3.Su - per - cal - i - frag - il - is - tic - ex - pi - al - i - do - cious!

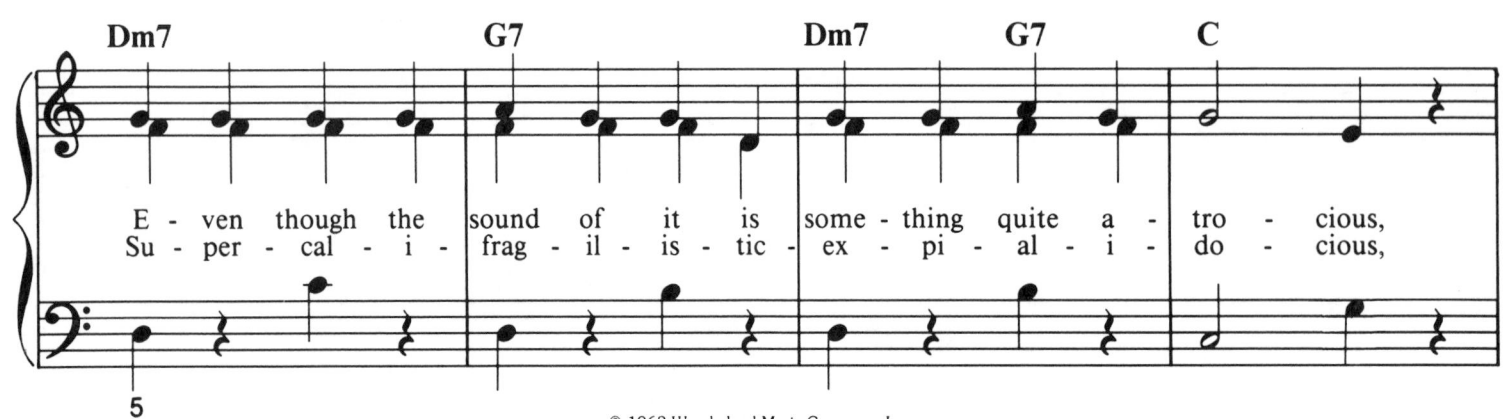

E - ven though the sound of it is some - thing quite a - tro - cious,
Su - per - cal - i - frag - il - is - tic - ex - pi - al - i - do - cious,

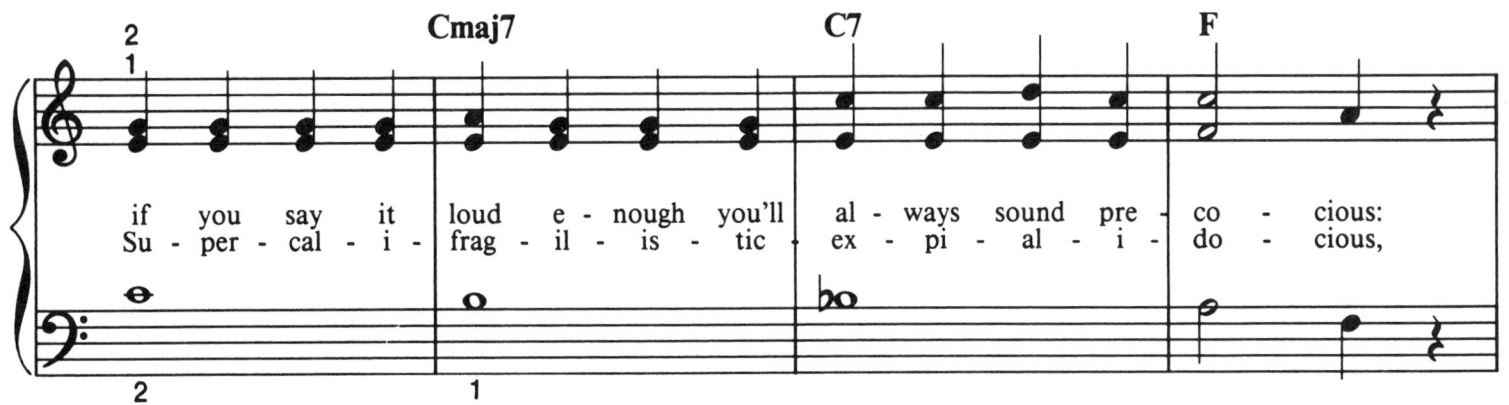

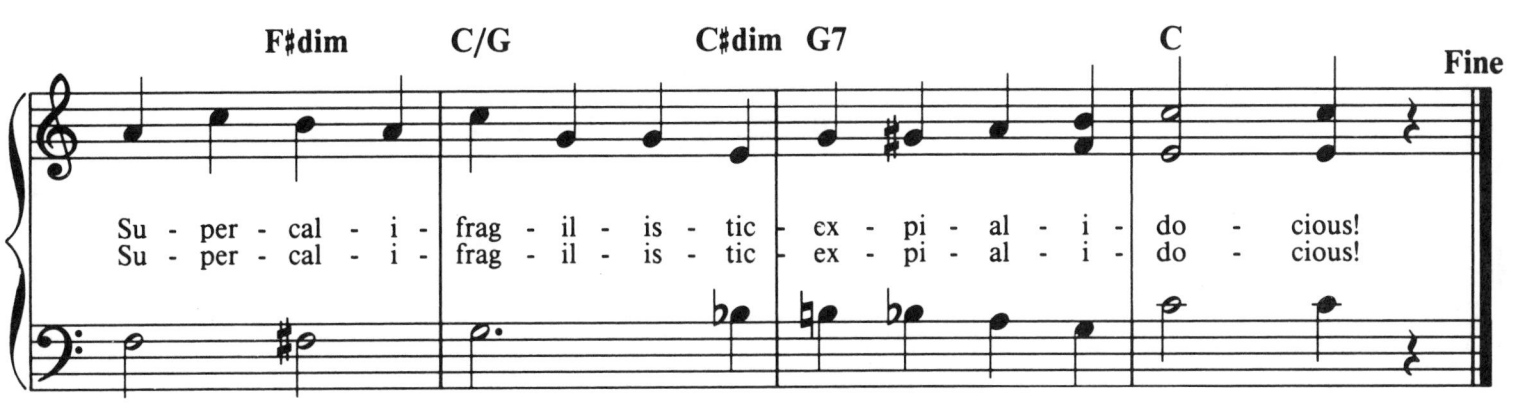

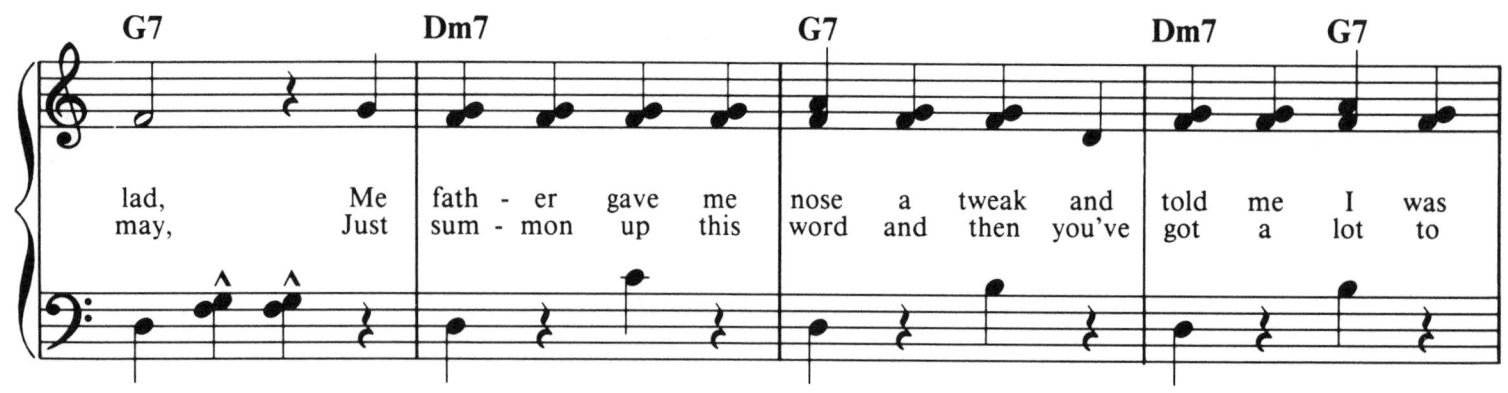

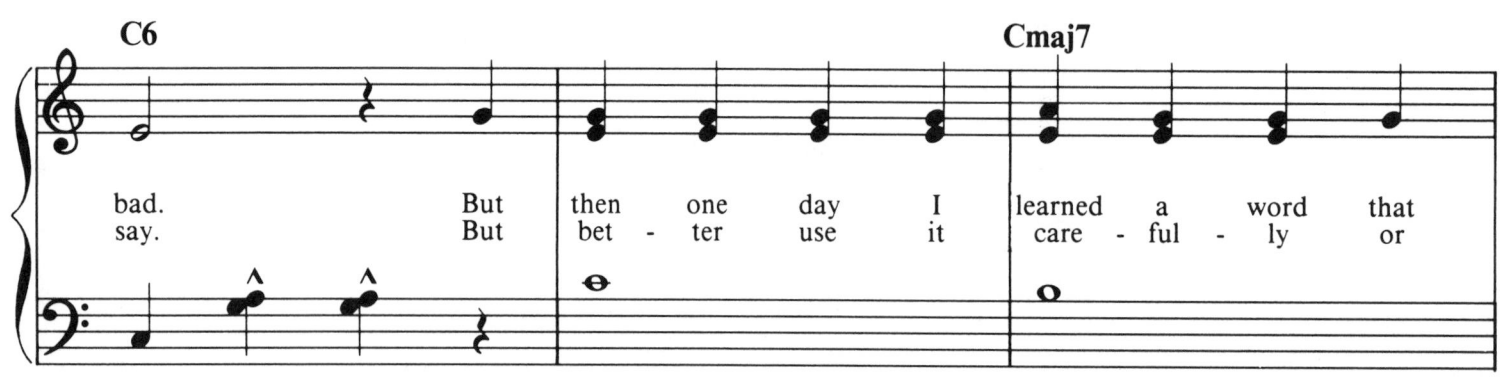

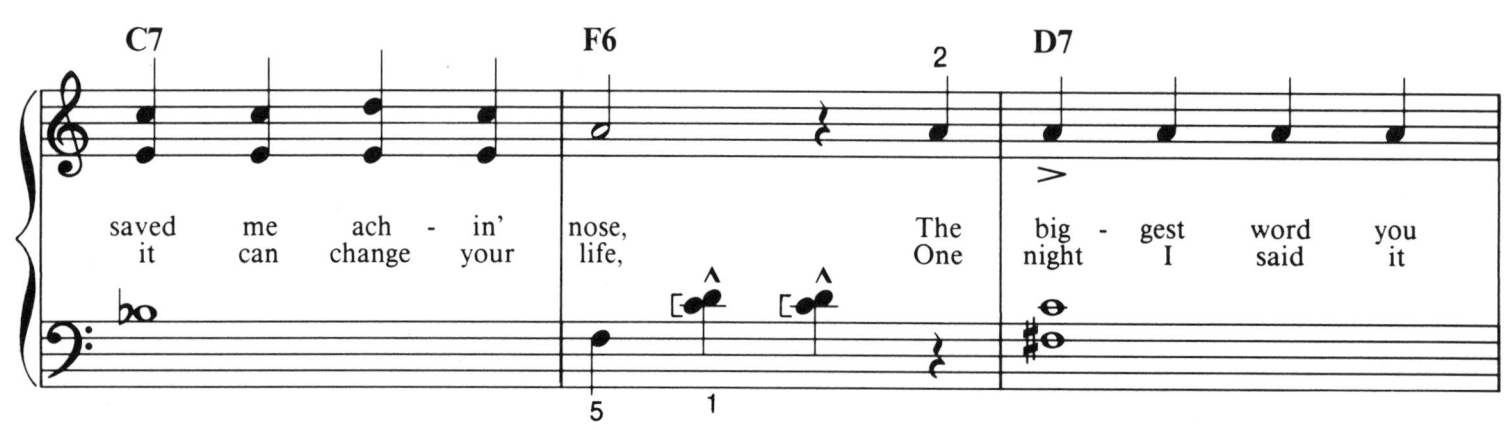

TOMORROW
from the Musical Production ANNIE

Lyric by MARTIN CHARNIN
Music by CHARLES STROUSE

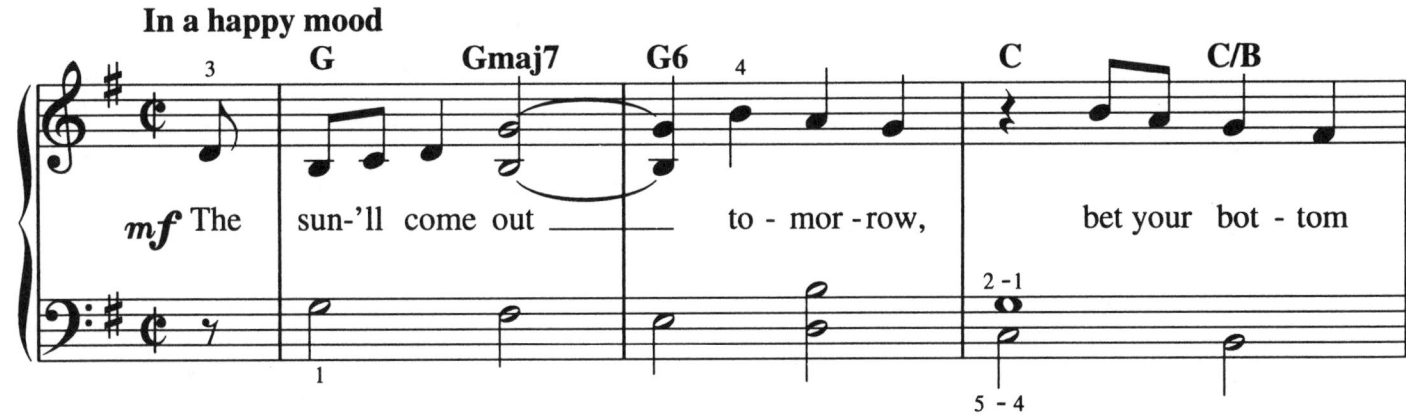

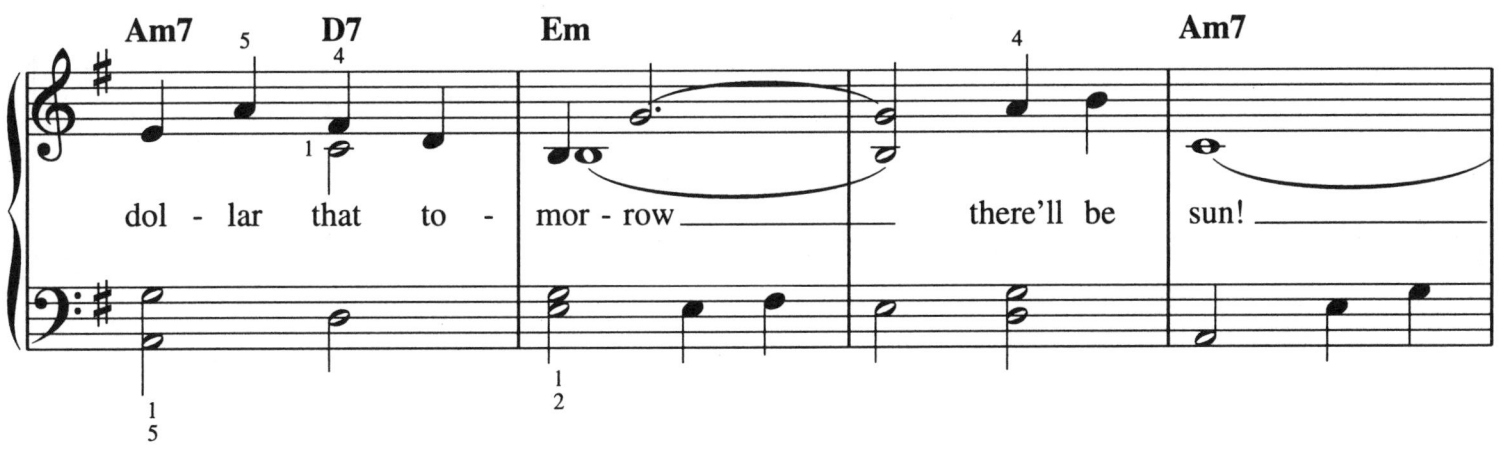

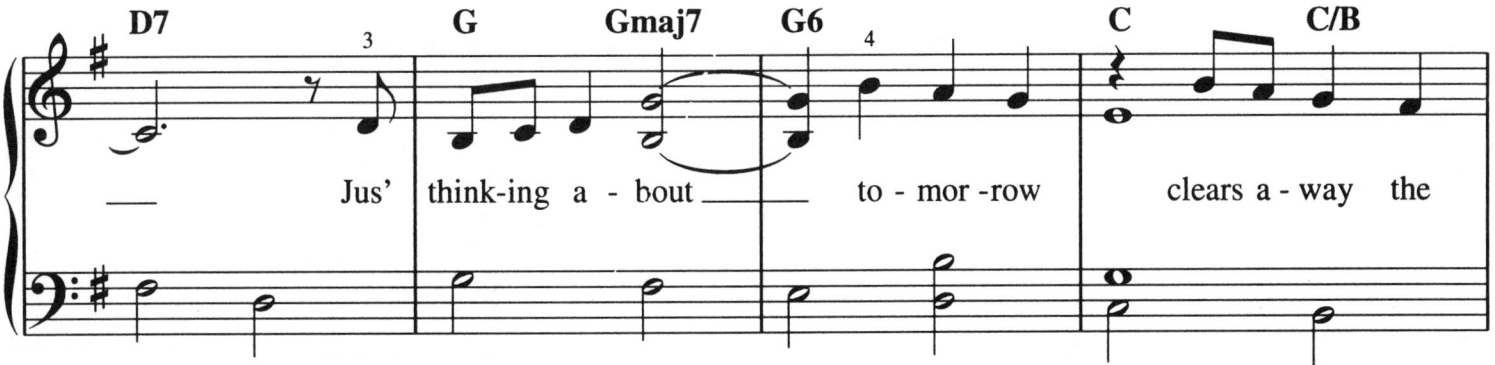

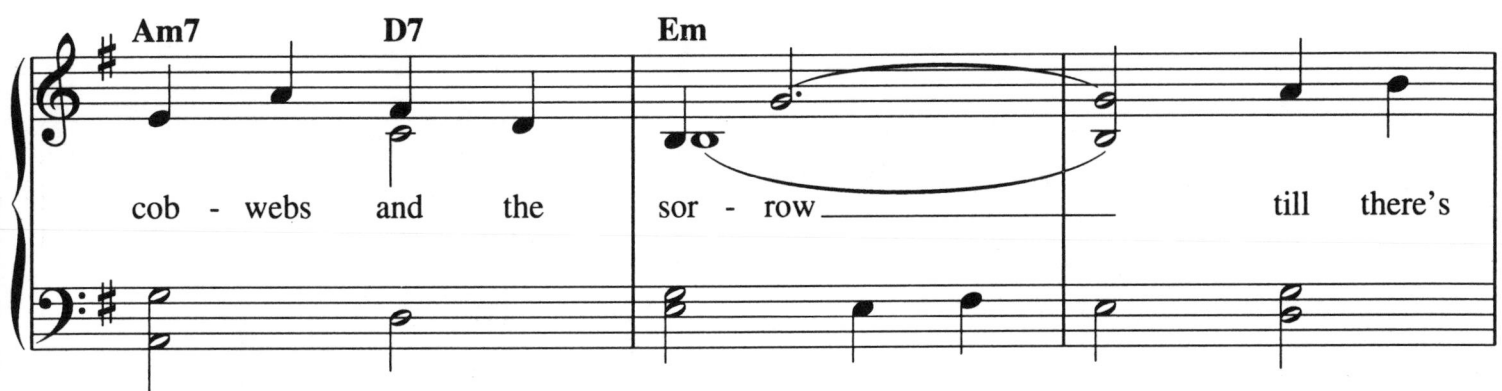

none._____ When I'm stuck with a day that's

gray and lone - ly,_____ I just stick out my chin and

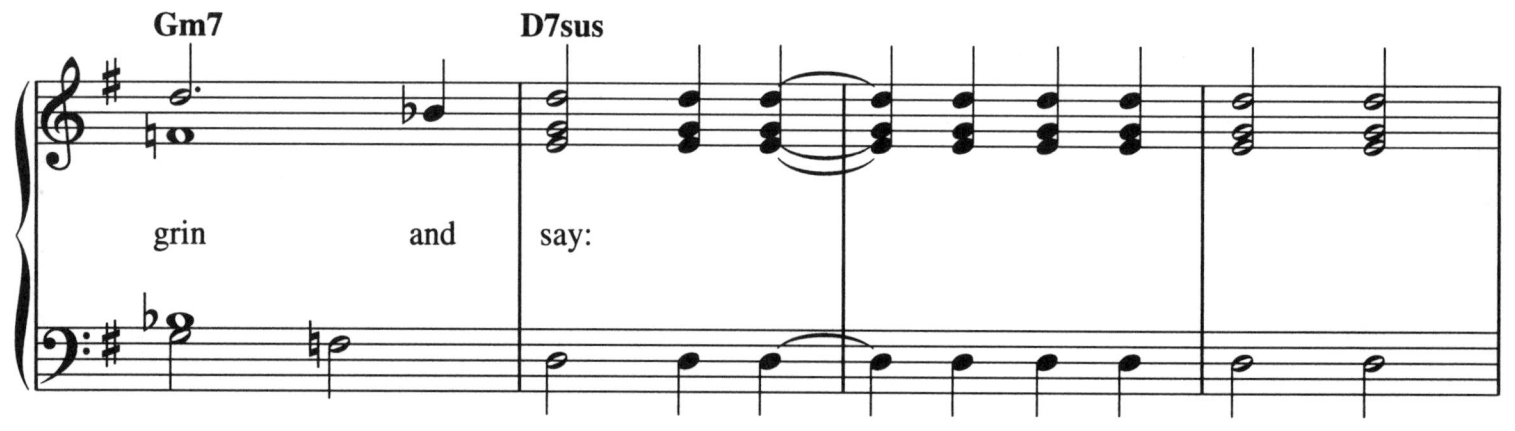

grin and say:

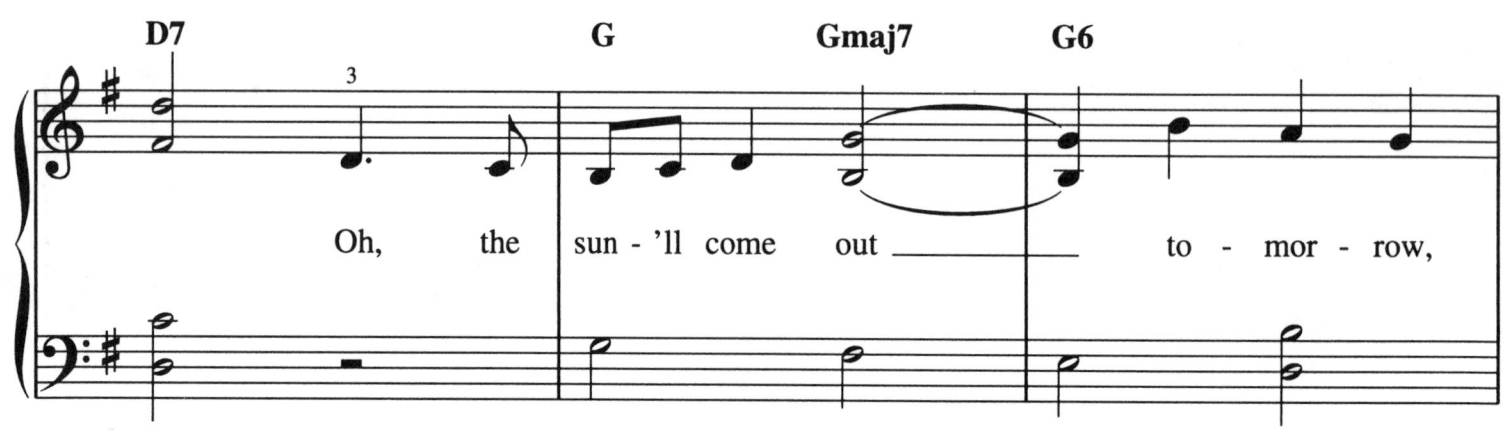

Oh, the sun - 'll come out _____ to - mor - row,

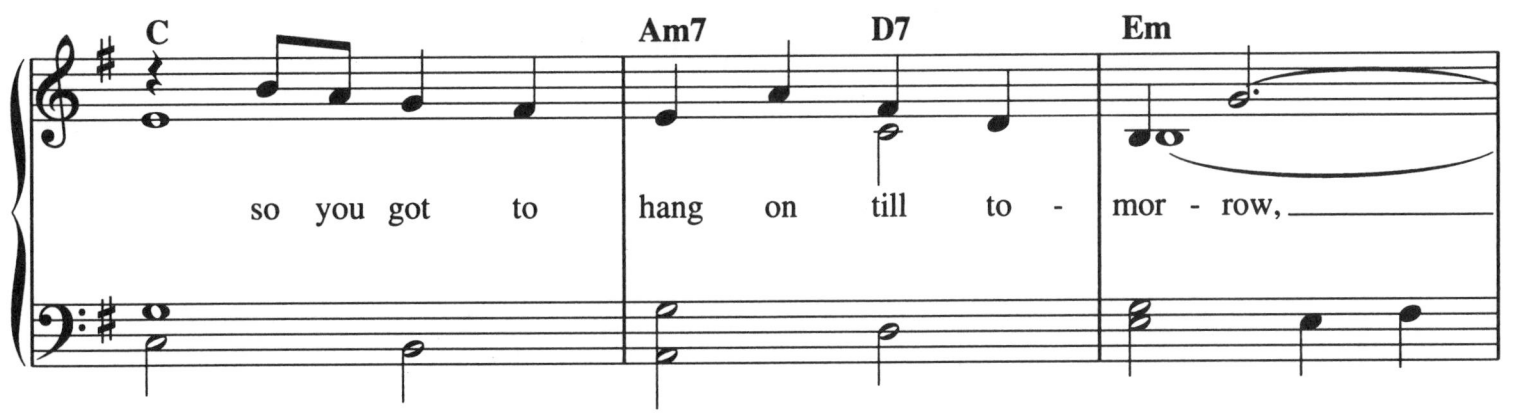

so you got to hang on till to - mor - row, ____

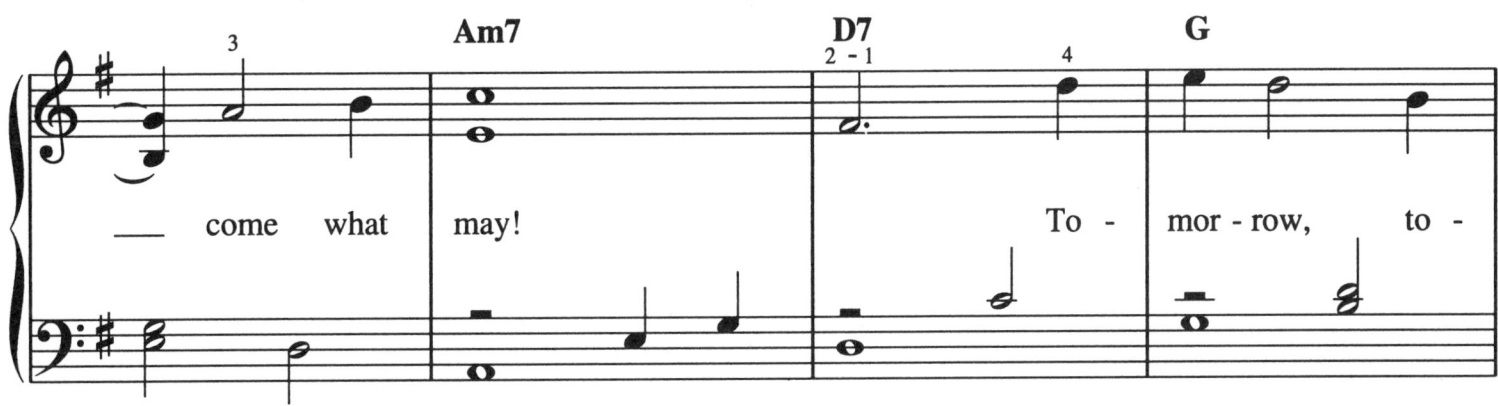

____ come what may! To - mor - row, to -

mor - row, I love ya, to - mor - row, you're

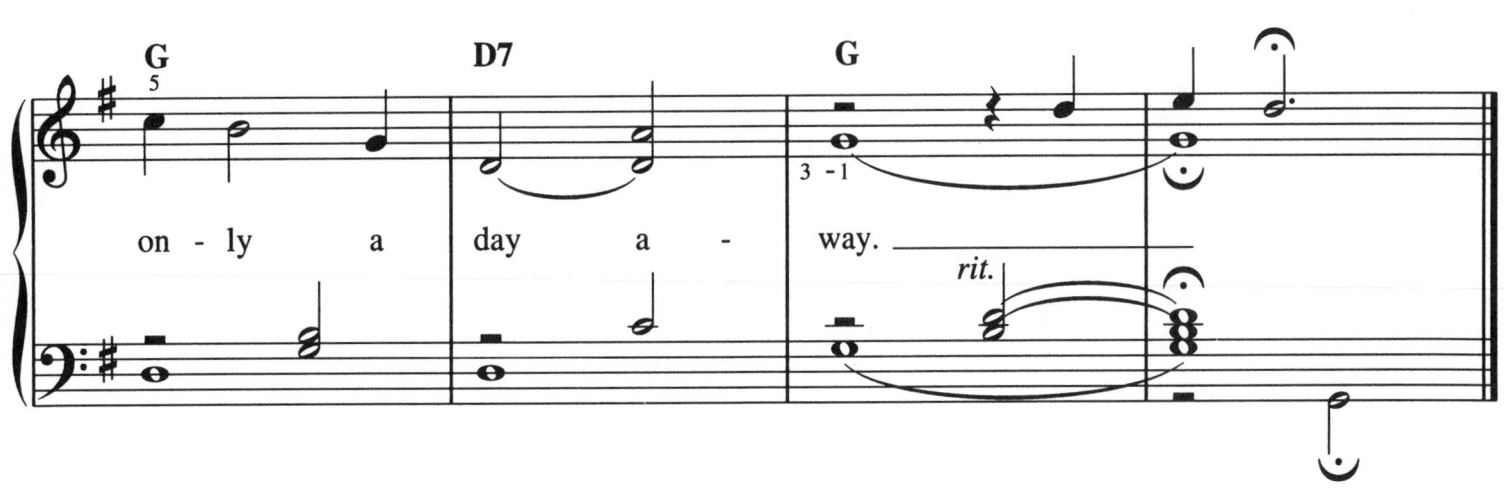

on - ly a day a - way. ____

rit.

TEN MINUTES AGO

from CINDERELLA

Lyrics by OSCAR HAMMERSTEIN II
Music by RICHARD RODGERS

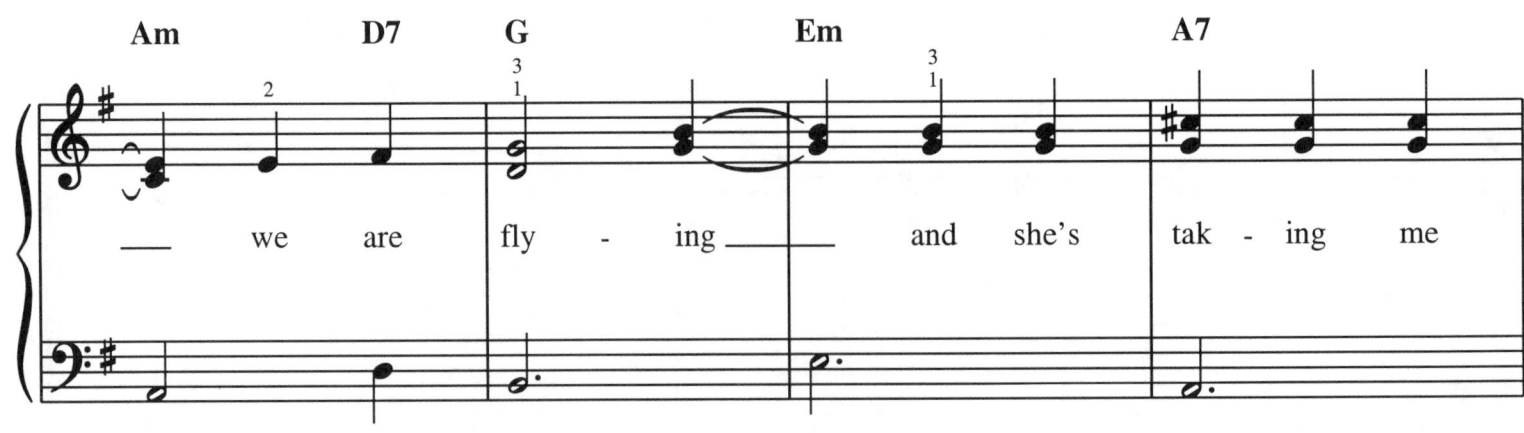

we are fly - ing _____ and she's tak - ing me

back to the skies. In the arms of my

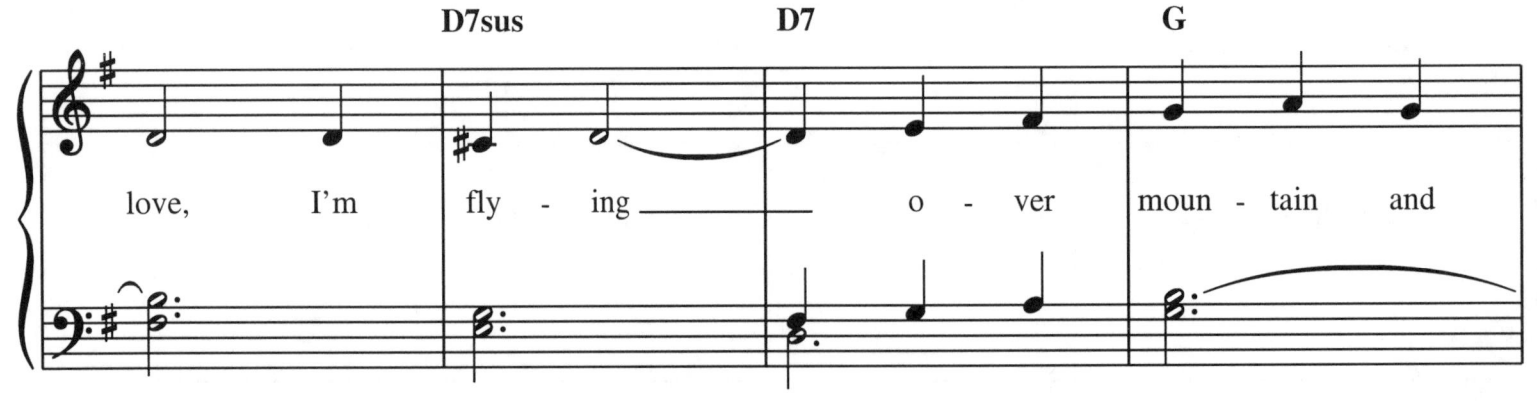

love, I'm fly - ing _____ o - ver moun - tain and

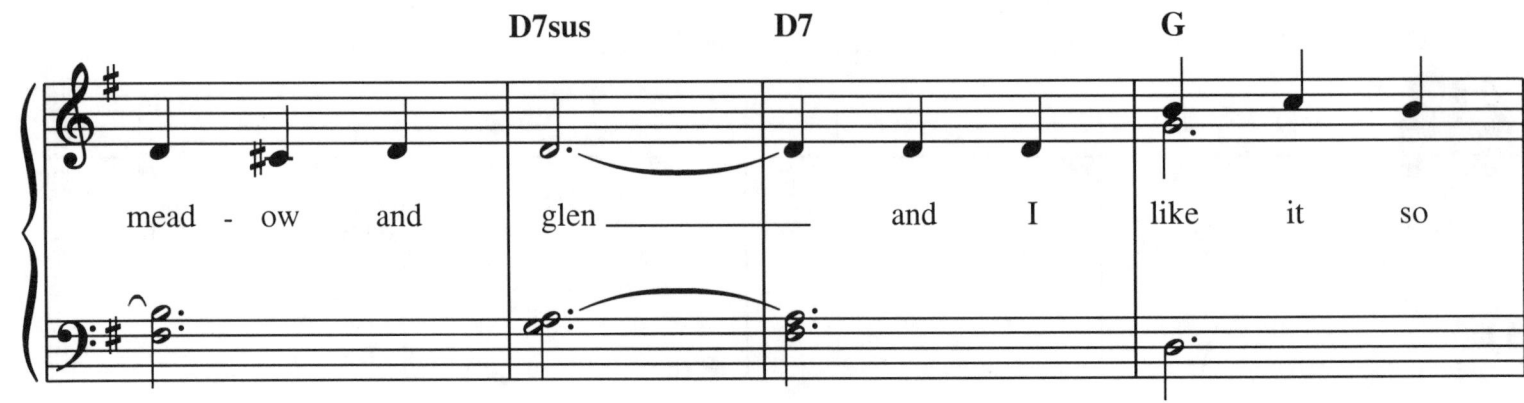

mead - ow and glen _____ and I like it so

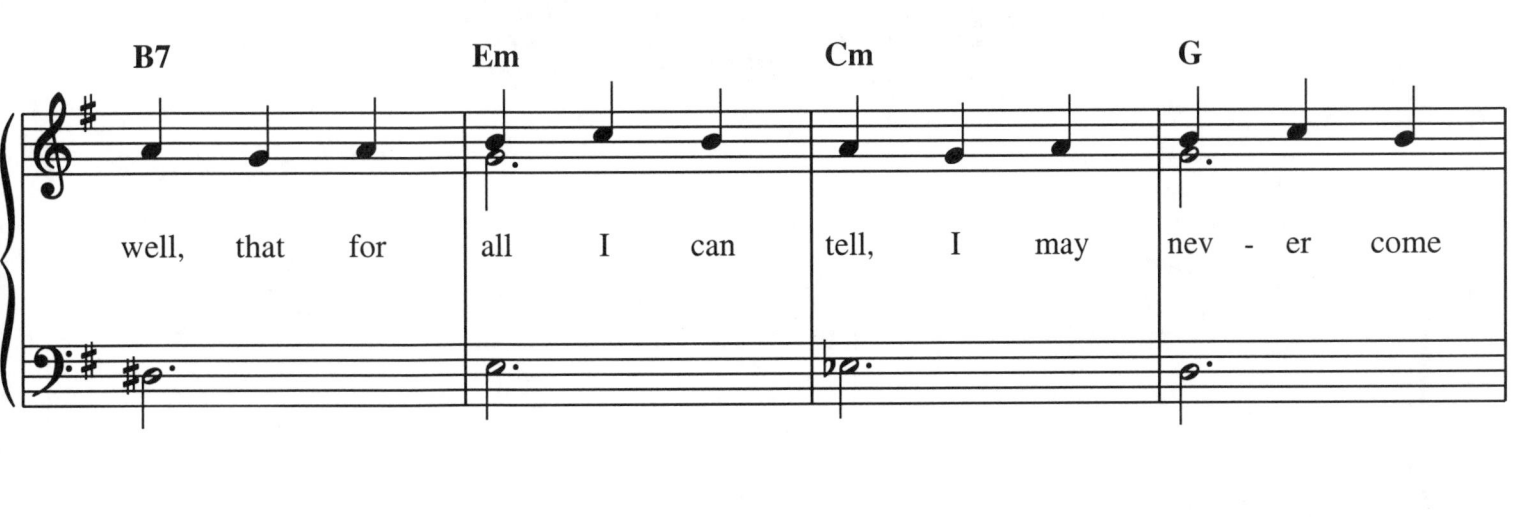

well, that for all I can tell, I may nev - er come

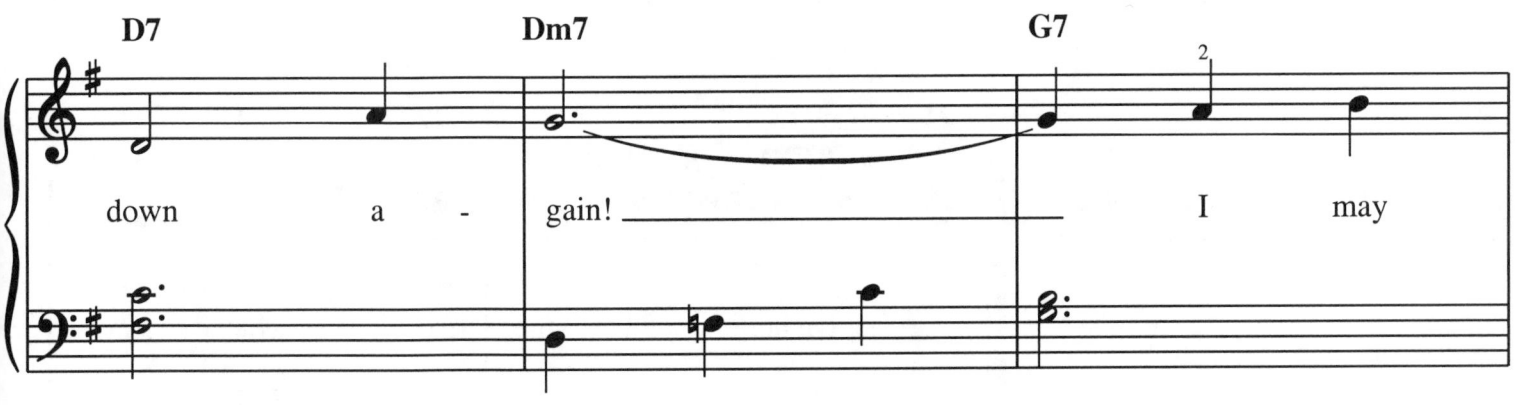

down a - gain! _____ I may

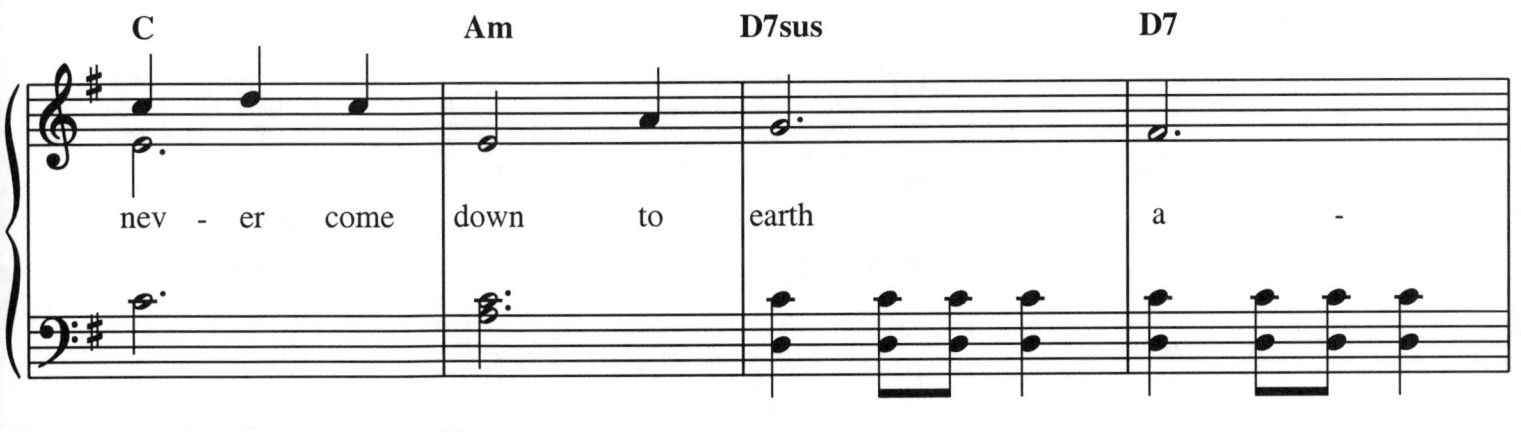

nev - er come down to earth a -

gain.

UNDER THE SEA
from Walt Disney's THE LITTLE MERMAID

Lyrics by HOWARD ASHMAN
Music by ALAN MENKEN

The sea - weed is al - ways green - er
Down here__ all the fish is hap - py

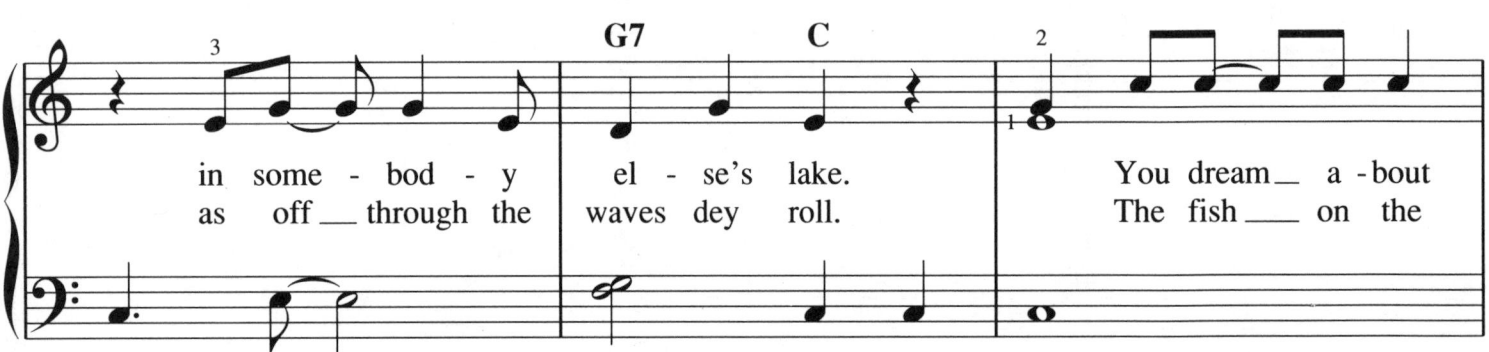

in some - bod - y el - se's lake.
as off __ through the waves dey roll.

You dream__ a - bout
The fish __ on the

go - ing up there.
land ain't hap - py.

But that __ is a
They sad__ 'cause they

big mis - take.
in the bowl.

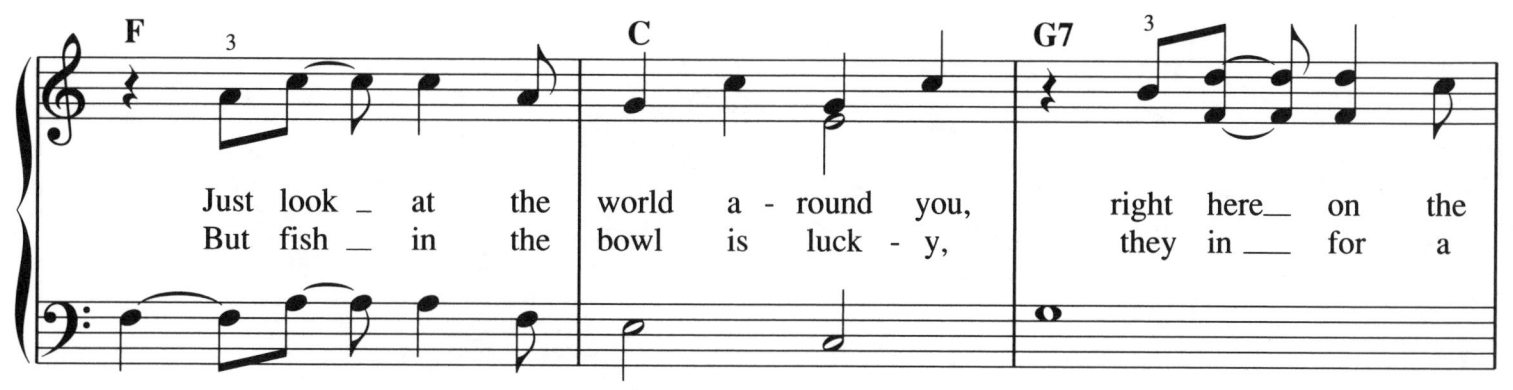

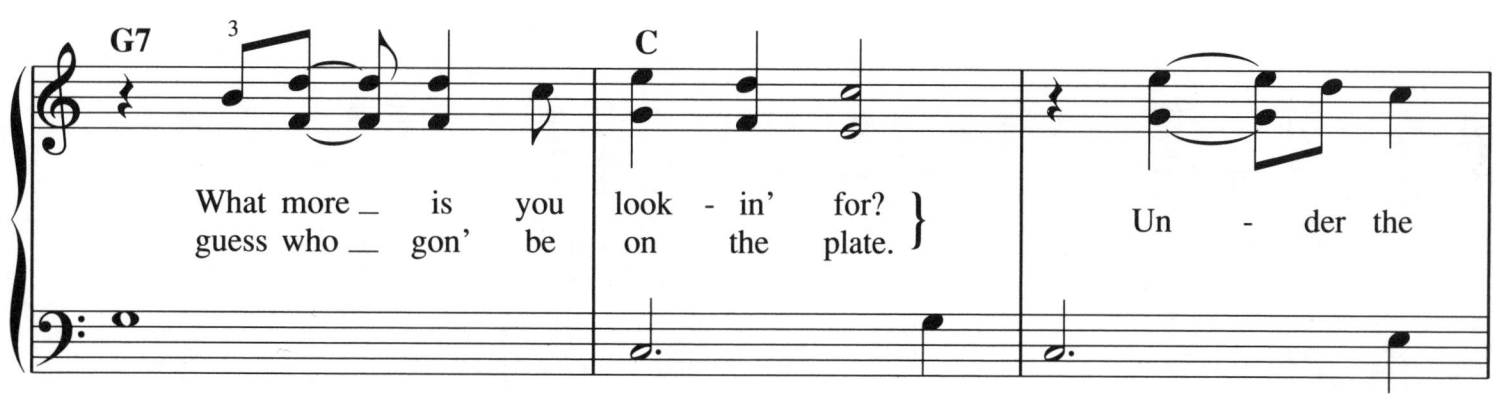

102

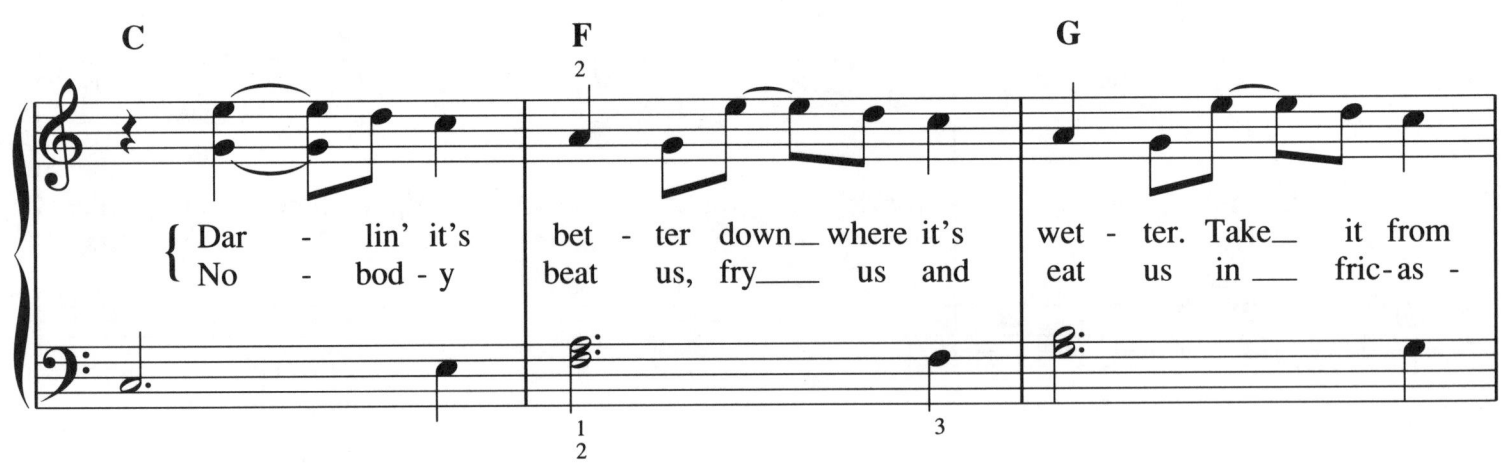

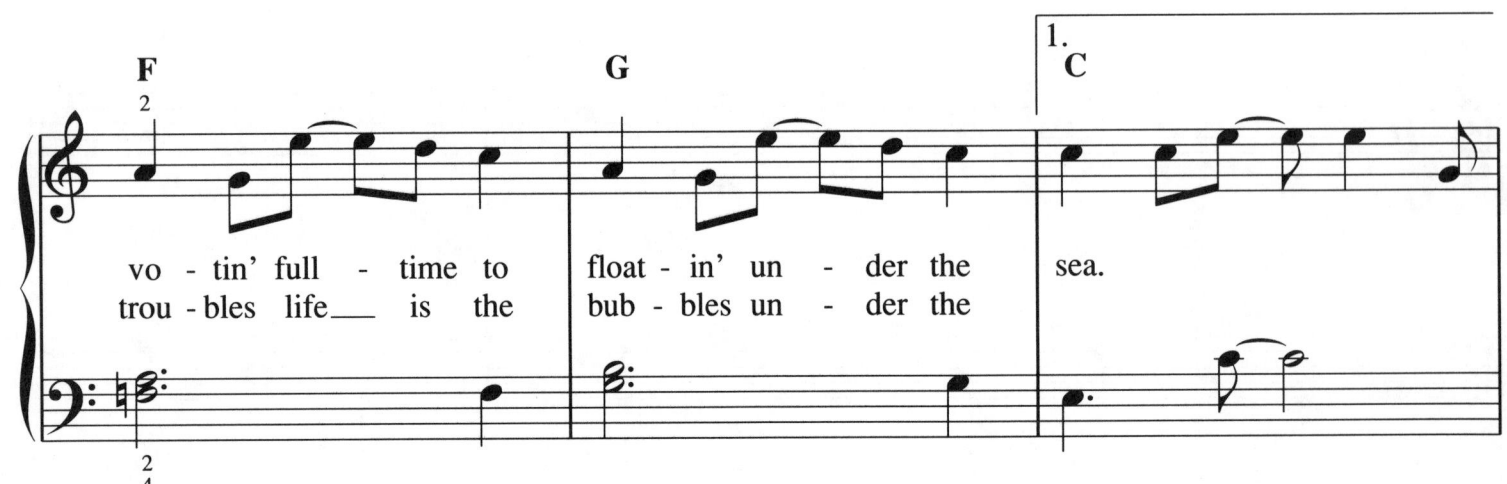

sea.   Un - der the   sea.

Since life   is   sweet here we ___ got the   beat here nat - u - ral -

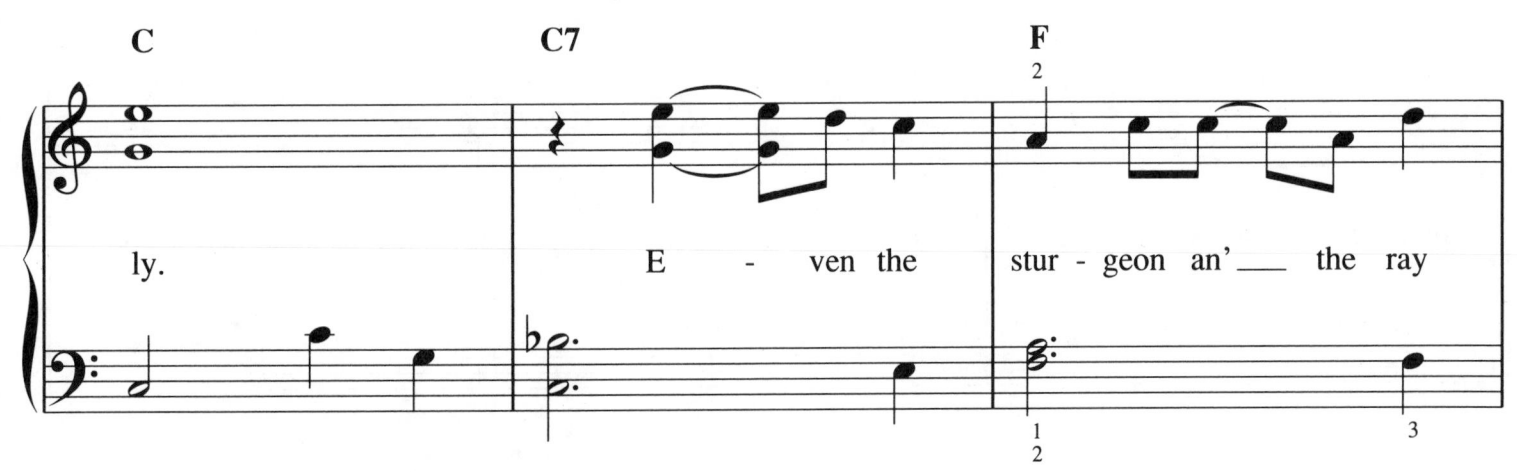

ly.   E - ven the   stur - geon an' ___ the ray

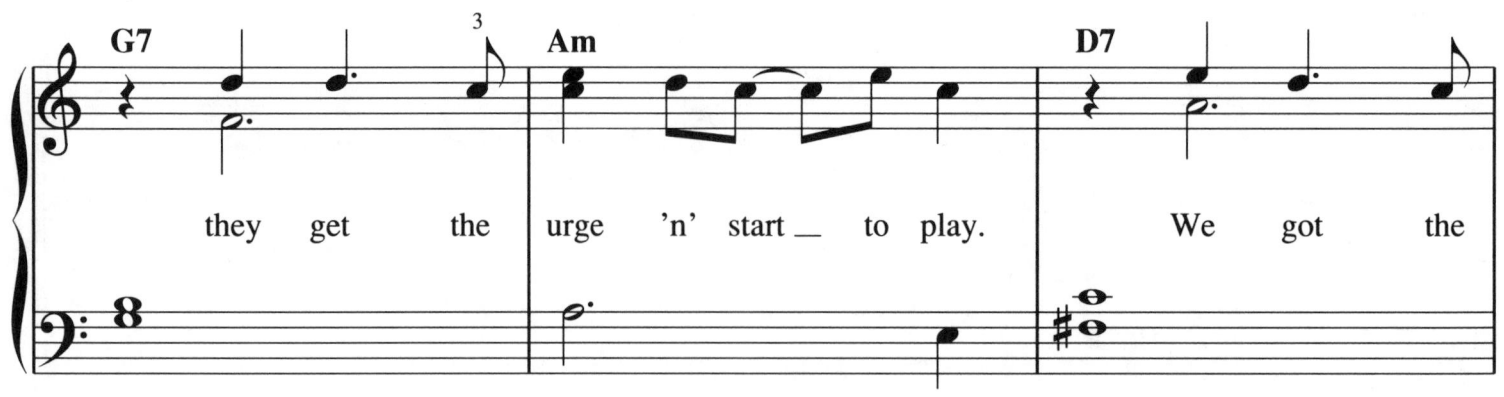

they get the urge 'n' start __ to play. We got the

spir - it, you __ got to hear it un - der the sea.

The newt play the flute. The carp play the harp. The

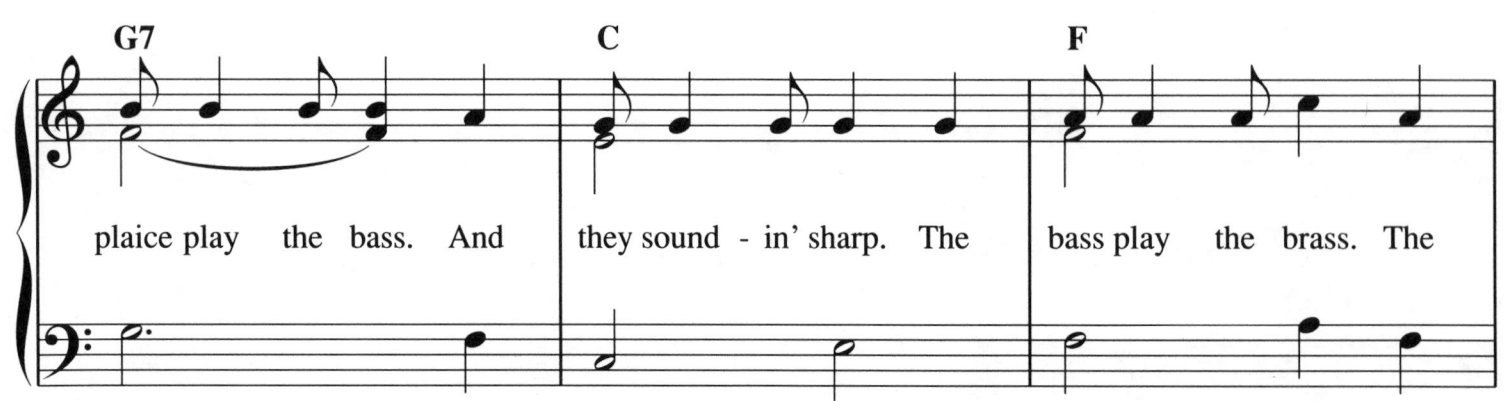

plaice play the bass. And they sound - in' sharp. The bass play the brass. The

chub play the tub. The fluke is the duke of soul. The

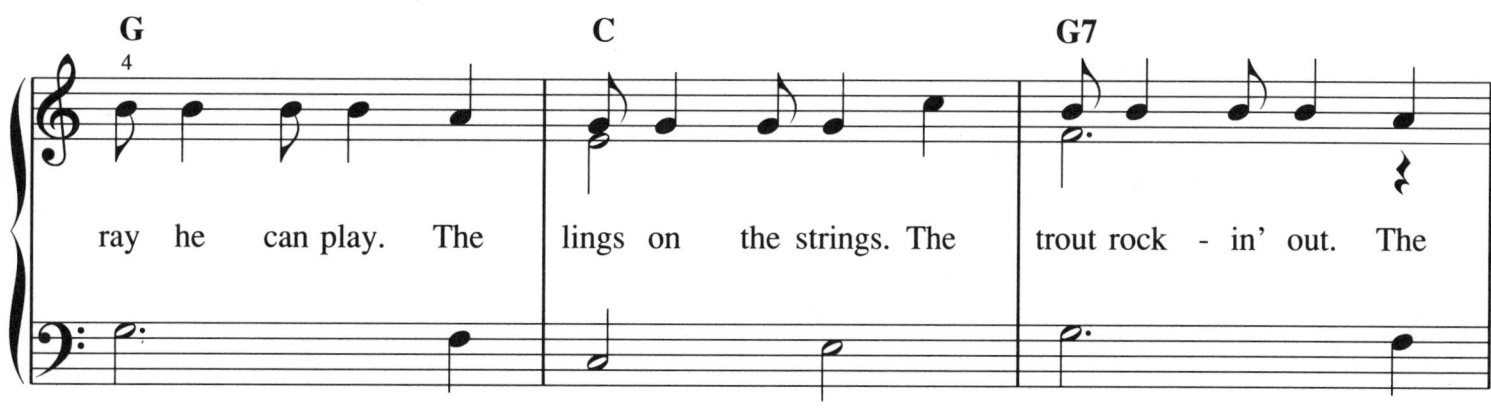

ray he can play. The lings on the strings. The trout rock - in' out. The

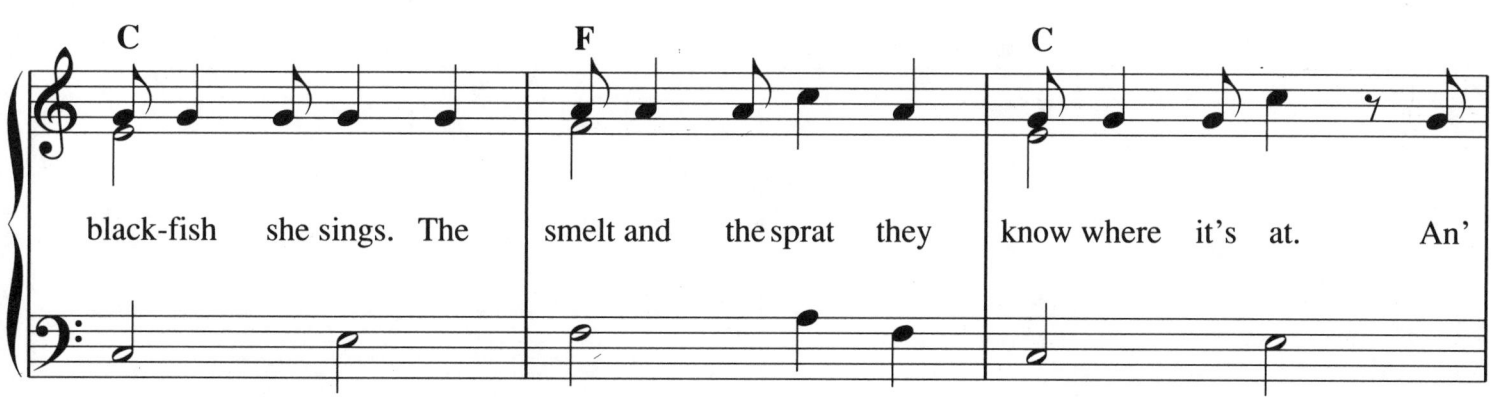

black-fish she sings. The smelt and the sprat they know where it's at. An'

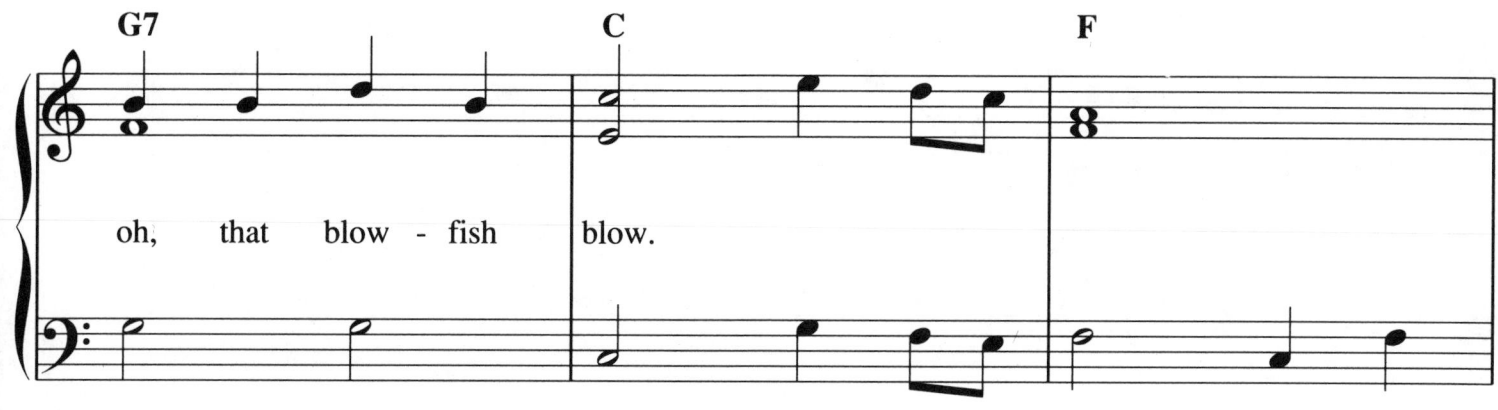

oh, that blow - fish blow.

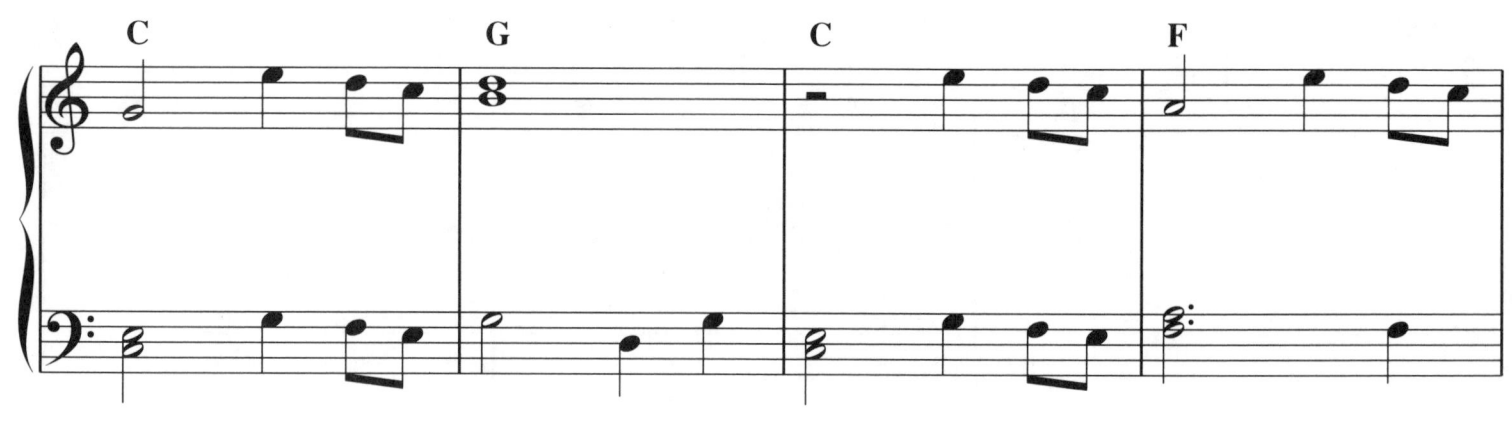

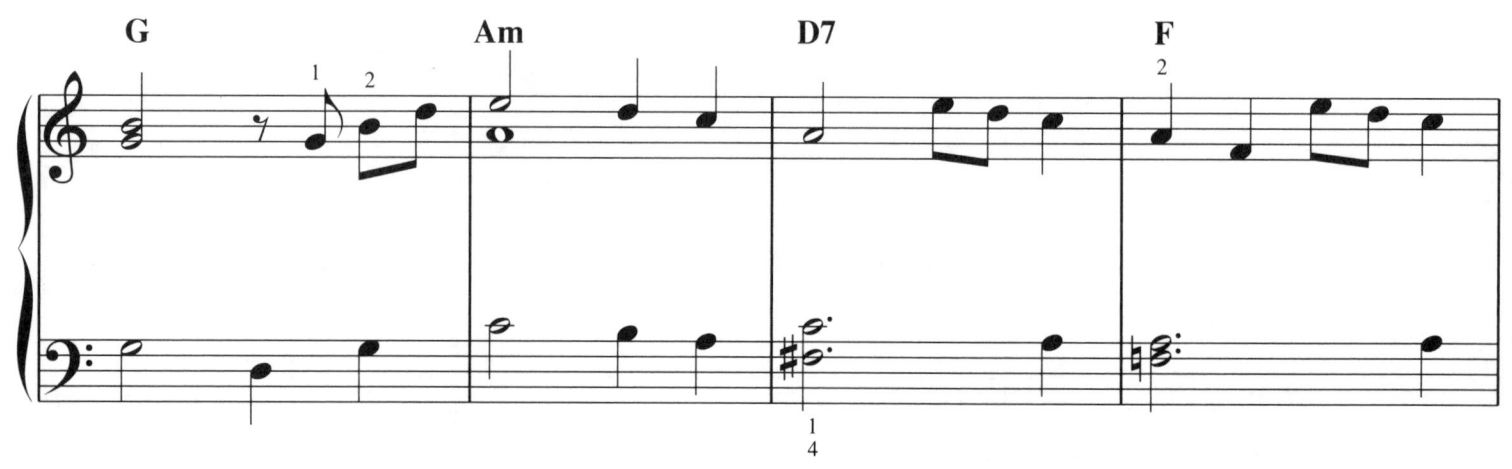

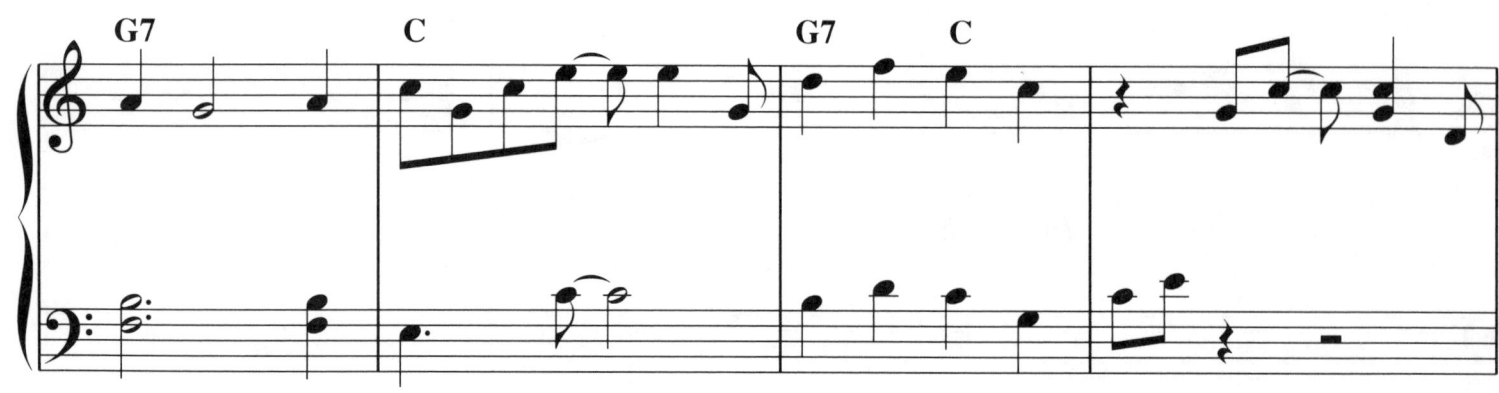

Un-der the sea.
Un-der the

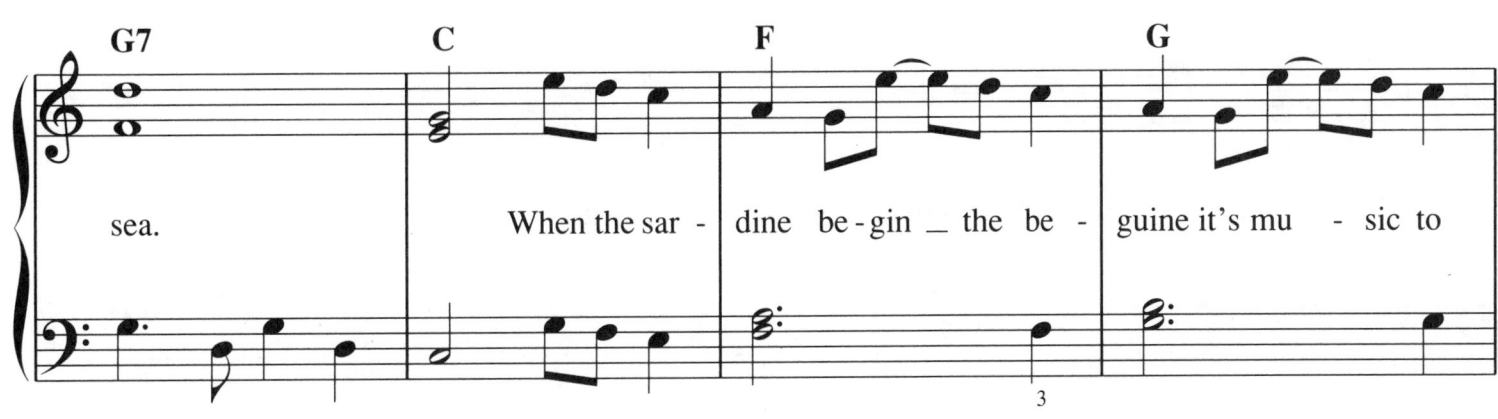

sea.
When the sar - dine be-gin _ the be - guine it's mu - sic to

me.
What _ do they got, a lot _ of sand.
We got a

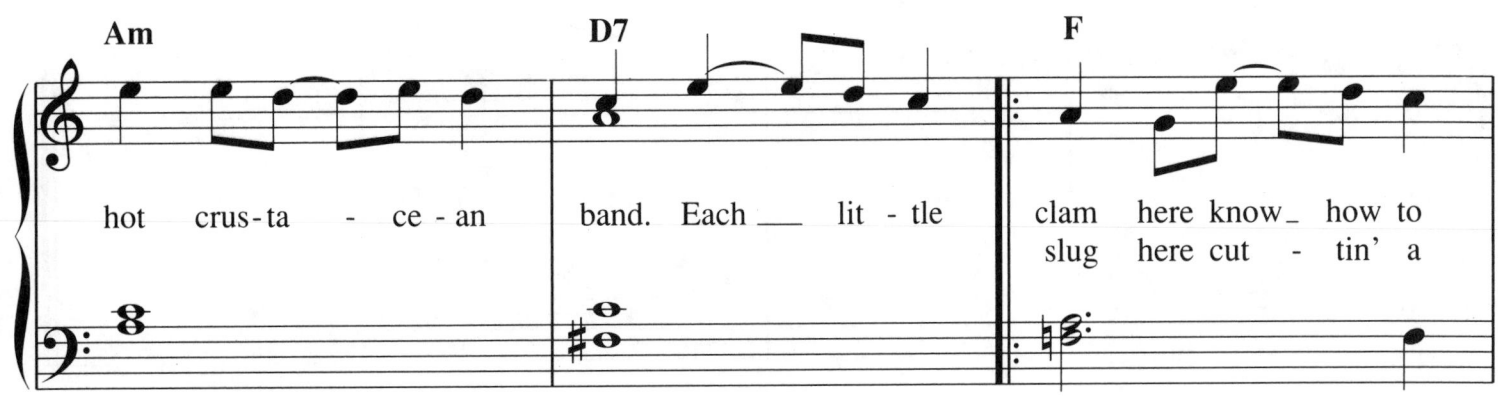

hot crus-ta - ce-an band. Each ___ lit-tle clam here know_ how to
slug here cut - tin' a

jam here un - der the sea.
rug here un - der the sea. Each lit - tle
Each lit - tle

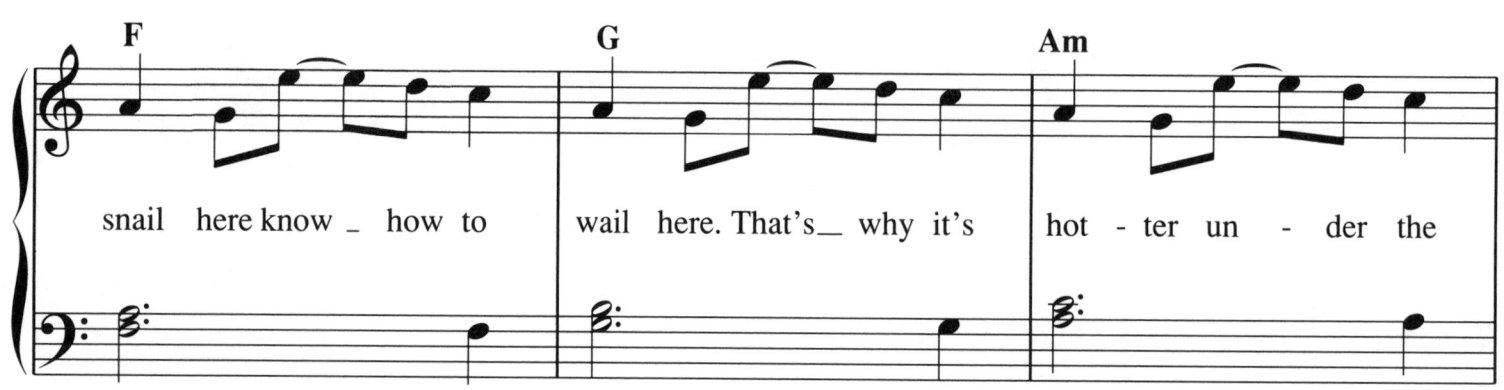

snail here know _ how to wail here. That's _ why it's hot - ter un - der the

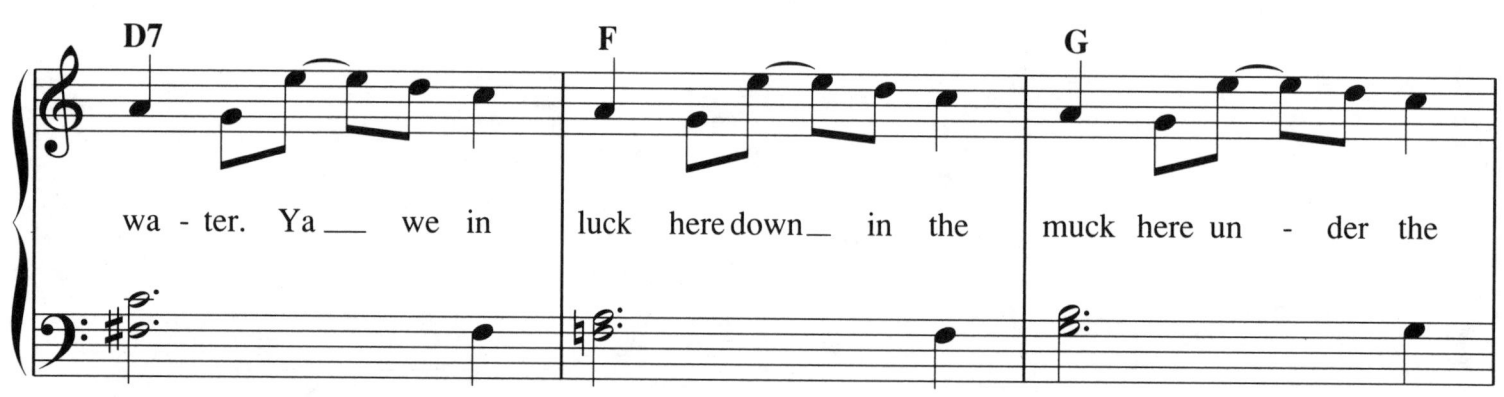

wa - ter. Ya _ we in luck here down _ in the muck here un - der the

sea.

WHEN YOU BELIEVE
(from THE PRINCE OF EGYPT)

Words and Music Composed by STEPHEN SCHWARTZ
with Additional Music by BABYFACE

Slowly

with pedal

Man - y nights we've prayed with no proof an - y - one could hear.
In this time of fear, when prayer so of - ten proved in vain,

In our hearts a hope - ful song we bare - ly un - der - stood. Now
hope seemed like the sum - mer birds, too swift - ly flown a - way. Yet

we are not a - fraid, al - though we know there's much to fear.
now I'm stand - ing here, with heart so full I can't ex - plain,

WHERE IS LOVE?

from the Columbia Pictures - Romulus Film OLIVER!

Words and Music by
LIONEL BART

Slowly

Where _____ is love?

Does it fall from skies a - bove? Is it un - der-neath the

wil - low tree ___ that I've been dream - ing of?

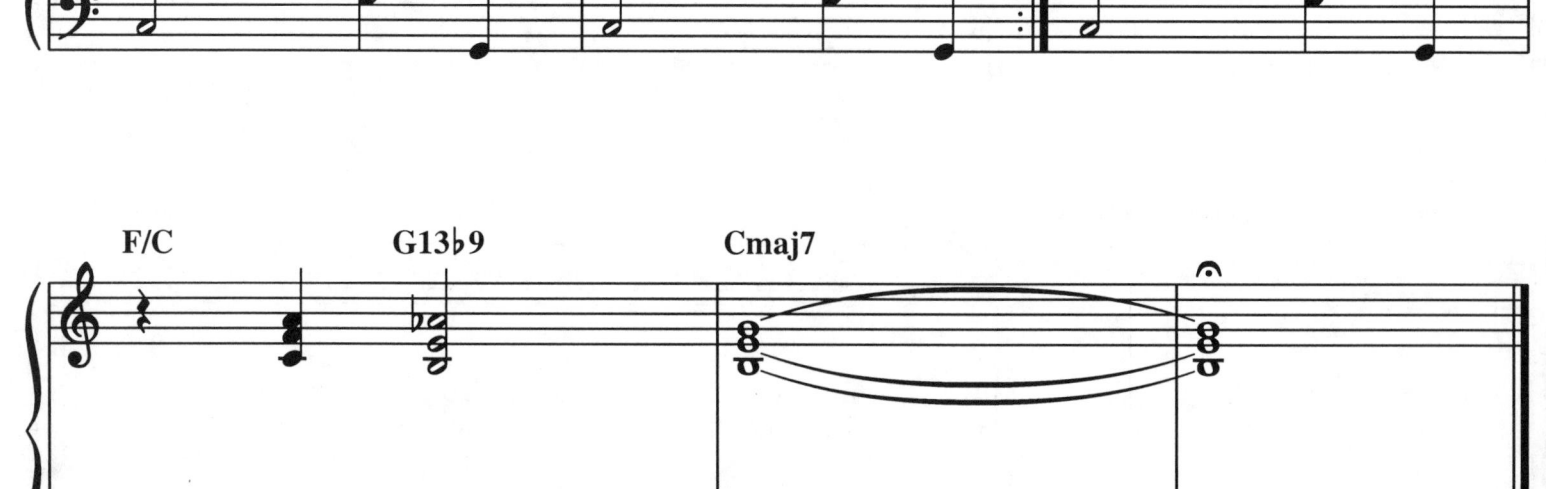

Dm7   **G7**   **Cmaj7**   **Cm7**   **F7**   **B♭maj7**   **B♭6**

till I am be-side the some - one who __
when I see the face of some - one who __

I can mean __

Amaj7   **C♯dim**   **Dm7**   **Am**   **Dm7**   **G7♭9**

some - thing to? __   Where, _____   Where _____ is

1.   **C**   **F/G**   **Cmaj7**   **F/G**   **2.**   **C**   **F/G**

love? _____   love?

F/C   **G13♭9**   **Cmaj7**

WHO WILL BUY?

from the Columbia Pictures - Romulus Film OLIVER!

Words and Music by
LIONEL BART

118

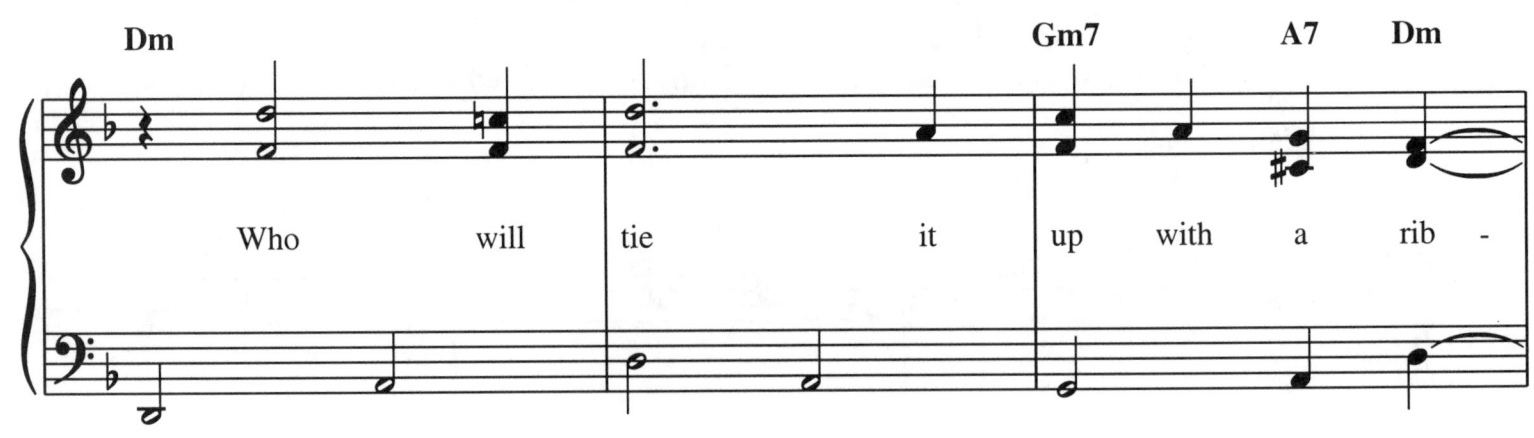

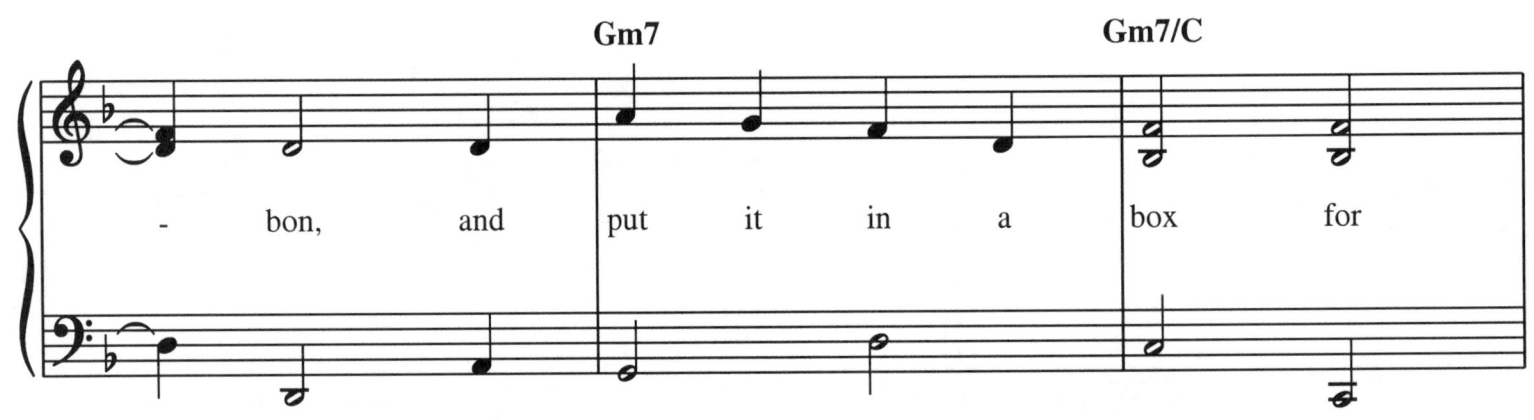

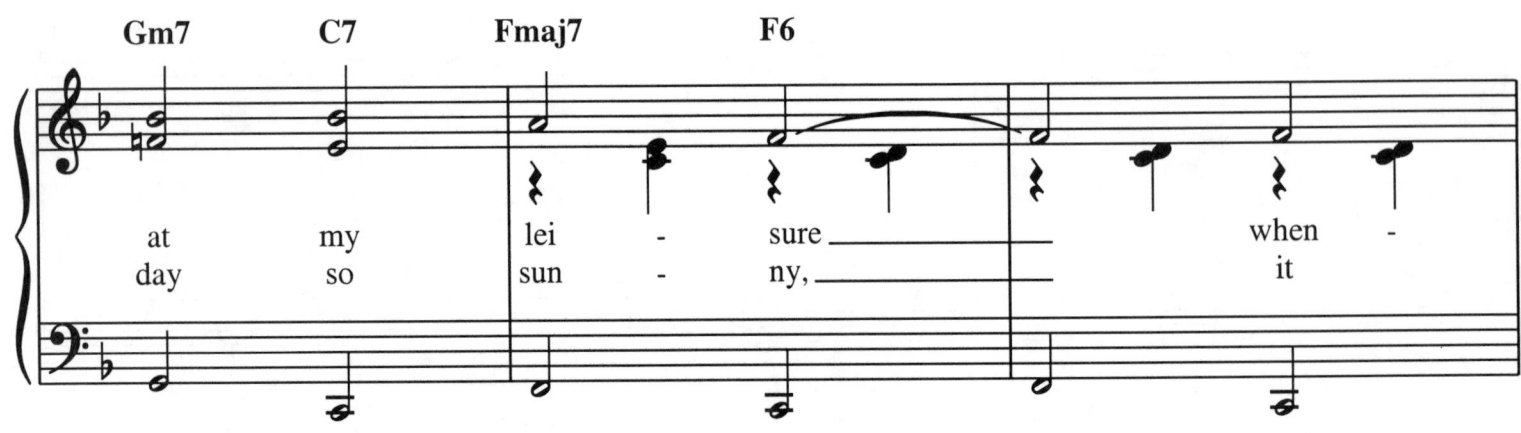

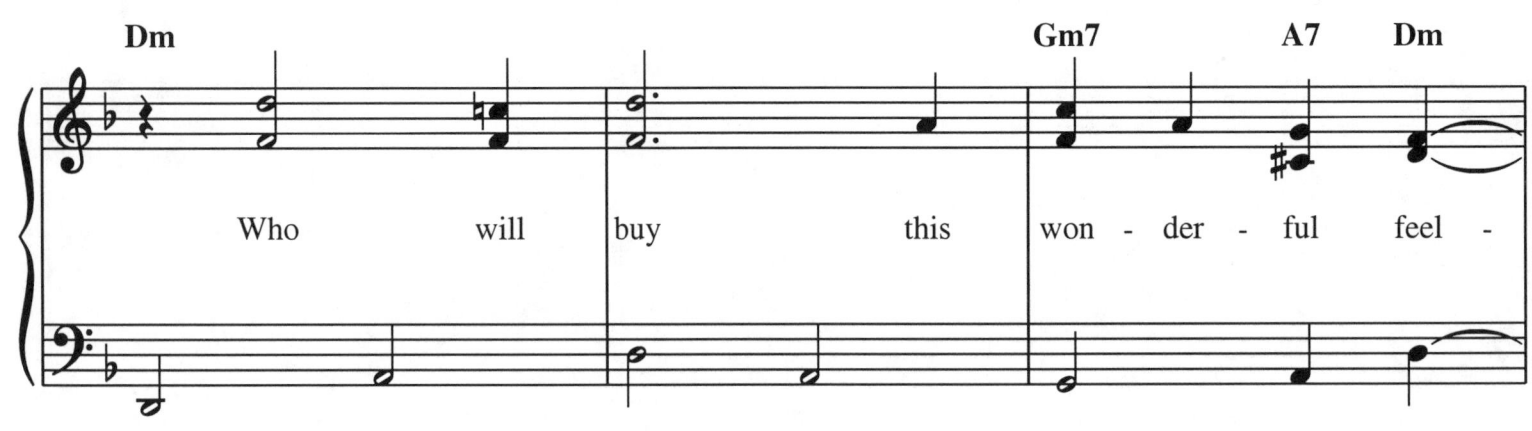

Who will buy this won - der - ful feel -

- ing? I'm so high, I

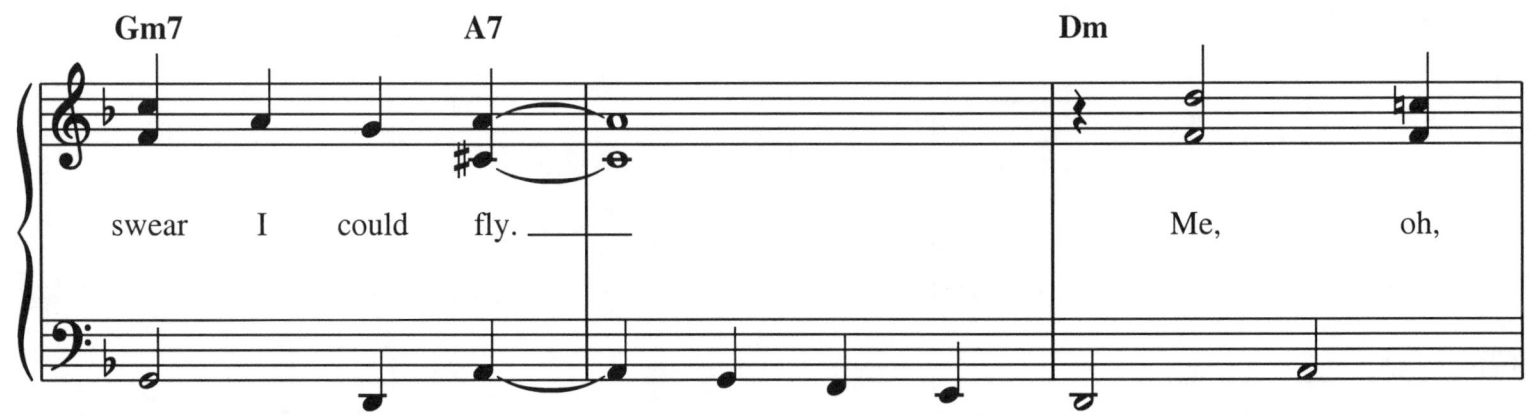

swear I could fly. Me, oh,

my, I don't want to lose it, so

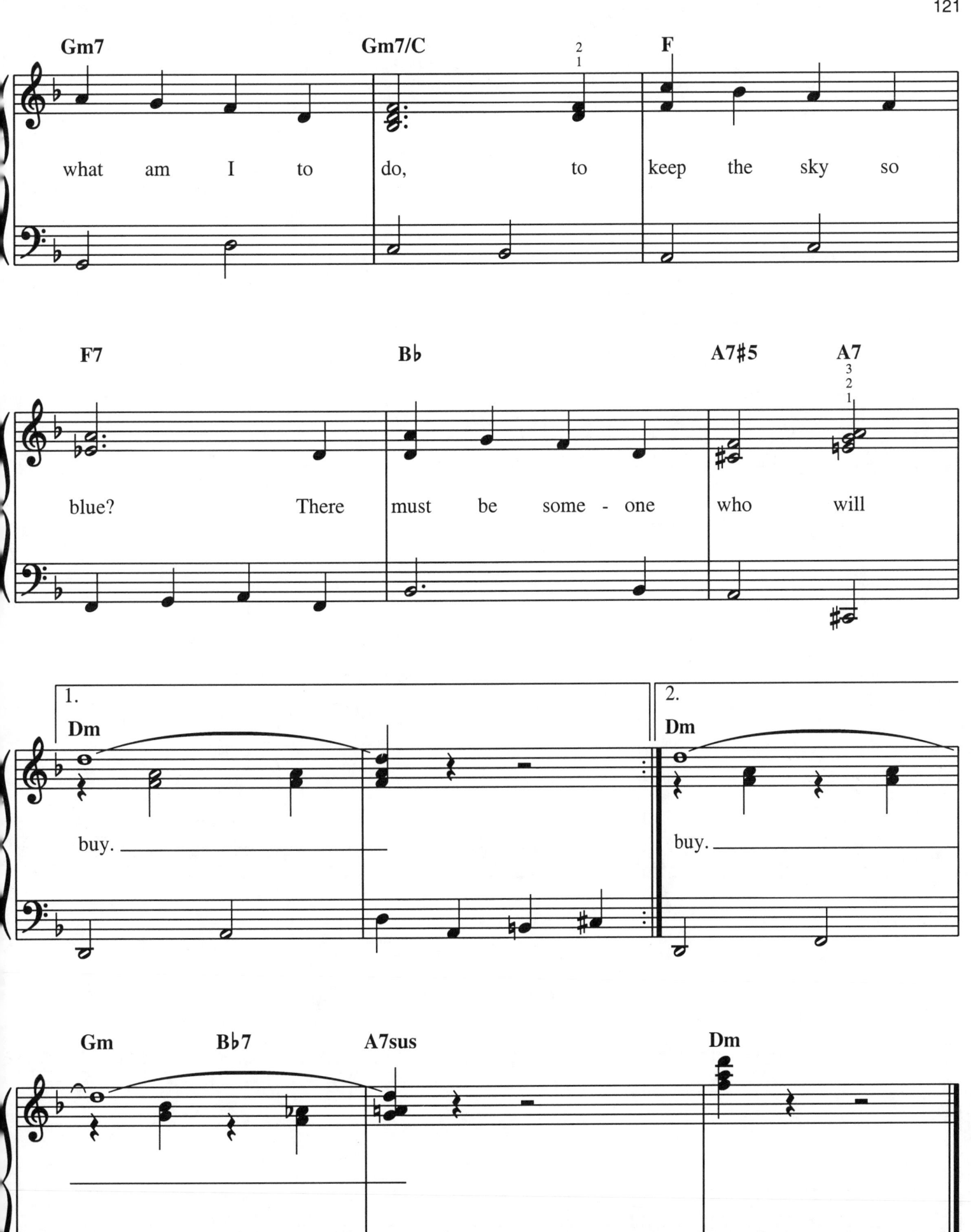

A WHOLE NEW WORLD

from Walt Disney's ALADDIN

Music by ALAN MENKEN
Lyrics by TIM RICE

Slowly and sweetly

With pedal

Aladdin:
I can show you the world,

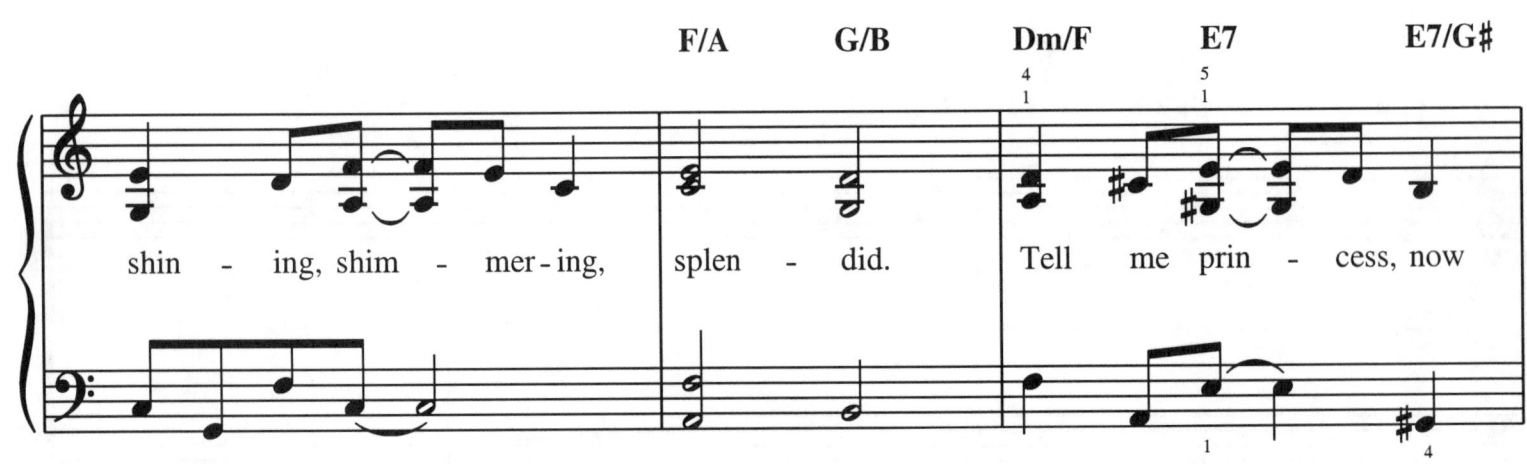

shin - ing, shim - mer - ing, splen - did.   Tell me prin - cess, now

when did you last let your heart __ de - cide?

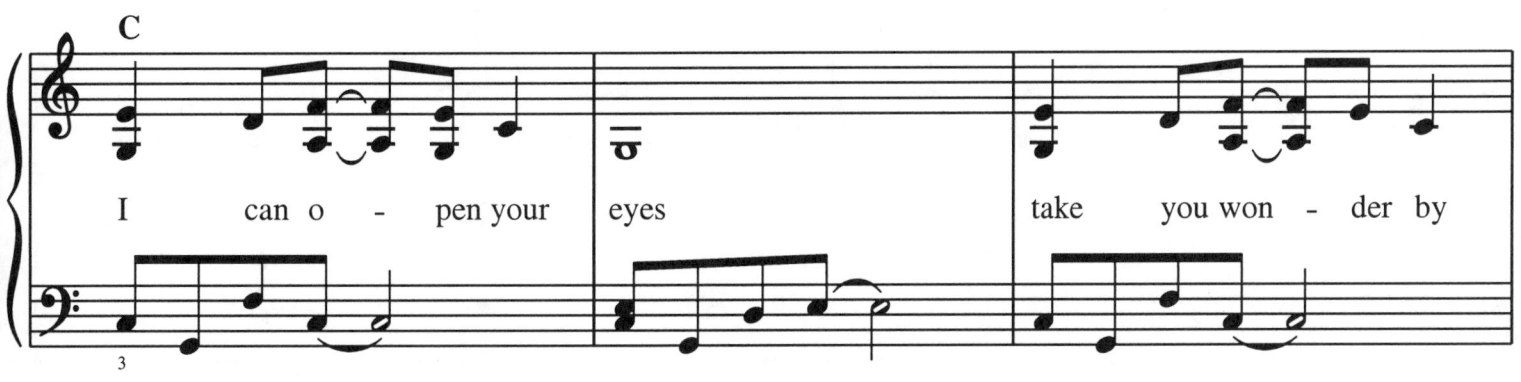

I can o - pen your eyes take you won - der by

won - der o - ver, side - ways and un - der on a

mag-ic car - pet ride. A whole new world

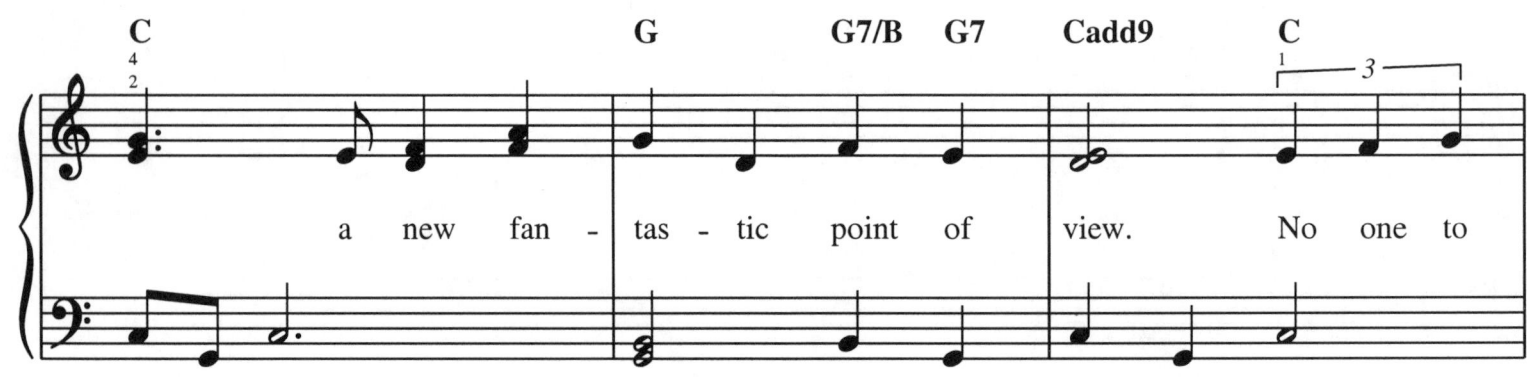

a new fan - tas - tic point of view. No one to

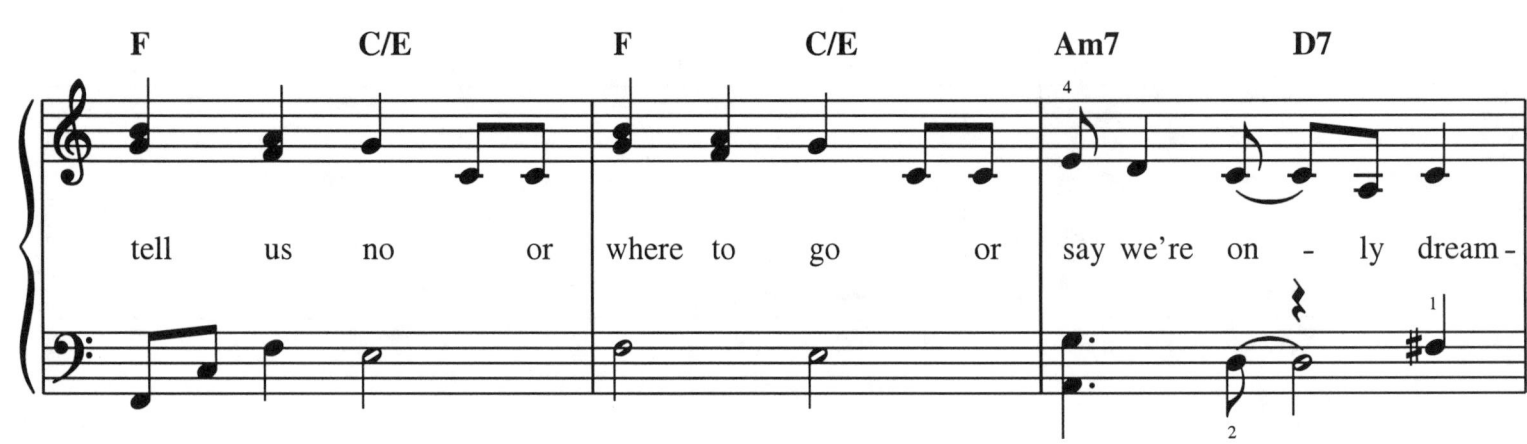

tell us no or where to go or say we're on - ly dream-

Jasmine:

ing. A whole new world a daz - zling

place I nev - er knew. But when I'm way up here it's

crys - tal   clear   that   now I'm   in   a   whole new   world with

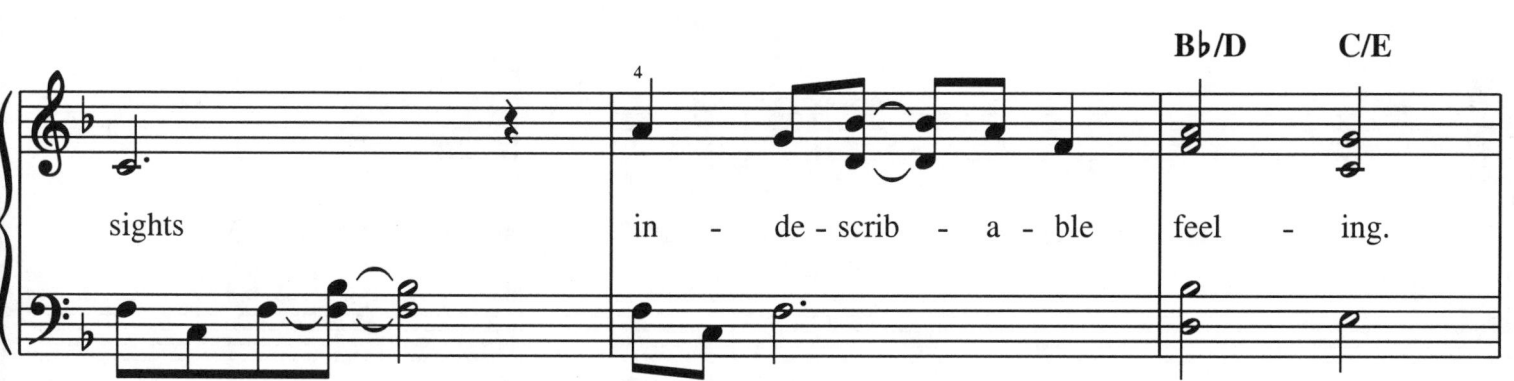

you.   Un - be - liev - a - ble

sights   in - de - scrib - a - ble   feel - ing.

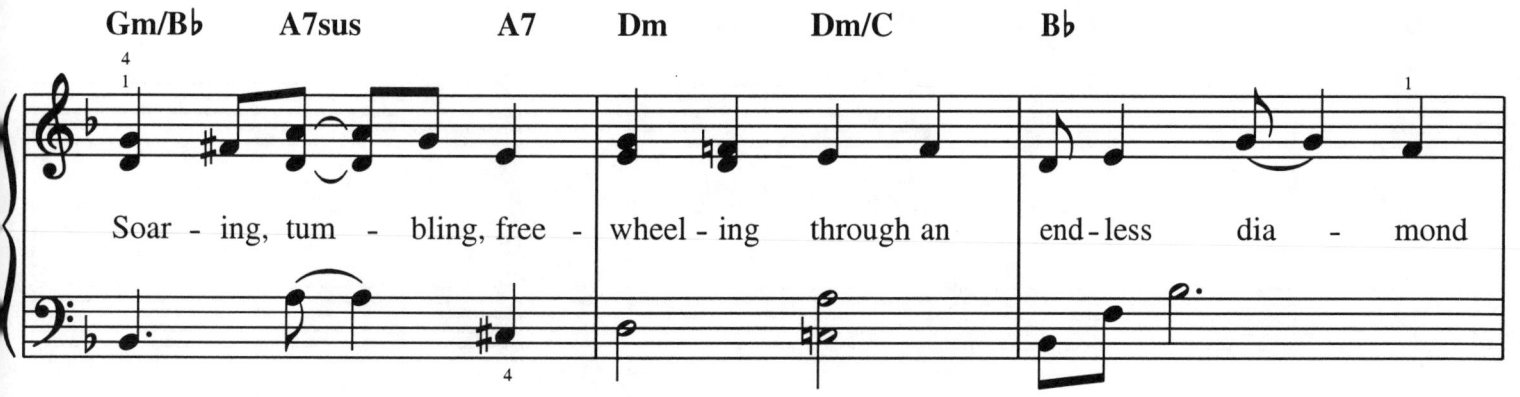

Soar - ing, tum - bling, free - wheel - ing   through an   end - less   dia - mond

F/C **B♭** **F/A**

Aladdin: A whole new world,   that's where we'll

Jasmine: A whole new world,

Gm7 **F/A** **B♭**

be.   A thrill - ing chase

that's where we'll   be.   A won - d'rous

C7sus **F**

for you and   me.

place for you and   me.

rit.   *L.H.*

WINNIE THE POOH
from Walt Disney's THE MANY ADVENTURES OF WINNIE THE POOH

Words and Music by RICHARD M. SHERMAN
and ROBERT B SHERMAN

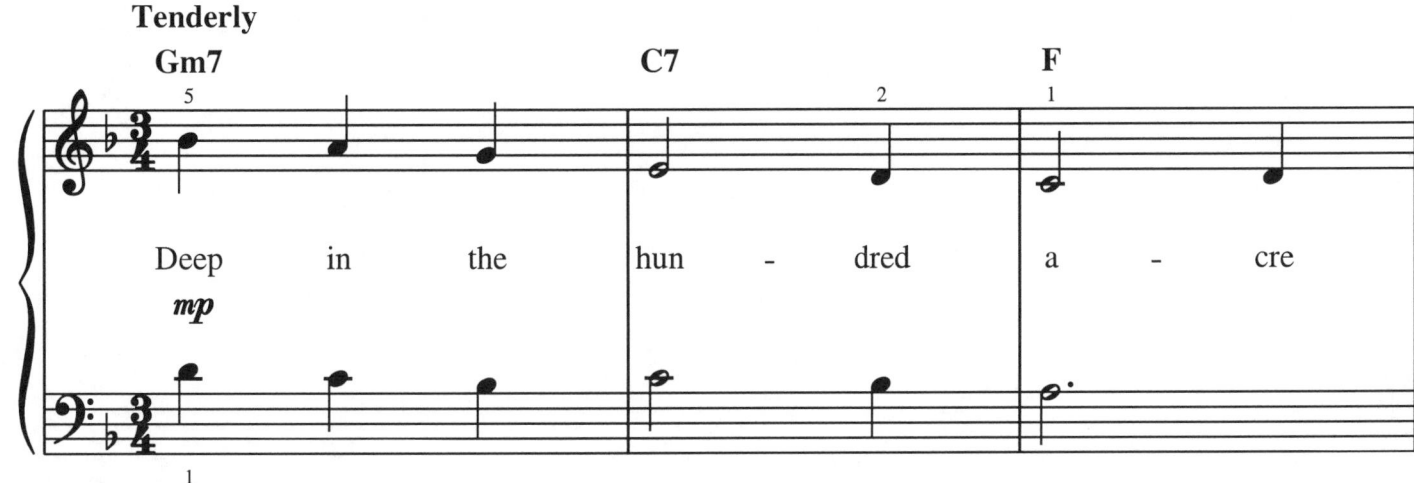

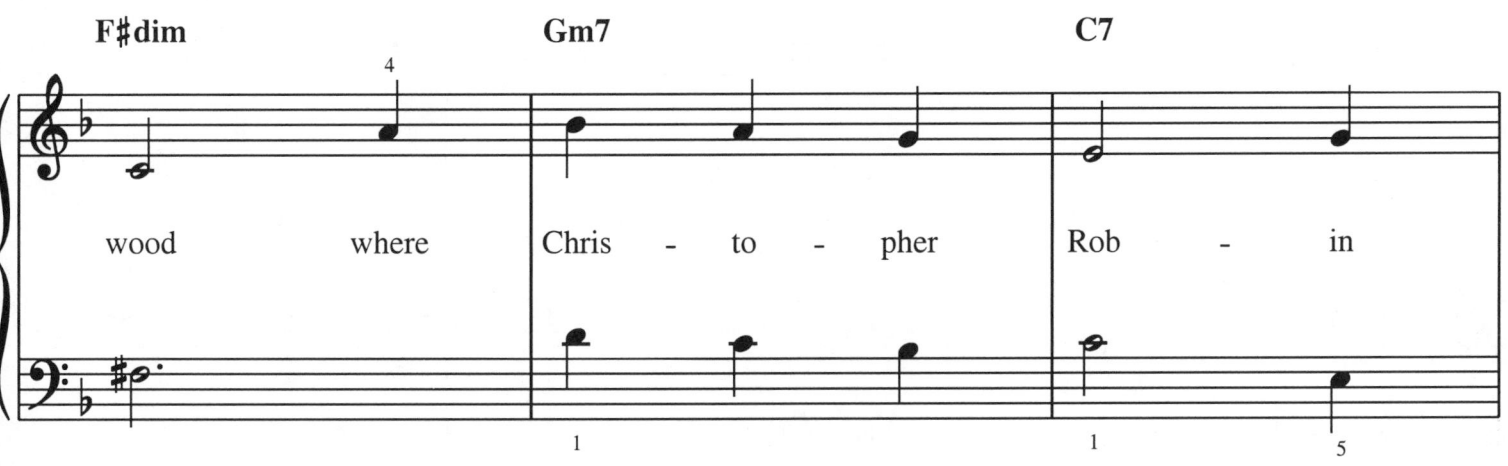

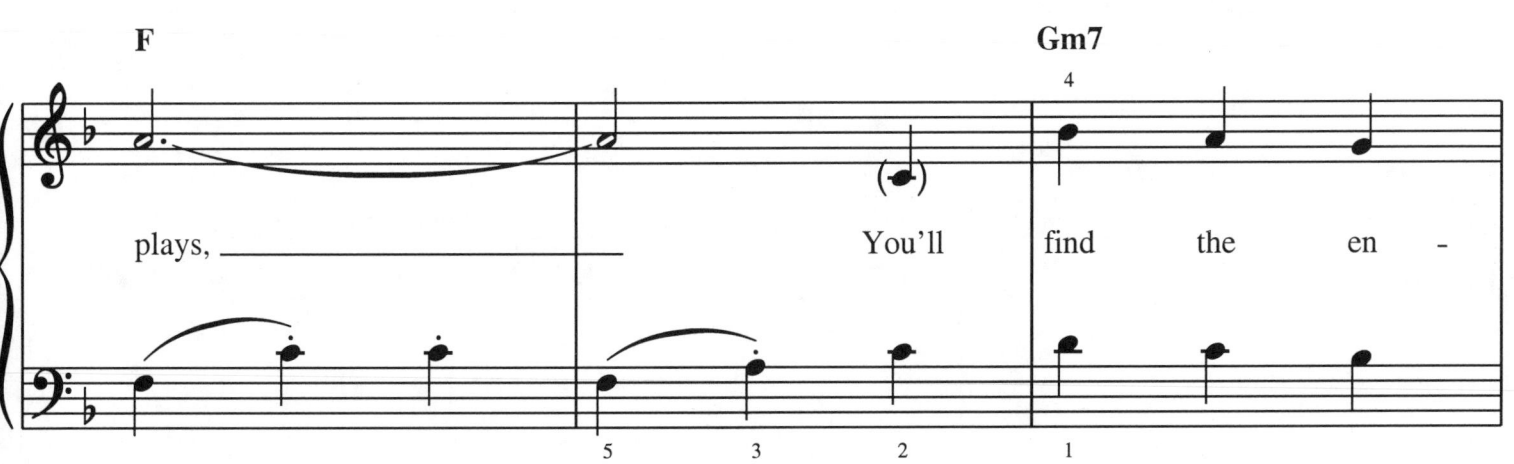

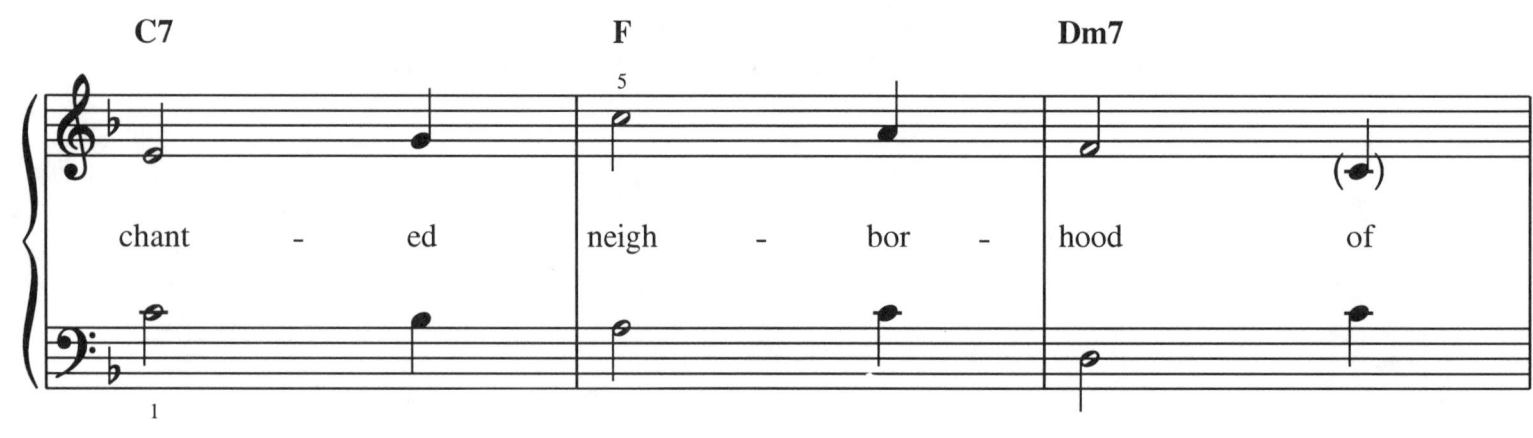

chant - ed neigh - bor - hood of

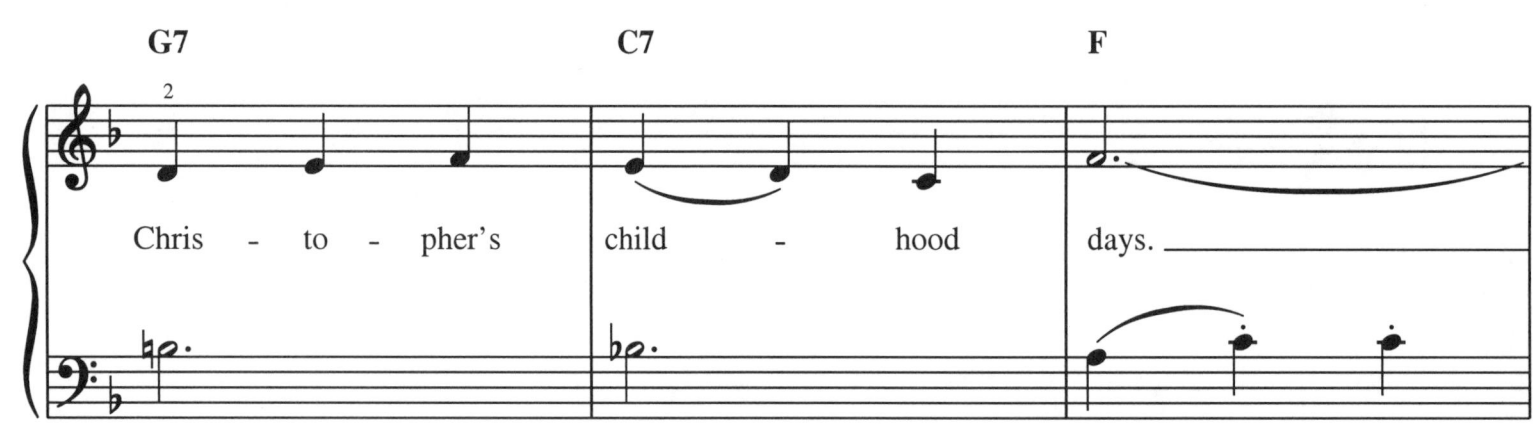

Chris - to - pher's child - hood days. _____

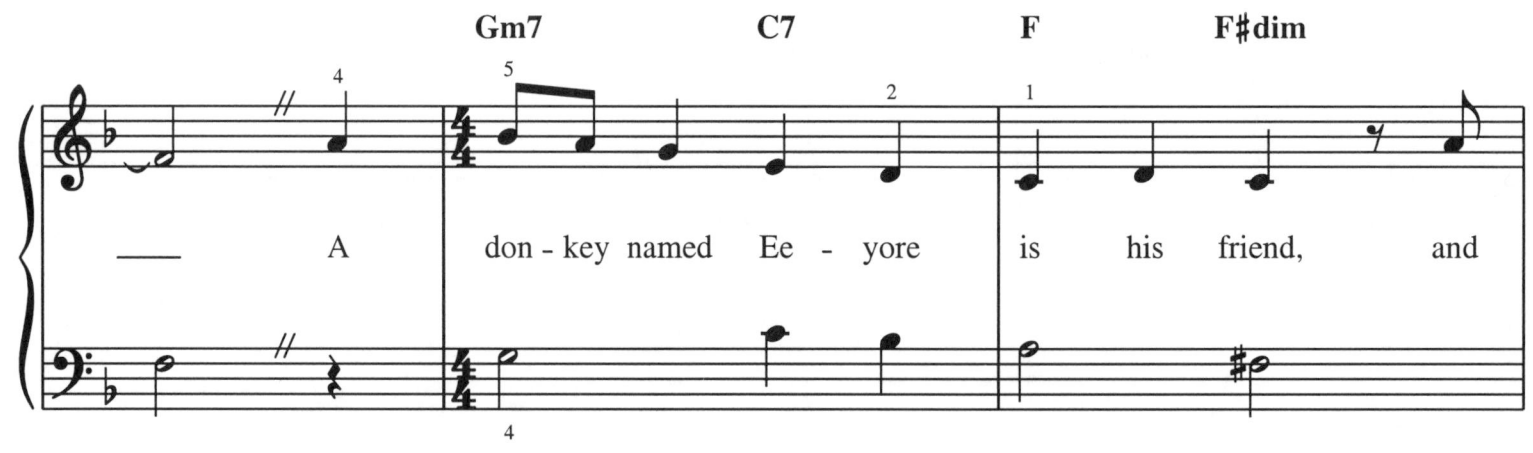

_____ A don - key named Ee - yore is his friend, and

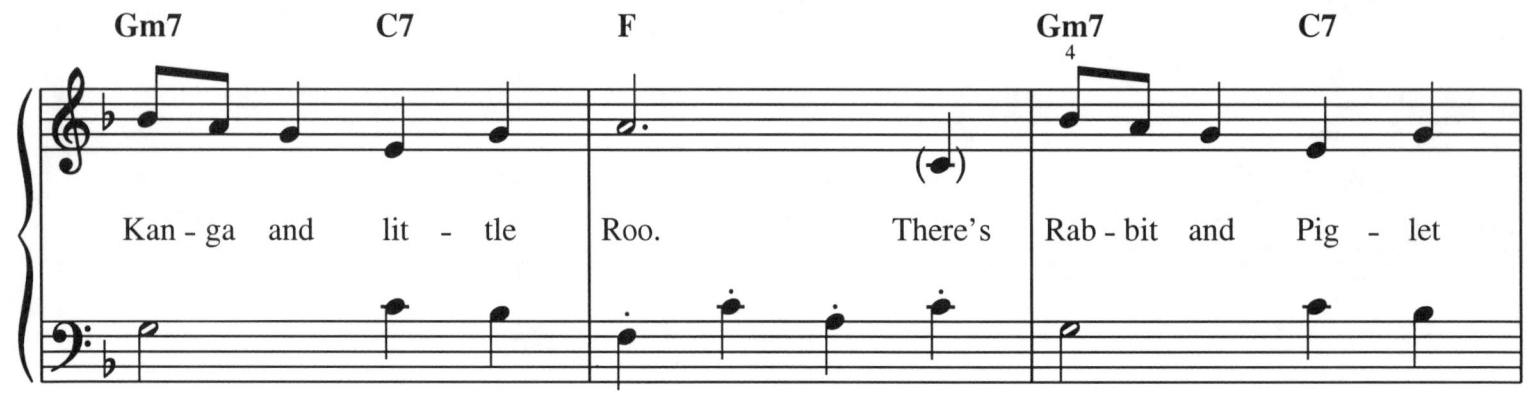

Kan - ga and lit - tle Roo. There's Rab - bit and Pig - let

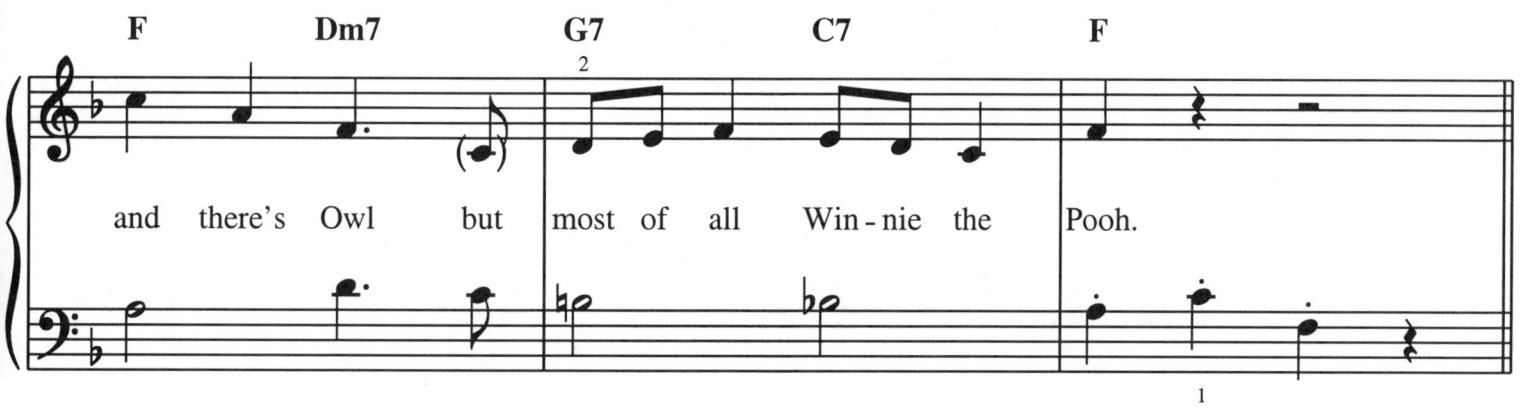

and there's Owl but most of all Win - nie the Pooh.

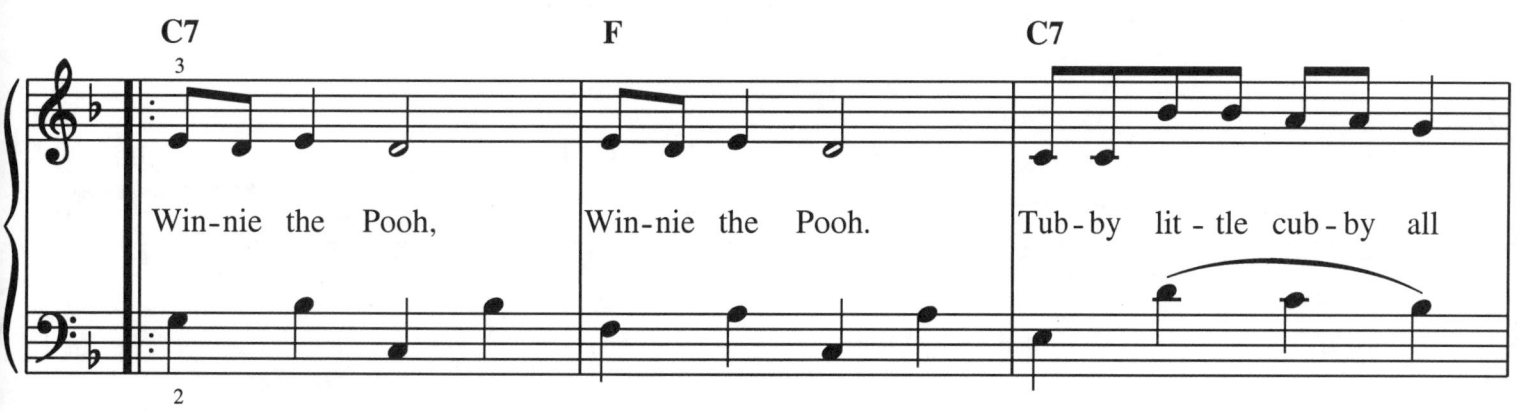

Win - nie the Pooh, Win - nie the Pooh. Tub - by lit - tle cub - by all

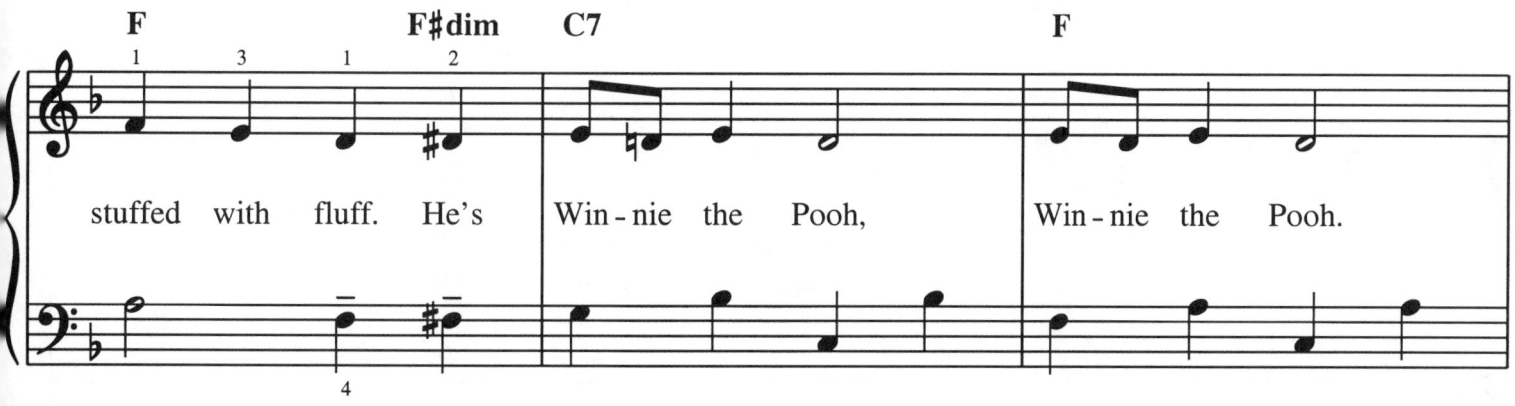

stuffed with fluff. He's Win - nie the Pooh, Win - nie the Pooh.

Wil - ly nil - ly sil - ly ole bear. bear.

YELLOW SUBMARINE
from YELLOW SUBMARINE

Words and Music by JOHN LENNON
and PAUL McCARTNEY

March tempo

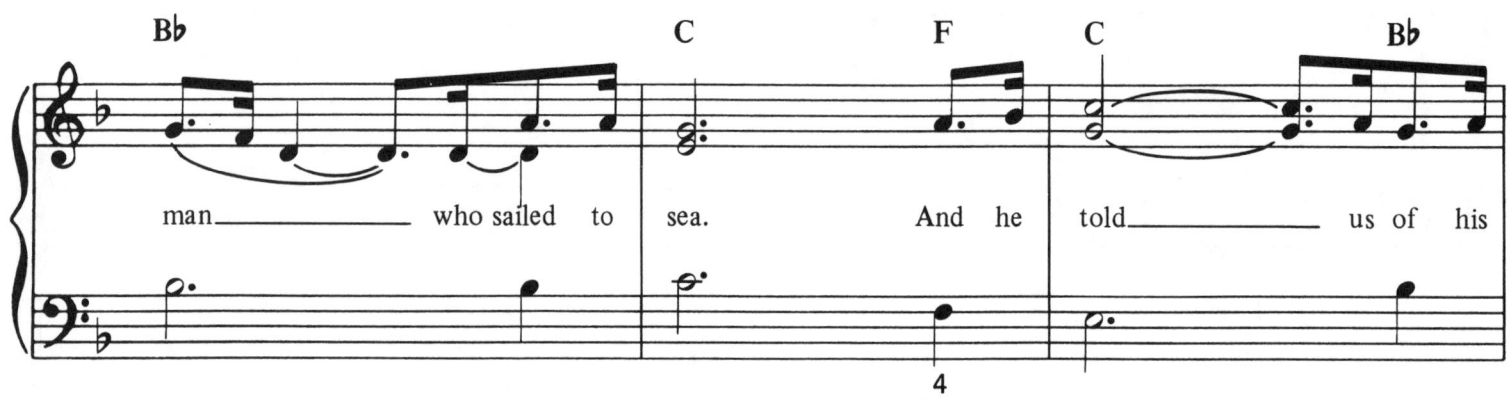

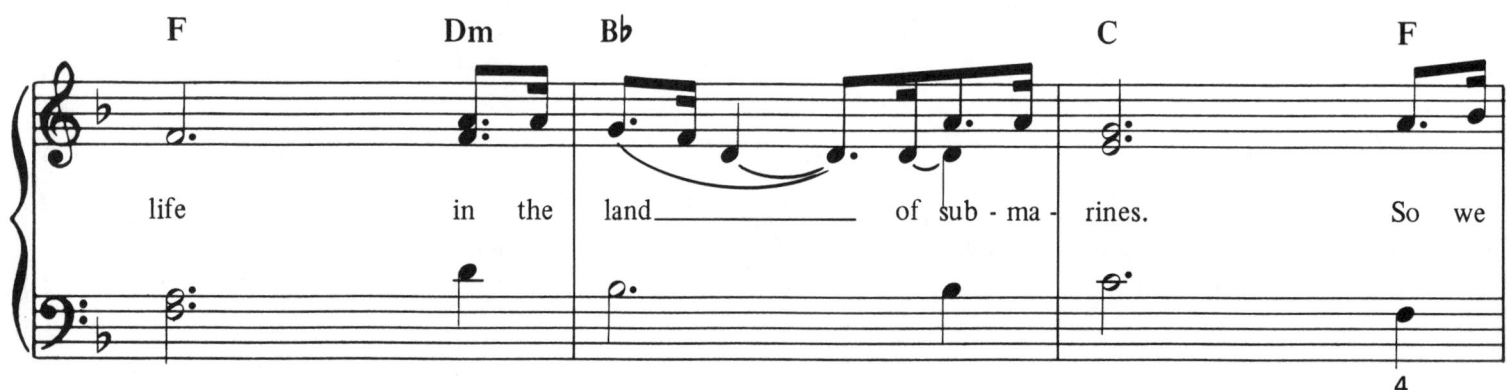

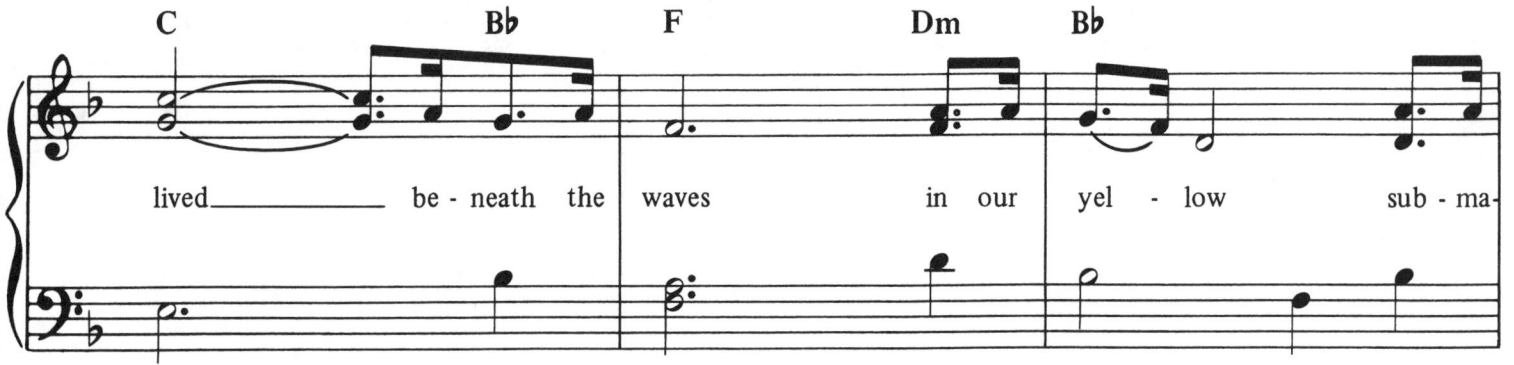

lived_____ be - neath the waves in our yel - low sub - ma-

rine. We all live in a yel - low sub - ma - rine,

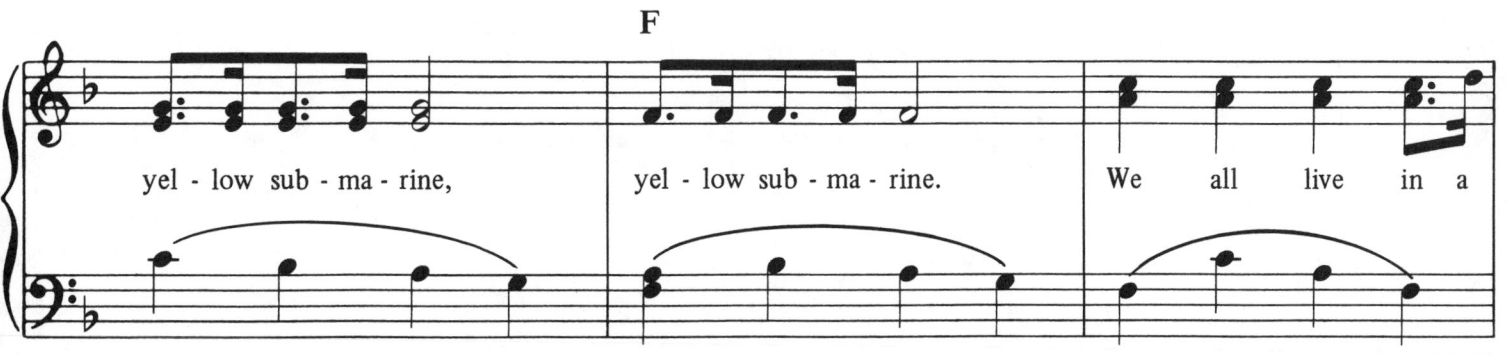

yel - low sub - ma - rine, yel - low sub - ma - rine. We all live in a

yel - low sub - ma - rine, yel - low sub - ma - rine, yel - low sub - ma - rine.

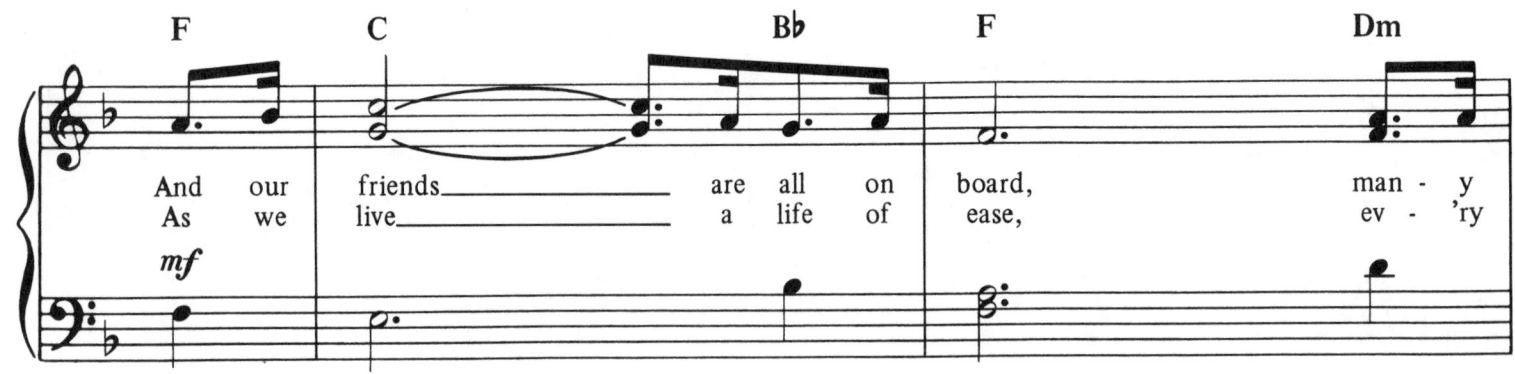

And our friends_____ are all on board, man - y
As we live_____ a life of ease, ev - 'ry

mf

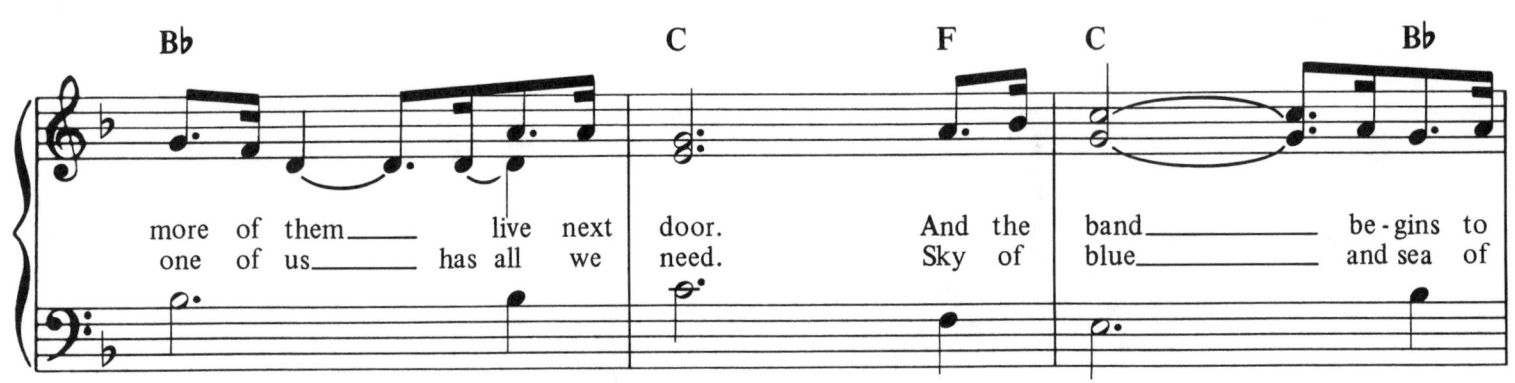

more of them____ live next door. And the band_____ be - gins to
one of us____ has all we need. Sky of blue_____ and sea of

1.

F   Gm7   C7   F

play:

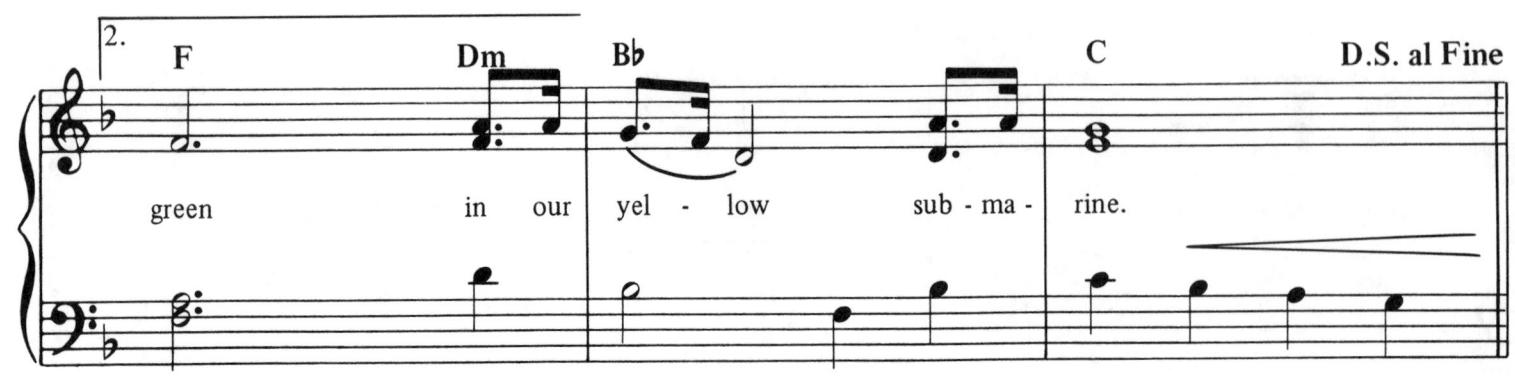

2.

F   Dm   Bb   C   **D.S. al Fine**

green   in our yel - low sub - ma - rine.

YOU'LL BE IN MY HEART

(Pop Version)
from Walt Disney Pictures' TARZAN™
As Performed by PHIL COLLINS

Words and Music by
PHIL COLLINS

138

ZIP-A-DEE-DOO-DAH

from Walt Disney's SONG OF THE SOUTH

Words by RAY GILBERT
Music by ALLIE WRUBEL

Blue - bird on my shoul - der, _____ it's the

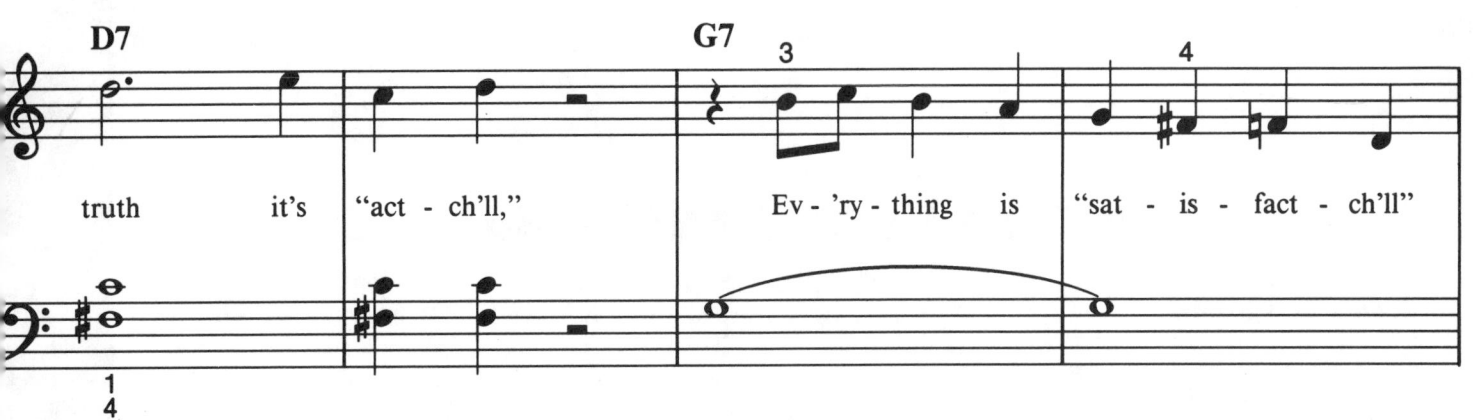

truth it's "act - ch'll," Ev - 'ry - thing is "sat - is - fact - ch'll"

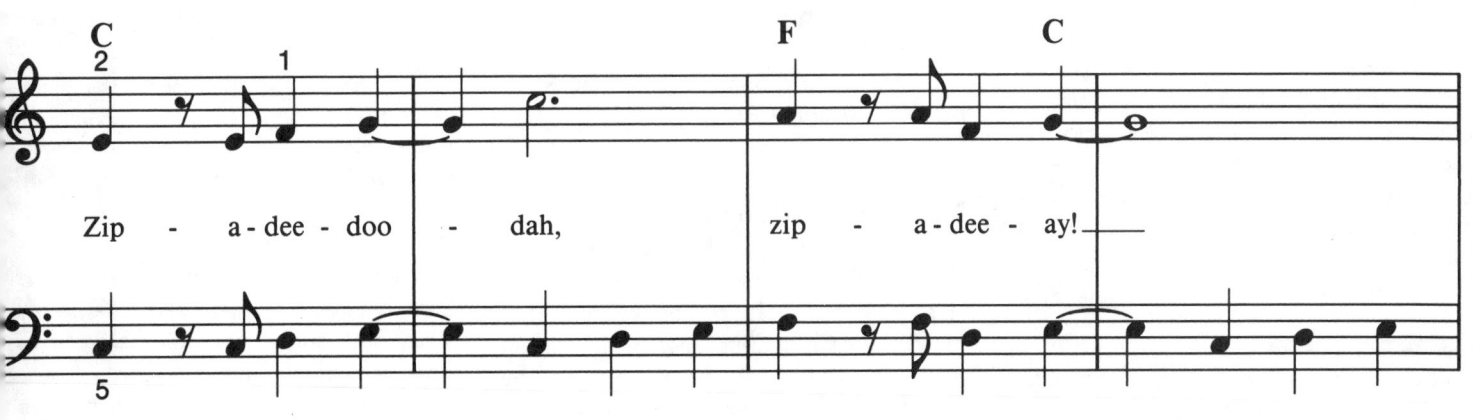

Zip - a - dee - doo - dah, zip - a - dee - ay! _____

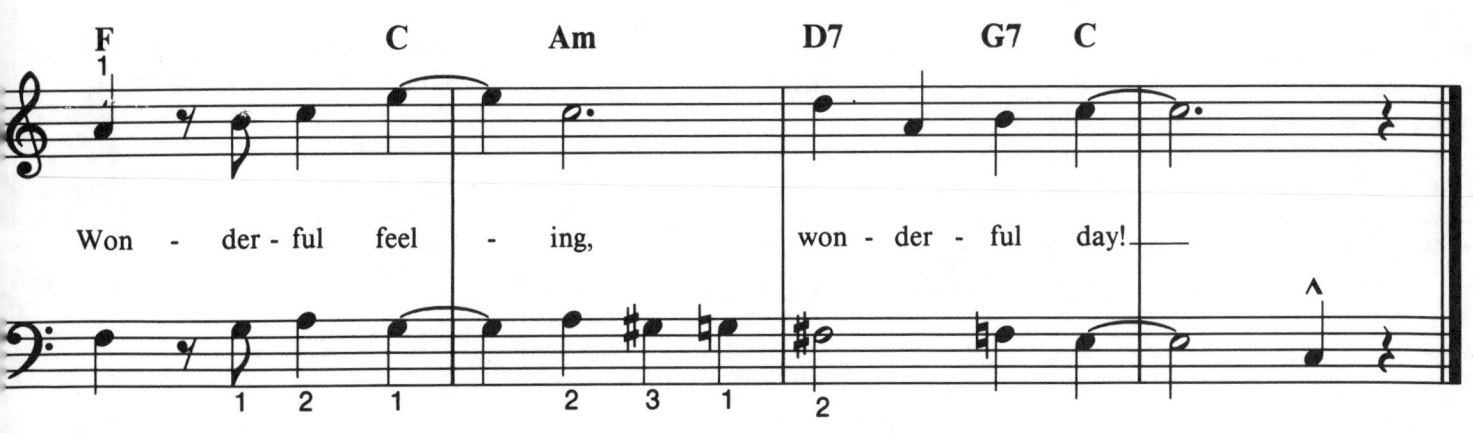

Won - der - ful feel - ing, won - der - ful day!

PIANO PLAYING THAT'S FUN & EASY

EASY PIANO BOOKS FROM HAL LEONARD

Irving Berlin's Children's Songbook
13 of his classics, including: Alexander's Ragtime Band • Count Your Blessings Instead of Sheep • Easter Parade • God Bless America • Happy Holiday • White Christmas • and more.
00306047 Easy Piano $7.95

Best Children's Songs Ever
A great collection of over 100 songs, including: Alouette • The Ballad of Davy Crockett • Beauty and the Beast • Eensy Weensy Spider • The Farmer in the Dell • Hakuna Matata • I'm Popeye the Sailor Man • Jesus Loves Me • On Top of Spaghetti • Puff the Magic Dragon • A Spoonful of Sugar • Twinkle, Twinkle Little Star • and more.
00310360 Easy Piano $19.95

Cartoon Tunes
15 favorite songs from Saturday mornings, including: I'm Popeye the Sailor Man • Jetsons Main Theme • (Meet) The Flintstones • Rocky & Bullwinkle • This Is It • and more.
00222570 Easy Piano $9.95

Children's Favorites For Easy Piano
49 songs children love to play and sing, including: AB-C-DEF-GHI • Bein' Green • C Is for Cookie • Do-Re-Mi • My Favorite Things • Rainbow Connection • Rubber Duckie • Sing • Somebody Come and Play • Won't You Be My Neighbor • and more!
00110014 Easy Piano $10.95

Disney's Silly Songs
Matching easy piano songbook to the album of the same name. 20 humorous songs, including: Baby Bumblebee • Little Bunny Foo Foo • I'm My Own Grandpaw • Three Little Fishies • When I See an Elephant Fly.
00290187 Easy Piano $9.95

Favorite Songs From Jim Henson's Muppets
15 favorite tunes including: Mah-Na-Mah-Na • The Muppet Show Theme • The Rainbow Connection • Rubber Duckie.
00356867 Easy Piano $10.95

The Disney Collection
Over 50 Disney delights, including: The Ballad of Davy Crockett • The Bare Necessities • Bibbidi-Bobbidi-Boo • Candle on the Water • Chim Chim Cher-ee • A Dream Is a Wish Your Heart Makes • Heigh Ho (The Dwarfs' Marching Song) • It's a Small World • Kiss the Girl • The Siamese Cat Song • Someday My Prince Will Come • Supercalifragilisticexpialidocious • Under the Sea • When You Wish upon a Star • Winnie the Pooh • Zip-A-Dee-Doo-Dah • and more.
00222535 Easy Piano $17.95

An Illustrated Treasury Of Songs For Children
56 traditional American songs, ballads, fo songs, and nursery rhymes for easy piano Each song is beautifully complemented wi full-color reproductions of famous artwor from the National Gallery of A Washington. Songs include: America, Th Beautiful • Clementine • The Farmer in th Dell • Hush, Little Baby • I've Been Workin on the Railroad • Jingle Bells • Oh, Susanr • On Top of Old Smokey • and more. wonderful gift idea for a parent or beginnir piano student.
00490439 Easy Piano $14.9

100 Kids' Songs
This terrific collection includes 100 song kids love: A-Tisket A-Tasket • Alouette Alphabet Song • America the Beautiful Baa Baa Black Sheep • Eensy Weens Spider • Hickory Dickory Dock • If You' Happy and You Know It • Jack and Jill Simple Gifts • Three Blind Mice • mar more!
00310572 Easy Piano $14.9

Willy Wonka & The Chocolate Factory
What child can resist this sweet collection 6 songs from their favorite movie, includir The Candy Man • Pure Imaginatic • Oompa Loompa Doompadee-Doo • ar more.
00222530 Easy Piano $6.9

FOR MORE INFORMATION, SEE YOUR LOCAL MUSIC DEALER, OR WRITE TO:

HAL•LEONARD® CORPORATION
7777 W. BLUEMOUND RD. P.O. BOX 13819 MILWAUKEE, WI 53213

Visit Hal Leonard Online at
www.halleonard.com

034